NEW HORIZONS IN JOURNALISM

Howard Rusk Long, *General Editor*

JIM ALLEE HART

The Developing

Views on the News

Editorial Syndrome

1500-1800

Foreword by Howard Rusk Long

Southern Illinois University Press

Carbondale and Edwardsville

Feffer & Simons, Inc.

London and Amsterdam

COPYRIGHT © *1970, by Southern Illinois University Press*
All rights reserved
Printed in the United States of America
Designed by Andor Braun
ISBN *0–8093–0455–4*
Library of Congress Catalog Card Number 79–112388

Contents

vi   *Contents*

Foreword

NEARLY EVERY NEWSPAPER in America, with a claim to re-
spectability, carries somewhere within its pages one or more
essays known as editorials. The subject may treat with any
topic of sufficient interest to challenge the attention of the
writer who, in turn, attempts to make his views interesting
to the readers.

There is a myth in journalism that the news pages are for
straight reportage, representing a free traffic in facts relating
to events, with any expression of opinion from within the staff
reserved for the editorial page or at least clearly differentiated
from that which passes as the work of the news writer. In fact
the more ambitious of American newspapers present an editorial page, or section. The purpose is to offer a corporate, or
institutional stance upon the issues of the day in the hope of
influencing or at least enlightening those who read the material wrapped around the advertisements.

An expression of opinion is a form of leadership. Therefore it is to be assumed that newspapers which employ a man,
or a staff of men, to write editorials aspire to a role in shaping
action of their readers in relation to decisions upon public
issues. Despite obvious efforts of management to make the
product of their "think tank" operation as forbidding as possible, newspaper editorials do carry great weight in the decision making process. It has been reported that no more than
10 percent of the readers of a metropolitan daily pay serious
attention to the editorials on any given day. But this collection of serious readers includes elected officials of local, state
and national government, representatives of foreign governments, most of the nation's decision makers in all fields of endeavor, as well as that elite sometimes called "opinion leaders"

whose interests and activities help to bridge the gap between the faceless majority and the decision makers.

A critic unimpressed by the negativism of newspaper convention is free to wonder if it would not be possible to attract a much greater readership to the editorial page and, by means of this larger audience, attain greater influence.

Today's editors are a quiet breed. If blood pressures ever rise in the sanctum, it requires nothing less than the intrusion of Spiro Agnew or the Black Panthers to project the reaction to the printed page. For the newspaper that has no competition in its home city it is much better that way. Blandness is a hallmark of corporate monopoly journalism.

Nor should the man whose involvement can be expressed in nothing more personal than the editorial "we" be expected to become even a paper tiger. At a time when the electronic media permit the Elite Pharmacy to take credit for the weather report and a staff announcer to byline the time of day, print journalism still keeps its brightest minds hidden behind the convention of the anonymous editorial offered as an expression of institutional policy. Yet who is foolish enough to believe that a corporation ever had an idea; or the bankers on the board of directors for that matter?

It is a game among teachers of journalism to name the ten greatest newspapers. Yet who can match his list of the "ten greatest" with the names of the men who preside over the editorial pages? Editorial cartoonists are known by name and work throughout the land but the men who build and maintain the quality and vitality of the editorial page upon which these cartoons appear, at times, must produce credentials in order to pass the security guard at the office door.

With the weeklies things are a little better, although, here too, convention is honored more often than it is flouted. At least the editor is a man in his own right in the community. His personal influence in day to day association with other community leaders may outweigh his influence as an editorial writer. Even so, some of the best editorial writing and some of the most vigorous editorial leadership in American journalism is to be found among the small town and suburban weeklies, as well as in the growing number of those flourishing in the shadow of metropolitan dailies. All the readers of the *Vineyard Gazette* of Edgartown, Mass., are aware that the unsigned editorials are the work of Henry Beetle Hough, perhaps the ablest writer of the weekly press. But James Reston, of the New York *Times,* who now owns the *Gazette,* signs HIS copy when it appears on the page alongside the work of Mr. Hough.

The signed column, in fact, must be included in any consideration of the newspaper editorial. Walter Lippmann, so-so editor of the long defunct New York *World,* set the fashion when he opened shop in the *Herald Tribune* with a regular contribution printed under his name. In this way a conservative newspaper was able to obtain the viewpoints of an established writer of liberal leanings without compromising the integrity of institutional policy. Walter Lippmann wrote for Walter Lippmann and not for the management of the *Herald Tribune.* The experiment opened the door to freedom of expression for writers smarter than their bosses and at the same time, by means of syndication, provided ready-made conflicting opinions for the growing number of monopoly newspapers faced with pressures for concessions to the pluralistic viewpoints of their captive audience.

Today when it is difficult with some newspapers for writers to earn as much as the printers and when it is possible for the publisher to buy the work of a dozen syndicated columnists for less than the salary of a topflight editorial writer, there are those who hold that the day of the editorial is passing. The electronic media now have their own editorials. Television, we are told, will determine the outcome of future presidential elections. As we face up to the inevitable changes promised by technology, who knows what forms persuasion will take in the future? Meanwhile we know so very little about the development of the editorial as we know it today and as it may be found in the old files of newspapers long dead.

Students of American literature keep alive for their poetry, their novels, and their commentary the names of editors virtually forgotten for their contributions to journalism. Political historians and the biographers perpetuate the names of other editors who particiated in decisions which shaped their times. We know of editors, James Franklin and Peter Zenger for instance, who went to jail for publishing their defiance of authority. We know that his editorials caused Elijah Parish Lovejoy to be killed by a mob at Alton, Illinois and that William Brann, editor of the *Iconoclast*, was assassinated in Texas. We know much about the men, little of their product and how it developed.

Benjamin Franklin tells us that he polished the quality of his composition by rewriting essays from the *Spectator*. Powerful "editorials" from the pulpit were commonplace before printing was invented. The bard, the minstrel, the balladeer, along with the learned men of their times, all in some way contributed to the form of expression that finally evolved on our side of the Atlantic as the American newspaper editorial. Certainly it was no simple evolution, as Professor Jim A. Hart, demonstrates in this first offering from his monumental effort to record the history of the American newspaper editorial. Much of his research for this volume is based upon the published British materials of the seventeenth and eighteenth centuries. And with this prodigious effort he brings us only to the year 1800 a date significant because at this time the newspaper editorial, as we know it, was first becoming recognizable.

The serious student will ask that this volume be the prologue to greater things. Read carefully and join me in experiencing the excitement of Professor Hart's exclusive (who else had the energy to undertake the labors involved) story of the development of the newspaper editorial.

Howard Rusk Long

Carbondale, Illinois
February 22, 1970

Preface

TELEVISION NEWSCASTERS with their practice of interlarding views with the news have influenced newspapers in the same direction. This trend away from restricting opinion writing to editorial pages or sections of the newspaper is a return to the earlier practices of news-opinion writing which are discussed in this book.

I have attempted to show the slow evolution of the editorial and to examine historically certain formats, styles, and purposes which have been used to comment on written news. The forerunners, precursors, sources, roots, and derivations of the editorial pointed to such obvious lineal ancestrage as ballads, pamphlets, newssheets, newsletters, and newsbooks. Perhaps this study could have gone back to the old Roman *Acta Diurna,* but the relationship seemed rather tenuous; therefore it was decided to begin with handwritten materials in the early sixteenth century and from there to trace news-opinion writing to 1800, when the editorial had begun to emerge in a somewhat definite form.

I am grateful to Dr. Howard Rusk Long for his suggestions, understanding, and encouragement during my long, but exciting task. I am obligated to the University of Rochester Library for making available the films of three thousand early English newspapers. Mrs. Elizabeth Husson, director of the Microtext and Duplicating Service at that institution, was most helpful and very kind to me. I am also indebted to the staff of Morris Library at Southern Illinois University for making other film and source material available.

Jim Allee Hart

Carbondale, Illinois
July 1969

Views on the News

1. In the Beginning

When English émigrés began arriving on the shores of North America in the first quarter of the seventeenth century, even the first crude newspapers had not been printed in the mother country. It would be almost twenty years before the first printing press would arrive in the Massachusetts Bay Colony and seventy years before Benjamin Harris would dare to publish his abortive *Publick Occurrences Both Forreign and Domestick*. But undoubtedly many of these early settlers, perhaps most of them, had seen copies of the crudely printed newsletters and newsbooks that had circulated in England. It is not inconceivable that a few copies may have been tucked away in the possessions of arrivals on almost every boat that touched shore. As a matter of fact, two men aboard the Mayflower, William Brewster and Edward Winslow, had published in Holland and surreptitiously sent to England newssheets designed to foment revolt against civil and ecclesiastical rule.

Although Scotch, Scotch-Irish, French Huguenots, and Dutch were settling along the Atlantic coast, English culture would prevail. And for more than a hundred years, the writing of news and views in the colonies would be patterned on that in publications in the mother country. It is necessary, then, to know how opinion writing in relation to news events developed in England, if one is to comprehend the emergence of the editorial as a distinct part of the American newspaper.

In the first half of the sixteenth century, when printing was still in its incubation period, views and news were disseminated through two types of written communication—handwritten newsletters and handwritten news ballads. Because few Englishmen, other than ecclesiastics, could read or write, the need for either type was limited. In London, the average man

depended on his daily visits to the Old Exchange, to Westminster Hall, or to the Gothic nave of St. Paul's to learn, no
doubt, as much opinion as news. Those who desired more information than they could garner in their daily gossip sessions
relied on letters from friends and from hired agents, known
sometimes as "intelligencers." Among the latter were retired
or disabled sea captains who haunted the market places to collect news for their country subscribers. Ministers of state, particularly those out of the country, depended on correspondence
from their friends. Big trading companies employed men to
write newsletters that passed freely between headquarters and
branch offices.[1]

Toward the end of the century, such handwritten letters
of news, commissioned by a person or by a group interested in
political and economic events of the day, had become quite
common. Since neither the writer nor the reader differentiated
between news and comment, these early news chronicles combined the narrative of the event with commentary. In fact,
they were so interrelated that the opinion element—the moralizing and the propagandizing of interest groups—cannot be
disentangled entirely from the news report.

John Chamberlain was a typical writer of these newsletters. A well-to-do Londoner of the merchant class, he was not
a professional "intelligencer." [2] But like the hired letter writers
of that day, he frequented St. Paul's to talk, seek news, listen
to rumors, and hear commentary on events. Then he would go
to his residence and painstakingly write to Sir Dudley Carlton,
who was a British ambassador on the Continent. Chamberlain told about and commented on trials and executions; births,
deaths, and marriages of royalty; poverty in London; duels,
disasters, and strange happenings; and naval engagements.

Once when he reported that "ships from Dunkerke" had
been so near Yorkshire that "beacons" were fired, he explained
that "huge levies of money," to be used in raising an army,
and a national loan of "150,000ᴸⁱ" make many of our citizens
shrincke and pull in theyre hornes." And he added that if the
English were "driven to these shifts alredy God knowes how
we shall hold hereafter." [3]

It was in this letter, too, that Chamberlain asked Carleton
to keep their correspondence confidential so that there would

be no danger to the letter writer. "I am so used to libertie and fredome of speach when I converse or write to my friends that I cannot easilie leave it," he wrote. This danger to liberty and freedom of writing opinions would haunt news writers for nearly two hundred years.

When Chamberlain reported the trials of the Earls of Essex and Southhampton, he thought the latter "spake very well" but "somewhat too much" when he "descended to intreatie" and seemed "too loth to die before a powde ennemie."[4] Chamberlain also labeled as "an odde fray" a duel between Thomas Hutchinson and Sir German Poole, in which one man lost three fingers and the other the end of his nose.[5] In a later letter, he revealed his contempt for Catholics with this question: "Here were three seminarie priests hanged and quartered the last weeke, but what is that among so many?"[6]

Although the comment element of such private letters may have influenced somewhat the actions and decisions of one person and a few friends to whom the recipient may have shown the letters, it was perhaps the newsletters passing between offices of trading companies that reached and influenced the most people. The Fugger newsletters are examples. The Fuggers were a German banking family who had offices or paid letter writers in nearly every port in Europe and in England.

Unlike the Chamberlain letters which often wandered over a dozen events, the commercial-interest communications usually covered only one event. Comment in some of these letters was wedged in the middle of the report, which itself was liberally sprinkled with biased adjectives and phrases. Midway in a letter from Madrid describing the death of Don Carlos, the writer noted that the event was "unpleasant tidings for the country."[7] A writer from Paris interrupted his narrative of student riots, in which the aged Queen Mother of France had been assaulted with unsheathed swords and insulted in "obscene, foul, and lewd terms which it would be shameful to repeat," to say that the reason for the occurrence "had not been imparted to me, neither what devilry drove" the students to "such disorderly conduct."[8]

Sometimes such comment was interwoven into an otherwise factual statement, much in the manner of a modern reporter writing a news analysis story. In the midst of a description of the Battle of Lepanto, in which the Christian Armada defeated that of the Turks, these sentences were injected:

> Thereupon the Turkish Commander began preparations for battle with joy, and took aboard twelve thousand men over and above the soldiery he had in the Armada. Thus thanks to divine Providence and Fate, he robbed himself of an advantage contrary to all usage of sea Warfare.[9]

In many Fugger newsletters the event was described first and the comment reserved until the end. In a gruesome report of the murder of the Admiral of France and his family, the letter writer moralized in the last paragraph that "potentates do not permit themselves to be trifled with, and whosoever is so blind that he cannot see this learns it later" to his sorrow. Further, he predicted that the event in time would cause a "great uproar, as it is more probable that many a one at present regarded" as innocent of the crime would prove "party to this game." [10]

A short Fugger letter from Seville reported that twenty-four galleys filled with Moors had arrived at that seaport. The Moors were to be distributed throughout the country. In this way, the writer said, Spaniards would become more "tainted and intermixed with Moors than heretofore," and they and the Jews would be "the noblest and strongest races, for they multiply like royal rabbits." [11] And a letter from Antwerp, which told of soldiers and Calvinists mutilating pictures and altars in Belgian churches and cloisters, ended: "But as Catholics and Calvinists cannot keep peace with the Lutherans and Anapapists it will ill serve the promoting of commerce and many persons will leave this town." [12] Placing such editoriallike utterances at the ends of news accounts would be used by authors of colonial newspapers more than a hundred years later.

The other type of handwritten communication which played a predecessor role in the eventual development of the editorial was the ballad. As a craving for information spread among the English people, ballads of news came to serve the poorer people as the handwritten newsletters did the wealthy and the aristocratic.[13] Probably sold in London streets in the early sixteenth century,[14] handwritten ballads gave news in verse. But often they contained more comment on than report of an event. More sensational than the newsletters, they moralized about monstrous births and other weird events.

Although handwritten letters would survive well past the middle of seventeenth century as the main communication medium for the aristocracy, who feared the printed word, the coming of the printing press to England would bring the printed newsletter and the broadside news ballad to London streets. As the handwritten newsletter was the predecessor of the printed newsletter, so was the handwritten ballad the predecessor of the printed ballad. And as it will be seen, both contained seeds of the future newspaper editorial.

2. FROM EDICT TO NEWSBOOK

CENSORSHIP IMPOSED by royalty slowed the development of printing in England and deterred the use of printed comment on news events. There has never been a period when the power structure of a country has really liked comment on or criticism of its conduct, but dislike for this type of utterance in the sixteenth and seventeenth centuries was violent and unconcealed. Repressive measures, varying from censorship to suppression and from fines to death, were common for those who engaged in writing, printing, and distributing the news with its interwoven commentary on public affairs.[1]

In 1476, William Caxton established the first press in England at the sign of the Red Pale in the Abby precincts at Westminster. Other printers soon followed him to England from France, the Low Countries, or Germany. They were welcomed at first by the government not only because they brought a much needed skill to the islands but also because the administration saw a need for printing its edicts and proclamations. As Caxton did, these printers worked outside the city or in a "liberty" in London.[2] And their work was so appreciated that in 1484 Parliament passed an act which exempted printers, booksellers, bookbinders, and illuminators of whatever country from restrictions imposed on other types of foreign labor.

Fifty years later, though, so many native Englishmen had been trained as printers that this act was repealed. Then, during the reign of Queen Mary, the Stationers' Company, a printer-publisher organization, was granted a royal charter. This company had the power to track down and punish purveyors of heretical and treasonous writings. It was controlled by the highest ecclesiastical tribunal, the Court of High Commission, which did the actual licensing of printers and their output.[3]

Both church and government worried about the dangerous possibilities of the printed word. The church feared the
heretical doctrines of Luther—a potent force in the social
upheaval on the Continent.[4] Even though such theological,
heterodoxical concepts could be spread by word of mouth,
they would travel faster if they were printed in books and
pamphlets which could be passed from one person to another
and read and reread. Similarly, the government feared criticisms of its actions. Both church and governmental officials
must have hoped that the licensing of the Stationers' Company
and the ensuing steady stream of royal proclamations against
seditious and heretical books and pamphlets would maintain a
status quo in the country.

But licensing could not quite staunch progress. By 1620,
printing of news with its interlaced and accompanying commentary had manifested itself in several forms—all eventually
to play a part in the evolution of the newspaper editorial.
These included the ecclesiastic edict and royal proclamation,
the religious and political pamphlet, the newsletter, the broadside news ballad, and the newsbook, which came to be called
the coranto.

With religion and politics the main preoccupation of the
people during this period, there was little licensed printing
that was not religious or governmental in nature. Ecclesiastic
edicts and royal proclamations, printed on one side of a small
sheet of flimsy paper, were published by the Crown's printer.
Sometimes the sole purpose of a royal publication was to sway
public opinion. When Henry VIII wanted to maneuver the
Pope into granting an annulment of his marriage, he obtained
from learned bodies in Europe opinions on the sinfulness of
marrying the widow of a brother. These he had printed and
distributed through his kingdom. Later he repeated this process when he wanted to foment opinion against a general religious council proposed by the Pope.[5] In purpose, these documents were a kind of editorial.

Pamphlets, which could be, and often were, no larger
than a folded sheet of typing paper, began to appear occasionally in the early part of the sixteenth century. Authorized
by the Crown and published by the royal printer, these political,
or governmental, pamphlets were written by such men as Sir

Francis Bacon and William Day, who were in the confidence of the royal court. Their printed opinions were those that would best serve the interest of the nation's power structure. They used such events as the trials of Sir Walter Raleigh and of Catholic offenders to justify the Crown's actions.[6] This purpose was evident also in a 1553 pamphlet under the imprint of the Queen's printer. It gave the last words of "John late Duke of Northumberlande upon the scaffolde," at the time of his execution.[7]

Because of sanctions imposed on printers who dared to mention state affairs, there was little pure political pamphleteering in England at this time. Barnaby Rich was one of the few men who dared to write political propaganda. In tracts published between 1578 and 1610, he set down his ideas of what was wrong with Ireland. Evidently his publications were designed to arouse hatred against France by reciting old grievances against that country.[8]

Interestingly, the first stirrings of what was to develop into the editorial paragraph appeared in some of the early governmental pamphlets. They had prefaces addressed to the reader. As early as 1611, an anonymous tract, relating the proceedings of the House of Commons and including a speech given before that body, had such a preface. In it, the writer explained that he had come to the defense of the House which had resisted the King's complaint against its actions.[9] Use of "Dear Reader" prefaces for comment on news would increase as news publications developed.

The religious pamphlet, so much a part of early American printing, probably originated during the reign of Henry VIII, when the Catholic-Protestant controversy spilled over into print.[10] Both sides used the press to carry on a kind of pamphlet warfare. Their polemical and dialectical tracts were fanatical, dolorous tirades on passing events, on memorials to martrys, or on justifications of the ways and works of one or the other side of the controversy.

During the reign of Queen Mary, who favored the antichrists, reformers used presses on the Continent and secret presses in England to barrage the public with their viewpoints. Under Queen Elizabeth I, the Protestants, with the upper hand, used the licensed London presses to memorialize martyrs

of Queen Mary's time. Later dissenting Protestant sects, hated
by the power elite almost as much as were the Papists, kept foreign presses busy. Tracts published in the Catholic interest
were laced with invectives and warned readers of the malice
and cruelty of Protestants. Those published in the Protestant
interest were vituperative in kind.[11]

Even titles of such publications were liberally endowed
with opinionated adjectives in an attempt to influence public
opinion. One read: "John Niccols Pilgrimage, wherein is dis-
plaid the lives of the proude Popes, ambitious Cardinals, lech-
erous Bishops, fat-bellied Monks, and Hypocriticall Jesuits."[12]
Usually introduced by biblical texts, the main argument was
interwoven with Latin and biblical phrases and filled with long,
dull sentences.

Curiously, clergymen, who contended that printed news
was dangerous, used current happenings in their sermons. Such
public affairs events as a jesuistical conspiracy against the
Crown or the execution of the Earl of Essex were excuses for
sermons that were designed to justify state or church actions.
Clergymen had no trouble in finding a licensed printer to publish these sermons which were probably sold in bookstores.

Other religious pamphlets were written to instruct. In a
1613 pamphlet, the Reverend John Hilliard, writing of the
death by fire of one John Hitchell, said that the fire was
heaven-sent and that his only purpose in writing the tract was
"to rouse up the sloathful, carelesse, and instruct the filthy for-
getful, to behold the wonderfule workes of the Lord."[13] And
the Reverend John Field used the Sunday deaths of eight people for an instructive religious pamphlet. They had been killed
when the scaffolding at a bearbaiting garden had collapsed.
Field blamed the deaths on civic authorities for allowing the
desecration of the Sabbath, and he argued that the accident
was not caused by rotten lumber, but by a wrathful God.[14] An
early example of criticism of authority, this pamphlet may
have set a precedent in subject matter for the slowly developing editorial.

By the time printing, publishing, and bookselling had become an established industry in England, the more speculative
printers were daring to transform handwritten newsletters into
print. Each was printed by a member of the Stationers' Com-

pany and registered by that organization prior to sale and sometimes prior to printing.[15] At first these were broadsides— a single letter printed on one side of a small sheet of paper.

In the printing of newsletters and even in their format, English printers were following in the footsteps of those on the Continent, just as colonial printers would follow in the footsteps of English printers. Almost all of the early news broadsides and later newsbooks were translations of French and Dutch broadsides and newsbooks. During the reign of Queen Elizabeth I, several books of news (mere pamphlets) telling of affairs in Spain and Holland were translated, printed, and sold on London streets. They told of military campaigns, battles, and political maneuvers. As with all news accounts of the time, they were infused with comment.[16]

Sometimes printed newsletters, like some pamphlets, were prefaced by an address to the reader. In 1607, the writer of an account of the King's speech explained to the "gentle reader" that so many different versions of the speech had been printed that he had been permitted to print what he hoped were the "substantiall reasons and arguments" uttered by the King. He did not dare to maintain that his version was the "true and full relation of all his Majestie spake" because it fell far short "of the life of his Majesties eloquent phrases, and fulnesse of the matter." [17]

The same type of introduction was used by the royal printer, Robert Baker, when he published a newsletter that reported the Gunpowder plot to blow up Parliament. In his address to the reader, he called the plot the "most barbarous and damnable treason" and said that it was necessary for men to understand the "abominable and detestable conspiracy." [18] And a letter reporting bloody rioting in Devonshire and Cornwall against enclosing public lands, was introduced with a long harangue in objurgation and with grim prophecies of what would happen when the King sent forces to quell the disturbance.[19]

Such newsletters were undoubtedly written by men close to court. Their introductory quasi editorials may or may not have been written by the printer. But in form they were surely only a few steps behind the introductory essay which Daniel Defoe in the next century would be using in news-

papers. And the Defoe essays have been called the true progenitor of the editorial.[20]

If one was not a crown printer, he did not often dare to
publish minority versions of news happenings. If he did, he
was likely to face the same punishment as two printers who
in 1556 were forced to pay the royal printer forty pounds
each for printing a newsbook.[21] Still by the turn of the century,
news accounts, termed "relations," written by people in close
sympathy with government or with "in" religious sects, had
become a part of every bookseller's wares. Also by this time,
a few printed newsletters had appeared under such fictitious
names as "Andreas Philopater." [22] Use of pseudonym would
come to be an accepted practice by later English journalists
and early colonial opinion writers.

Respectable and sober-minded Englishmen read the
longer pamphlets and newsbooks. They learned of official
transactions, rebellions, trials for treason and heresy. In long
digressive editorializing sentences and pious statements, they
were warned against blind obstinancy and against blasphemous, idolatrous, and superstitious beliefs.

Those of the lower classes who could read favored the
single-sheet broadsides. Here they read of court marriages,
tournaments, murder and other crime, miracles, monstrous
births, witchcraft, plague, acts of God, and sporting events.
Stories of tournaments usually contained encomiastic comment.
Relations of crime, often compounded of lamentation and
repentance by the culprit, exhorted the reader to avoid the
same end. Miracles were a sign of God's mercy and were used
as a call to repent.[23]

Almost any event could be and was interpreted in the
approved morality of that period. In a broadside describing
Siamese pigs appeared this comment: "Almighty God sendeth
amongst us, that we should not be forgetfull of his Almighty
power, nor unthankful for his great mercies so plentifully
poured upon us." [24] When the plague devastated London, it
was said to have been caused by the sinfulness of God's
chosen people. The cure was repentance and retribution.[25]
Floods, fire by lightning, and earthquakes were attributed to
a jealous God.

The broadside ballad provided still another form for

printing news opinion. Though their special appeal was to the lower classes, everybody probably sang them. The sixteenth century narrative ballad was composed, printed, and sold immediately following an event. Frequently after an event was printed in a newsletter, the publisher would hire a ballad writer to versify on the happening. Such songs have been called political journalism in rhyme.[26]

Ballads about the burning of the Globe Theater were in existence the next day, and two ballads and three newsbooks about an earthquake were in print forty-eight hours after the event.[27] Infused with tedious morals, the poems were more commentary on events than records of them. Deaths brought out obituary ballads with pious contemplations and commentaries on the vanity of worldly goods. Songs about the execution of criminals were filled with obvious warnings to avoid the same pitfalls.[28]

In that one apparent aim of the topical ballad was to express opinions on current events, it resembled somewhat the purpose of the modern editorial article. Although the sixteenth-century news ballad was the only printed medium which could serve as a forum for laity to express individual opinions, many may have been written by experienced commentators on public affairs. They were sung to a popular tune of the time, and their popularity would continue well into the next century.

As newsbooks from Europe gained popularity in England, English printers (men who distributed by wholesale and retail the products of their own presses), booksellers (men who imported books and sold them wholesale and retail), and undertakers (men who were paid by another printer or by a bookseller to produce books for them to sell) were quick to see the financial advantage of having the European newsbooks translated.[29] They frequently hired translators for this work. Explanatory or editoriallike prefaces, added by the translator, the sponsor, or the undertaker, were often quite partisan. Like a book in appearance, these publications were really pamphlets of four, eight, or twelve quarto pages. In England they were known as corantos.

The first of the newsbooks, *Mercurius Gallobellicus,* was a semiannual publication, written in Latin and published in Cologne. Its tenor favored the Catholic viewpoint.[30] A number of single-sheet corantos with Protestant sentiments appeared sporadically. Some may have been compilations of two or more European newsbooks.[31] They bore such names as Courant, Newes, Mercury, Post, Gazette, Intelligencer, Diurnal, Occurrance, Passage, Account and Proceedings.

As the demand for these newsbooks increased postmasters in European towns began collecting news items in their areas and forwarding them to central transmission points.[32] There these dispatches were assembled into professional newsbooks, consisting of a series of short paragraphs. Each paragraph was headed with a rubric specifying the place of origin and the date of the event. They were then shipped to England where they were translated, printed, and sold.

Such newsbooks had no continuity of publication date or even of name. But these forerunners of the English newspaper carried elements of opinion in their biased reports of events and in their moralizing prefaces. In October 1621 a great fire destroyed much of Paris. A newsbook account of this event began with this paragraph, typical of the pious comment of the times:

> God whose goodnesse and clemencie is incomprehensible, to our humane thoughts and imaginations, doth not always discharge the arrowes of his wraith upon miserable sinners; who . . . have stirred up and provoked his wrath against them. . . . But when he seeth that they waxe worse, and are hardened in their sinnes . . . then he rouzeth up himselfe with the scourge of adversitie, and dischargeth the fury of his wrath against them, to make them turn unto him. . . . Then (I Say) he employeth the great forces of the heavens, and the elements, thereby to heale the vicer of their vices, that wallow and take pleasure in sinne, as a Sow delighteth to wallow in mire.[33]

Edward Aggas, a bookseller in London for at least thirty years, was active in publishing news from abroad. Sometimes he translated for others. Of the news accounts from France before 1600, about half were published by Aggas; John Wolf, who was said to have five presses; William Wright; and John Field.[34]

Sometimes the English printer received several accounts of the same event. In at least one instance, an account of the coronation of Henry IV of France, Thomas Nelson, printer, or his translator tried to combine the accounts. In a preface, readers were advised:

> Whatsoever other discourses of this argument that may peradventure come to thy handes are false, counterfeit, and rashly published, but this is true, perfect and written at leysure, with all order requisite. Thus much I thought good to give thee to understand, least otherwise, where thou seekest for truthe, thou mightest be abused with falsehood.[35]

Occasionally accounts of foreign events drew rebuttals from Englishmen. Sir Thomas Baskerville and Sir Robert Mansel were apparently outraged by news accounts which they believed cast aspersions on them. Sir Robert wrote his own account. In his preface, he told his readers that he thought it was his "dutie both to you, and to the State" to correct "a report very vulgar in many mens mouthes in the Citie" and to clear himself of the charges.[36]

The report of an event itself was liberally dotted with comment and pious asides. One newsbook, *Lamentable Newes out of Monmouthshire in Wales,* contained five pages. But the account was so enshrouded in speculation and admonishments that it was more an opinion publication than one of news.

The demand in England for news accounts of events in Europe was heightened by occurrences in central Europe. Princess Elizabeth, daughter of King James I, was a favorite with the English people. She had married Frederick, Elector Palatine. In November 1619 he had accepted the Crown of Bohemia. The resulting storm soon took on the appearance of a Catholic-Protestant war. About this time two printers in Amsterdam, Pieter Van der Keere and Broer Jansz, began publishing corantos in English and exporting them to London. Usually these were translations of Dutch newsletters, but they contained accounts of major political and military events. Most were slanted to the Protestant viewpoint and minimized Catholic victories.

Pieter Van der Keere published the first of these newsbooks on December 2, 1620. It was printed on a single sheet of small folio size and contained six items. Although the evident purpose of these accounts was to give the news, there were occasional interspersed sentences of opinion. This coranto has been called the first English newspaper, although it had no name and was not printed on English soil.[37] It was like a newspaper in that its six items had rubrics. The accounts were not newsletters, but like newsletters, they did predict. They could not be called editorials, but they used certain phrases, such as "it is feared" and "Wee understand," that would become characteristic language in early editorials.

Newsbooks printed in English in the Netherlands never contained any news or comment from England because it was dangerous for booksellers to handle publications that mentioned home affairs. King James viewed with disfavor any public discussion of state affairs and in 1621 banned the importing of these corantos into England. His actions followed the appearance in London of a newsbook which had been printed in Germany and which contained a report of one of his speeches. The King ordered all copies seized for their "foul and untrue matter." [38] But there may have been another reason for his action.

English printers were beginning to issue their own newsbooks. The King may have believed that he could better control the content of corantos published in England. He also may have decided that English printers might as well make more profits by printing using their own presses for the printing of the corcantos.

Among the printers and booksellers who were involved in these first coranto ventures were Samuel Butter, Nicholas Bourne, Thomas Archer, Nathaniel Newberry, and William Sheffard. The most prolific of these was Butter. The son of a bookseller, he was the leading figure in the publication of the first newspaper to be printed on English soil. It was almost entirely a translation of news reports from abroad and followed the format of the Amsterdam corantos.[39]

Shortly after the King banned foreign corantos, six issues of a coranto were printed in London "by authority" either for Butter or for Bourne. The following year a series of newsbooks, usually called the first English newspaper, succeeded these. The pattern for infusing news accounts with biased comment and pious observations, however, had been set. The next quarter of a century would find newsbook writers, pamphleteers, and balladeers even more concerned with writing opinions.

3. Corantos

The first English corantos to be published on a time continuum were sold in London in 1621, only a year after the Pilgrims had landed at Plymouth Rock. During the next thirty years corantos would be replaced by diurnals; and they, in turn, would give way to mercuries. The story of the development of opinion writing in these publications and in pamphlets and news ballads during the second quarter of the seventeenth century is really the story of England during those turbulent years of social unrest, of internal political strife, of religious reform. It is the story, too, of the Englishman's struggle for a free press—a struggle that would be echoed in the American colonies.

Bankrupted by the wasteful policies of a vacillating James I, torn by two civil wars during the even weaker reign of Charles I, and agitated by the policies of an interregnum government, England became a breeding place for a corrupt and scurrilous press. Its influence would color English journalism for years and would eventually influence colonial journalism.

When the first six issues of corantos printed in England were apparently well received by the public, news pamphlets, springing up like dandelions, emerged from the grimness and obscurity of London alleys, from where, out of fear of the licenser and the king, they were sneaked into the streets. Between 1620 and 1624 nearly a thousand of these publications were printed. It has been estimated that an average of four hundred copies of each issue were required to sate the appetite of the English, who were hungry for news of the Swedish-German War.[1] Readers must have thought the corantos, with their eight to twenty-four 6 by 7½-inch pages, a great improvement over the old single-sheet newsletters of the early part of the century.

Until 1632, when the Star Chamber banned the printing of all gazettes and newsbooks from foreign parts, news reports in English corantos came from Continental news publications, from private letters, and from stories related by travelers in London. But the English corantos differed from Continental news publications in that the English publisher or printer maintained a continuous and close contact with his readers. In what can now be termed an "editorial notice" or an "editorial aside" (the term "editorial" was not then known), the reader was sometimes severely berated, sometimes told to moderate his grief, and often told to trust in God.[2]

Although corantos came to be known conversationally as "weekely newes," "weekely relationes of newes," or "weekely currants," they actually had quite long titles displayed over the first, or title, page of the publication. It was here that the undertaker or printer, or both, following a practice already established, exposed religious bias by using descriptive or opinionated adjectives. If the Protestants in the Continental wars won a skirmish, on the title page it was a great battle; if they lost, the Catholics had won by a lucky chance. If a favorite general led the winning forces, he was forced to slaughter the enemy; but if he lost, the opposing general was a bloody tyrant.[3] One coranto typical of the era was entitled: *More newes from the Palatinate; and more comfort to every true Christian, that either favoreth the cause of religion or wisheth well to the King of Bohemia's Proceedings.* Titles for many years would continue to have the slanted words of pro-Protestantism.

A Current of Generall newes . . . was the best known and longest lived of the corantos. First issued May 18, 1622, it was published by Nicholas Bourne and Thomas Archer. But Archer, who the year before had been "laid by the heels" and imprisoned for adding to an individually produced newsbook after it had been licensed, soon was replaced by other publishers. By October, a kind of syndicate had been formed by Bourne, Archer, Nathaniel Butter, William Sheffard, Nathaniel Newberry, and Bartholomew Downes. For two years one or more of these men issued this weekly coranto under a monopoly license. Then Bourne and Butter (today the acknowledged father of the regular newspaper press) emerged as the leading partners.

Earlier, in July 1622, Bourne and Archer seemed to have employed Captain Thomas Gainsford as a compiler of items for the coranto.[4] A veteran of the Irish wars, Gainsford translated, wrote, and compiled foreign corantos and private letters into a continuous narrative. He included reports of "warlike preparations" by nations, council and diet meetings, proclamations and edicts, oppression of Protestants, deaths of popes and kings, murders, and miracles. Only in rare instances did he use an item of English news, and this information probably arrived by way of Holland. He was careful to introduce these reports with such phrases as "it is rumored" or "we hear." Sometimes he added official documents and copies of private letters to English gentlemen.[5]

But the hand of Captain Gainsford as a commentator on events soon became apparent in his prefaces. Usually his utterances were shallow and commonplace, and certainly piously pro-Protestant; but this man, who has been called the "grandfather of English editors," [6] was trying to tell his readers how to judge the news. One of his first quasi editorials appeared in the July 3, 1622, issue of *A continuation of the warres* . . . , one of the longer newsbooks published by Bourne and Archer. "Now courteous Reader," he wrote toward the end of the publication, "having heard the truth of the matter, moderate your griefe, and doe not discourage a young brave warrior, by lamenting for some small losse by him sustained, seeing . . . that many times it happeneth, that those that one day have the worst, the next day have the better hand. Wherefore let us trust in God." [7]

That Gainsford early was judging the information that he gathered for the corantos was apparent when he addressed the reader in the July 15, 1622, issue of *The strangling and death of the greate Turke*. He could not help wondering, he wrote, "at the shameless reportes of strange men, and weake certificates by *Corantos* from foraine parts." It was especially disconcerting to read printed accounts that spoke of "so many thousand slaine, the Prince kill'd, Sigismond defeated, and the whole Army put to flight" when there never had been "any such matter, nor any set Battaile fought."

Not only did Gainsford appear to doubt the accuracy of foreign corantos, but by means of the editorial "we," he also expressed a dim view of his London competitors.

> Wee should also present you with the French newes, but that for some, who neither know what both past before, not how business depended one on the other, have patcht up a Pamphlet with broken relations, contradicted newes of Sea-fights, and most non-sense Translations of matters of State; we cannot but informe you how you have been wronged, and we are prevented by those who would thrust out any falsitie if they were persuaded that the novelty would sell it.[8]

Occasionally the compiler explained the news to readers in parenthesis within a statement, as: "They write from Vienna, May 18, That some Rebels of the Emperours (so the Letters call them, by which you may understand some great men of Hungarie and thereabouts) are gathering to gather very strong."[9]

Often, however, Gainsford did not bother with the parenthesis and merely added an explanation or an evaluation of the news. In *More newes of the Affaires of the World* . . . (June 10, 1623), in a report that Count Mansfield had been destroyed by "treacherie," he added: "but of this we confesse that we have nothing from beyond the sea." And in *The newes and affaires of Europe* . . . (January 15, 1624) he reported that the last letter from Vienna seemed "to be more intelligent, and by way of discourse afford you reasons why Bethlem Gabor consented to a parley concerning cessation of arms."

These editorial asides and comments resulted in news accounts that thoroughly mixed fact with interpretation, still an overriding characteristic of news writing. But perhaps the Gainsford device that came nearer to the editorial was the address to the reader, or preface, which appeared, when it was used, on the verso side of the title page. Its location always on the left-hand page and its essaylike utterances are characteristic of modern editorial page practices. One such told the "Gentle Readers" that there were two sorts of them. One group wished "well to the Emperor and his proceeding"; the other murmured and repined "that the Palatine's cause and Bohemia's business thrives no better." Since there seemed no way of satisfying both groups "with any report or newes" that concerned either side, Gainsford said that "to avoid partiality and take an eaven course," he would follow his customary procedure "of searching and opening the Letters that came from beyond the seas and so acquaint you with their secrets." Then if "any of you all either out of deeper apprehension, or quicker capacity, find fault with the newes for tenuity or small variety, or impertinent matters to expectation," he should blame the "Letters or the Time that affordeth no plenary satisfaction" and not him or the printer who were so willing "to please or pleasure you." [10]

In the summer of 1624, however, Gainsford died of the plague. In his two years with the Butter and Bourne publication, his contributions to the developing newspaper and opinion news writing were outstanding. For his news judgments and his compilations efforts, he can rightfully be called "the grandfather of English editors." Perhaps, too, for his editorial notices, "addresses to the reader," and editorial asides he can be called the great grandfather of the newspaper editorial.

A few weeks after Gainsford's death, Butter and Bourne found a new compiler for their coranto. But he was no Gainsford. His "addresses" did not have the flavor of the captain's writings. Cause of this, however, may have been trouble with the censor. In 1626 the new compiler added to translated letters sentences that indicated he did not dare report all he knew "lest trouble should ensue." [11] His editorial notices were used merely to correct printing errors in previous issues.

By June of the following year, authorities had become suspicious of all foreign news. Apparently, compilers and publishers were being extremely careful not to print any news report that could contribute to deterioration of England's relations with European countries. During 1628 Butter and Bourne published fewer issues. At this time the Protestant cause on the Continent appeared hopeless; and readers, perhaps tired of reports of lost battles and only false and vague rumors of victories, seemed to lose interest in newsbooks.

But in mid-1631, when the Swedish army began its march into Northern Germany, Protestant victories began increasing and the demand for news publications jumped. It was about this time, too, that Butter and Bourne found another compiler, William Watts. A learned and well-traveled clergyman of Caius College, Oxford, Watts was apparently stimulated by the successful campaigns of Gustavus Adolphus. It was evident in the wording of the title page and in his "reader addresses" that he was not trying to hide his Protestant sympathies or his Catholic antipathies.

Like Gainsford, Watts used the editorial "we." On the verso of the title page (September 2, 1631) he told his "Impartial Reader" that he was concerned about the Catholic slant to news from Europe. "In our last avisos," he wrote, "wee printed several passages of the late good successes and victories of the King of Sweden against Monsieur Tilly, as wee received them from foreine" sources. They had been "published by us without addition or substraction." But some readers, Watts reported, had called these passages lies and had maintained that the King had been killed, or at least taken prisoner, and his army defeated. Now the compiler was publishing a confirmation of his earlier passages, "against which let the most barking curr open his mouth and say as formerly God grant him [Adolphus] the multiplication of like victories and good successes until all his enemies be vanquished, and a general peace settle in all parts of Germany. Amen."

In the meantime, Butter and Bourne, as publishers, had made two advances. One was the continuation of a device used in a fewer earlier Continental newsbooks. In the third year of their coranto, the two men had assumed a pseudonym. Where the title page had read "printed for N. Butter and Nathaniel Bourne," after December 30, 1624, it read "printed for Mercurius Brittanicus." The other device was standardization of their coranto's title. Although the two men had been able to publish their coranto almost every week since its inception, each issue usually had a different title. But by the time Watts had become compiler, the title always began with *The Continuation of our weekely (or Foraine) Avisos* . . . Even though standardization of titles would become a common practice, Butter and Bourne may have used it first as a kind of ploy in an attempt to differentiate their publication from those of their competitors.

As Gainsford had earlier indicated, rival corantos kept appearing on London streets. Some lasted one issue; some as many as ten. All had the usual mixture of fact and interpretation in their news accounts, but none had the commentary elements of the Butter-Bourne publication. When the writers of these rival newsbooks dared to comment, they usually confined themselves to innocuous, pious statements. " 'Tis most manifestly known to all the world," wrote one rival compiler, "that hatred, envy, and dissension reign mightily nowadays; the son is against the father, and the sister against the brother, and in general we are so exasperated one against another that if we could drown one another in a spoon, we would not fetch a pail." Therefore, he advised praying to "God that he will not judge us according to our deserts, but grant us everlasting salvation." [12]

The Butter-Bourne coranto must have been the talk of London because Ben Jonson used it as the background for his satiric play, *The Staple of Newes*. Although it is not one of Jonson's best plays, his description of the coranto office, his sharp sarcastic thrusts at "newes of doubtful credit" gathered at "Paul's, Exchange, and Westminster Hall" and at *Mercurius Britannicus,* who "dished out newes, were't true or false," his pun on the word "butter," and his ridicule of "honest common people," who gained "their pleasure in believing lyes that are made" for them in the coranto office must have delighted theatergoers. One character said that the very printing of "divers men's opinion" was newes to some people "that have not the heart to believe anything" unless they saw it in print. And another predicted that the press which had abused many would be reformed.

In 1625, the year this play was performed in London, James I died, and his son Charles I succeeded to the throne. The new King was married to Princess Henrietta Maria, sister to the King of France. Partially because of her Catholic influence, Charles, who strongly disapproved of public discussion of news events, resented flattering references in corantos to King Adolphus of Sweden. Besides, Charles was quarreling with Parliament, which he finally dissolved. Many stationers and printers, including Bourne, were fined and imprisoned. But when pro-Protestant newsbooks continued to appear, Charles on October 17, 1632, issued a proclamation banning all pamphlets of news.[18] This news blackout was to last six years. It would be nearly ten years before further significant development in newsbook editorializing would be discernible.

4. Diurnals and Mercuries

Butter and Bourne must have chafed under the newsbook restrictions imposed by Charles. They probably knew that Jan van Hilton, an Amsterdam publisher with Puritan beliefs, was printing newsbooks in English and smuggling them into the country.[1] These publications were only translations of Dutch corantos and newsletters about battles, but still the two English publishers undoubtedly missed the fairly lucrative income from their weekly coranto. It probably was not easy for them to see their potential profits going to a foreign publisher. Several times they petitioned the King for a new license. But not until December 20, 1638, were they granted a royal newsletter patent. Under its provisions they were given the exclusive right to publish in English for twenty-one years "all matters of History of newes of any foraine place or kingdom" on the condition that they contribute ten pounds annually to the repair of St. Paul's cathedral.[2] The newsbook blackout was over.

But the Butter-Bourne publication was never the same. William Watts still compiled the coranto; but he used little editorial matter, except in passages which he prefaced with "Some say" and "Most men are of the opinion." The publishers were careful to include on title pages the phrase "with privilege" or "with permission." Yet in a little less than a year they were in trouble with the censor. (The office of licenser of the press had been established by then.) Furthermore, competition was cutting their profits. As a result, Bourne quit the organization.

Butter continued to publish the coranto for another three years. Sometimes a month would elapse between issues. On one such occasion he complained in an address to "Courteous

Reader" that "the licenser (out of partial affection) would
not often let pass apparent truth." In fact, the licenser had
been "so cross" and altered so much of his copy that Butter
was "almost weary of printing." [3]

Competition from unlicensed newsbooks that were flood-
ing London streets must have made him even more weary.
To counteract, Butter reduced the size and price of his coranto. He told his readers on April 23, 1640, that if his
copies did not sell, "we shall be forced to put a period to the
Presse, and leave every man to the pleasing of his own fansie
by a more uncertaine restrained way of private letters, or
verball newes." More than a year later he complained that
other booksellers "obscured and villified his 'Forrein Oc-
curents.' " [4] Shortly afterward, the publisher did put a period
to his coranto.

The trouble with Butter's coranto was that it contained
only foreign "avisos," and by this time English readers were
no longer interested in foreign events. Civil war was approaching, and people were discussing ship money, subsidies,
papism, and Puritanism. The King had set out for Scotland,
and events at home were far overshadowing those on the
Continent.

Moreover, the time was ripe for the publication of newsbooks that told of happenings at home. In July 1641 the Star
Chamber had been abolished by Parliament, which Charles
had reconvened the year before. And for two years this body
was so busy with state affairs that it did not get around to
any censorship edicts. Also, it was encroaching on royal prerogative by allowing publication of its daily proceedings in
weekly chronicles. Its members had recognized the need to
counteract rumors and guide public opinion by presenting
their side of the parliamentary controversy with the King.
Thus were born the first English domestic newsbooks—the
diurnals, published under the imprimatur of the clerk of the
House of Commons. With them came the second phase in the
evolution of editorial comment.

The first of these semiofficial diurnals, *The Head of
Several Proceedings in the Present Parliament,* with an inside
title, *Diurnall Passages,* appeared in November 1641. Before
the end of the year, there were two other such diurnals

(weekly publications of daily happenings). And on January 31, 1642, a fourth and more enduring diurnal, *A Perfect Diurnall of the Passage in Parliament,* appeared. These early issues were basically neutral and contained a paucity of comment. Although there was an underlying tone of anti-Catholicism in reports of the Irish rebellion, the newsbooks lacked the asides and forthright comment of a Gainsford.[5] But there was such a demand for the inexpensive pamphlets of news that counterfeits and counter-counterfeits soon became common. Inevitably in this era when comment could not be segregated from fact, editorial comment began to crop up in shoulder notes, asides, and prefaces.

In March 1642 Parliament finally got around to passing a resolution to suppress newsbooks, but only two months later this edict was being ignored. In the summer London was threatened by the Royalist army, and by September the prevailing mood had become anti-Royalist. Followers of the King, sometimes called Cavaliers, were being described in parliamentary diurnals as "malicious and disaffected," "bloody-minded," and "malignant."

William Cooke (or Cook), a law publisher of Furnival's Inn, was the publisher of the aforementioned *A Perfect Diurnall.* When he hired Samuel Pecke, a scrivener with a stall in Westminster Hall, to compile his publication, he probably had no idea that his writer would develop into the leading journalist of the two prolific newsbook years, 1641 and 1642. Pecke, who was later to write for two other newsbooks, would be imprisoned twice for diurnall utterances that Parliament considered seditious.[6]

At first his "Courteous Reader" addresses and his anti-Royalists commentary had seemed rather mild. Even in the summer of 1642 his brief, sympathetic accounts of pro-parliamentary crowds rioting around Westminster seemed subdued and indirect. But by November of that year, he could end a lurid account of Royalist atrocities at Brainford with the comment: "It was very credibly reported that his majesty riding by some of the dead corps laughed and seemed to rejoice at their fall, and some other matters I forbeare to speak of, with hopes that it was otherwise." [7]

After one of his sojourns in prison, Pecke was back in

1644 writing *A Perfect Diurnall.* This time he was careful not to get involved in the parliamentary faction fights, but he was so anti-Royalist that he once blamed a Royalist-inspired plot for the Indian massacre of Virginia colonists.[8] He consistently wrote against the King, the Catholics, and the Irish. He even approved of an ordinance to kill all captured Irish rebels. But after he was reprimanded again in October 1646 for reporting too much detail about the negotiations between Parliament and the Scots, he toned down his editoriallike utterances. He pleaded for relaxation of tensions by telling his reader that the general question now was whether there would be peace or a new war, "for most think the old quarrel at an end." It would be a sad thing if the "Presbyters and the Independents" quarreled. "And there is more can be found to speak a word in season to reconcile the two." [9]

After the bloody London riots the following summer, Pecke was careful to stop all aside embellishments. Apparently, anxious not to return to prison, he adhered to new licensing regulations. Nothing in his news accounts could offend any faction, although he laced them with such innocuous commentary as, "There is not that division in the army our friends feared and our enemies hoped for." [10] By the time *A Perfect Diurnall* was closed in 1649, Pecke was confining his comments to praise of men in power.

In the meantime, Charles had not been long in realizing that he needed a press spokesman. When he fled London and established his headquarters in Oxford, he had carried a printing press with him. It was set up at Oriel College in the same building where his privy council met. From there, on January 1, 1643, the *Oxford Diurnall* was issued. In the next issue the name was changed to *Mercurius Aulicus.* It was published on Sundays, probably to irritate the Puritans.

But this was not the only element in *Aulicus,* as the publication was conversationally called, that irked the Protestant elements of the population. The utterances of its compiler, or author, became a thorn in their sides. John Birkenhead (or Berkenhead), already a known pamphleteer and balladeer, was an Oxford graduate and a protege of Archbishop Laud. He wasted no time in letting readers know that

Aulicus was a Royalist journal. In the foreword to the first issue, he said that the world had too long "been abused with falsehoods" by a weekly newssheet, "put out to nourish the abuse amongst people and make them pay for their seducement." Through *Aulicus* people would see that the court was "neither so barren of intelligence" nor its affairs "in so unprosperous conditions" as pamphlets made them seem. "It was thought fit," he wrote, "to let them [people] truly understand the state of things so that they may no longer pretend ignorance, or be deceived with untruths."

Birkenhead, assisted by Peter Heylin, the "proud priest," made a distinct contribution to the developing newspaper and editorial writing. They were the first to divide a news publication into sections. *Aulicus* had three parts: the news itself, comments on the news, and refutations of utterances in the parliamentary diurnalls. In the two opinion sections, Birkenhead apparently was trying to create dissension between Parliament and London, between individual members of Parliament, between the House of Commons and the House of Lords, between London business interests and the rest of the country, and between England and Scotland. Nothing seemed too absurd to escape his divisive attacks, as when he wrote in the fourth issue that the Lord Mayor of London had been illegally elected and, therefore, his orders should not be obeyed.

With an apparent pipeline to Parliament, Birkenhead abusively attacked the Earl of Essex and John Pym's leadership. A master propagandist, he used guilt by association, innuendo, and smear in his attempts to influence readers.[11] He claimed civilians and soldiers had lost confidence in the Earl of Essex, commander of the Parliamentary armies. A few issues later, Birkenhead criticized Cromwell, then a colonel in the Parliamentary army, by calling him "a bloody, greedy bore" who delighted in defacing churches.[12] And he called Pym's death in 1643 a happy event and said the "disease-laden body" made "a most loathsome and foul carkasse." [13]

Inevitably there were answers to *Aulicus,* especially after copies were either smuggled into London or reprinted on hidden presses there. Between spring 1643 and summer 1645, a dozen pamphlets and newsbooks attacked the Royalist publication. Among these was the newsbook, *Kingdomes Weekly Intelligencer,* compiled probably by Richard Collings. This publication generally praised Parliament, labeled the King's advisors as evil, and identified Royalists as Papists. Early attempts by Collings at anti-Royalists propaganda seemed somewhat clumsy. Later his arguments would become more reasoned. In 1645 he defended use of the *Book of Common Prayer* by writing that if the book was suppressed, people would hear no more about it. The difficulty, he said, was "in breaking off a people from Custome (a second nature), which once done they seldom think of returning to their flesh pots more." Many "Malignants" were "now convinced of their former errors in that particular, that should that Service be taken againe, they would be as great non-conformists as any." [14]

Ordinarily, though, Collings was no match for Birkenhead. His editoriallike utterances were too vague and platitudinous. Once he wrote that liberty was "a precious enjoyment," but if it was "not bounded and limited," it would run into "exorbitances." God had "given limits to the ocean," and without government, confusion would follow. "We are not to do what we will, but what we ought. It is imbecility to yield unto evils, but it is folly to ravish them." [15]

After the army occupied London, Collings, as other newsbook authors, often omitted his editoriallike openings, and his asides were concerned with events, not issues. In the few prefaces that he wrote, he was careful to be against sin and for God. He praised the occupying army and questioned the right of people to pry into state affairs.

Even in the early days of *Aulicus,* other newsbook compilers were more outspoken than Collings. The unknown author of *An Antidote Against Malignant Influence of Mercurius Aulicus* claimed that the purpose of his publication was to vindicate Parliament, its army, and London from aspersions cast on them by *Aulicus*.[16]

In June 1643 Parliament again had taken time to legislate against the outpouring of newsbooks, and Henry Wally had been appointed a prepublication censor of pamphlets and newsbooks. But again Parliament's ordinance had proved ineffective, particularly against the "scandalous Royalist pamphlets" coming from hidden London presses. As a result another spate of weekly newsbooks sympathizing with Parliament and attacking *Aulicus* had hit London streets.[17]

The *Parliamentary Scout* was one of the first of this new crop of newsbooks to be published. It was compiled and written by John Dillingham, whose style was usually too long-winded to be very effective. He used the standard anti-Royalist arguments, as when he wrote that "the people of England, had they been unanimous for their good, might have been the balancing power of Christendome, and the glory of the world," but now they had become "the slaves and villaines to French, Irish, and Papists." [18]

In spite of his style, however, Dillingham added a new dimension to his editoriallike comments. In his aside remarks and opening paragraphs he apparently tried to appeal to the less sophisticated Londoners and countrymen. Once in reporting a battle, he commented in an aside that the King's men fought as if they would be made barons and knights while Parliament's soldiers fought as if they were guarding "the libertie of our posterity."[19]

Dillingham's opening paragraphs in the *Parliamentary Scout* have been called the first of the leading articles—the term in British journalism for editorials.[20] Certainly these utterances can be called quasi editorials, as in such introductory sentences as: "Our Scout is much discouraged and hath thoughts of adventuring abroad no more. The reason is that he cannot be allowed to tell the truth" without being censured by a Royalist.[21]

As did other newsbook compilers of that era, to keep from being arrested, Dillingham had to apologize to his readers. Although he was able usually not to offend either side in the Cromwell-Manchester dispute or in the religious toleration issue, he could not conceal his liberalism in his asides. And he was imprisoned in February 1645. When he was released a few months later, he started another newsbook, the *Moderate Intelligencer*. He used asides in this publication to plead for better medical treatment of soldiers on both sides and for back payment of soldiers—a rare early example of news criticism on social inequities.

In June 1646 Dillingham complained that "so much

exception had been taken by one or the other" about his news-book commentary that he hardly knew "what to say or what to narrate." In such times it was good not "to hold arguments, only to ask questions." [22] From that point, Dillingham became even more cautious with his comments. As Collings did, he sprinkled the pages of the *Moderate Intelligencer* with platitudes and proverbs and used fewer and fewer editoriallike paragraphs. Finally he, too, was reduced to using such phrases as "some say," "others say," and "that no offense be taken, no more shall be said."

Another of the new crop of newsbooks, the *Weekly Account*, was first issued September 6, 1643. It was compiled and written by Daniel Border, who devoted a major portion of his publication to detailed refutations of recent arguments in *Aulicus*. His weekly quasi editorials were long-winded and filled with self-conscious piety. But he made a distinct contribution to news-opinion writing by giving opposing sides of a controversy in the same story. For example, in a story about the controversial Lilburne (August 20, 1645) he began with praise for Lilburne, then gave an "on-the-other-hand" discussion, and ended with a reprimand to Lilburne for being involved in politics. Too, on occasions Border wrote his commentaries in a kind of purple prose, typical of other newsbook commentators of the period. One such passage perhaps can be regarded as a forerunner of the nature editorial used by some modern newspapers:

> Walking this morning forth into the Wood alone, I know not whether to increase or allay my melancholy by the beautie and musicke of the Spring; there I might behold . . . the flowers. . . . The musicke was placed on every tree. . . . But tell me, Readers, is this not a Lazie and ungrateful speculation to regard the delights of Peace when Warre has almost covered this nation with fire and blood? [23]

By the summer of 1648 when his *Weekly Account* died temporarily, Border had stopped writing quasi editorials and asides.

Although both Dillingham and Border attacked *Aulicus* in their newsbooks, it was not until *Mercurius Britanicus*, Parliament's own propaganda journal, made its appearance that Birkenhead had a formidable opponent. *Britanicus* had two conductors—Captain Thomas Audley, later to become a deputy licenser of the press, collected information and Marchamont Nedham (or Needham) wrote it. Like Birkenhead, Nedham was an Oxford graduate, a lawyer, and a talented writer. Their scurrilous utterances were as poisonous as those that later appeared in American newspapers during the party press era. Birkenhead was known as the wittier and the livelier of the two; Nedham, as the greatest master of the invective.[24] The battle between the two continued for more than two years.

Nedham, who would later switch allegiance to the Royalists, used three-fourths of the space in *Britanicus* to answer and smear Birkenhead. In rough billingsgate, the former assaulted the Queen, indicted Charles for his pro-Catholicism, ridiculed lords and persons of quality, and refuted Birkenhead's name-calling. As time passed, Nedham grew even more abusive in his *Britanicus* comments. He praised generals with Presbyterian leanings, opposed freedom of speech, questioned the principle of religious toleration, advocated the remodeling of the army, and attacked the evil advisors of the King.

And he continued to insult Birkenhead. In one paragraph, Nedham addressed Birkenhead as a "mathematical liar," who framed "lies of all dimensions, long, broad, and profound lies," and who then played "the botcher, the quibbling pricllouse every week in tacking and sticking" the lies together. "I tell thee," Nedham continued, "thou art a knowne notorious forger: and though I will not say thou art (in thine own language, the sonne of an Egyptian whore), yet all the world knowes thou art an underling pimpe to the whore of Babylon, and thy conscience an arrant prostitute for base ends." [25]

In August 1645 Nedham dared to call for the arrest of Charles with a "hue and cry" in such offensive language that he and the licenser who had not censored the commentary were imprisoned. This was the end of *Britanicus*, but not of Nedham, as will be seen.

Still another newsbook compiler of the early 1640's was George Smith, the probable author of *Compleate Intelligencer and Resolver*, a weekly news publication that lasted four or five issues. Smith introduced the question-and-answer technique for commenting on news, a device that was to be used sporadically and more effectively by later journalists. In *Compleate Intelligencer*, he devoted a fourth of its eight to sixteen pages to asking and answering questions on news events. In his answers, Smith, a pious and garrulous man, favored aid to the Scots, persecution of Archbishop Laud, and unity of Presbyterians and Independents. In style and intent, his answers can be called precursors of the newspaper editorial. Once, for example in answer to a question of why the Lord General's Army advanced but suffered "the enemy thus at Tossiter and Reading," he replied that it was "not fit that his Army should expose themselves so in parties abroad as the Forces under other Commanders, because he ought to be a constant standing Bulwarke to the city and Parliament" and "keep up the reputation of our Affaires." [26] Smith also used questions and answers to open the *Scottish Dove*, another newsbook that he authored about this time.

One of the most vicious newsbook authors in 1644 was Durant Hatham. A Cambridge graduate and member of the lesser aristocracy, he was violently anti-Royalist. In the *Spie*, he swore to readers "never to leave hackneying" to the *Aulicus*, which would breathe its last in September 1645; and he vowed to turn an "errant Jockie for your sakes till his very posteriors became parchment and fret and peel like the scalp of any courtier." [27] He went so far as to attack the Royalists for sexual aberrations.[28]

By early 1645 newsbooks had become not only a profitable business but also a potent force in molding public opinion. London had a population of about five hundred thousand, and perhaps one-fourth of the adults there could read. John Rushworth, a lawyer, was now the licenser. Under him, the press was relatively free, and a new crop of newsbook authors appeared.

One of these was Henry Walker, who would become a leading newspaper author in the 1650's. He wrote vigorous anti-Catholic and anti-Royalist editorial asides in *Perfect Occurrences of Parliament*. His comments were conspicuously pious and vitriolic. Perhaps in the hopes of escaping punishment, he changed the name of his publication to *Public Occurrences* and followed in Butter and Bourne's footsteps by using a pseudonym, Luke Harruney.[29] However, as political tensions mounted in 1647, his comments and asides dwindled.

Richard Collings appeared on the scene with a new publication, *Mercurius Civicus*. It was as pro-Presbyterian and anti-Royalist as his *Kingdomes Weekly Intelligencer,* which he was still writing. In his *Mercurius Civicus,* which incidentally often carried letters from the American colonies, Collings was especially vitriolic in his attacks on the King. But in some of his lengthy asides he called for betterment of workhouses for the London poor and for education in handicrafts for their children. When rumors of impending censorship kept circulating, he said that "it was good worke" and would "coole the heate of the blood, and the ringworme of any who shall for private gaine have a desperate itch to insult and abuse the Kingdome." [30]

For the most part, in 1647 and 1648, Collings was able to conceal his views by ignoring controversial issues. But once in December 1647 he described Charles, who was then a prisoner on the Isle of Wight, as "overgrown with grief and hair." For this he was hauled before the Committee on Examinations. After that experience, Collings subsided and confined his remarks to attacks on Royalist mercuries.

In the fall of 1647, Gilbert Mabbott, assistant licenser, replaced Rushworth, his director. Mabbott was given extraordinary punitive powers. He could assess heavy fines on transgressing authors, printers, undertakers, and booksellers. He could have newshawks whipped for selling unlicensed newsbooks and pamphlets. Moreover, he was provided with two assistants, twenty deputies, and after January, soldiers. Many newsbooks went underground, but still arrests of compilers were numerous. However when the army moved north again the next summer, arrests and punishments lessened. And once again new mercuries appeared on London streets.

Among the new Royalist organs was *Mercurius Pragmaticus,* written by John Cleveland, a minor poet, and by Nedham, who, after a sojourn in jail, had changed sides. In this publication, Nedham praised anyone who had criticized Independents, derided Presbyterians, saluted Scots one day and snubbed them the next, and poked fun at "copper-nose" Cromwell, whose face was now "more toward an aristocracie than Zion." [31] Of the rebelling London masses, he wrote: "Good God, what a wild thing is Rebellion!" [32] In December

1648 Nedham deserted the doomed *Pragmaticus*; and early the next year he was back in jail.

Another new Royalist newsbook, *Mercurius Elencticus,* was written by George Wharton, an astrologer, who also spent considerable time in jail. He filled his publication with wishful prophecies, denounced Cromwell, and revered the King in customary long-winded sentences. When Charles was beheaded, Wharton wrote that the King had "yielded up his spotlesse soul with alacrity, courage, constancy, Faith, Hope and Charity . . . the Justice of the cause he dyed in." [33]

As other licensers before him, and as some who would follow him, Mabbott began authoring a newsbook. For his publication, he revived a title Dillingham had used earlier, the *Moderate Intelligencer*. Previously, Mabbott had contributed to a short-lived newsbook, the London *Post*. He had enlivened the dull military items that filled this publication with such forthright statements as: "It is vain to trust in Forces, Forts, or Castles, or Towers high as Heaven, for where neither the power of men nor the shower of Bullets can enter, the leane hand of Famine and pale Armie of Disease may." [34]

Now as compiler of the new *Moderate Intelligencer,* Mabbott contributed a simplicity to his editoriallike comments that foreshadowed modern editorial style. In the first issues, he had included reports of foreign events, but these were soon dropped; and Mabbott used all of his space to help the Liberal and Leveller causes. He packed opinion into lead paragraphs of one or two pages and scattered comments throughout his reports. He attacked Presbyterians for their connivance with the King and Charles for being responsible for the bloodshed of thousands. And he pled for a government of the people. "The laws of the government of this land being tirannous and arbitrary, and destructive to the freedom of the people, may be lawfully taken away by the people," he wrote. Until this "be done, the people of this nation are slaves and not Free men." [35]

When Cromwell came to power in 1649, he clamped down on weekly publications; only administrative organs were allowed. This news blackout would set back for many years the evolution of the newspaper editorial, which, during the 1640's had made remarkable strides.

5. PAMPHLETS AND BALLADS

WHILE INVENTIVE COMPILERS of corantos, diurnals, and mercuries were filling the pages of their publications with political commentaries and views of news events, that collateral ancestor of the newspaper editorial, the political and religious pamphlet, was spewing from secret and licensed presses like lava from a volcano. In the newsbook blackout years of 1632–38, pamphlets were plentiful; but it has been estimated that between 1640 and 1660 over thirty thousand were written and that during the turbulent years of 1647 and 1648, twenty-five hundred were circulated through England.[1] Newsbook authors, ministers, actors, politicians, and poets turned to pamphleteering and propounded ideas that later would become common mash for newspaper editorials.

In the 1620's and 1630's the pamphleteer wrote leisurely. He took time to develop his views and ideas; but as opposition to the Crown grew and factions developed within Parliament, scriveners who took few pains to be accurate frequently dashed off pamphlets overnight. Any current topic apparently was fit for discussion in these scurrilous and often treasonous publications.

In spite of the repressive Star Chamber decree in 1637, printing of papish and Puritan pamphlets on which the licenser would not dare place his imprimatur became a highly profitable business. Moreover, pamphlets from Scotland swept across the border like leaves before a windstorm.[2] All were tremendously influential on public opinion. Although they were most useful in cities, where they were read in shops, in drawing rooms, and later in coffeehouses, pamphlets also penetrated into the grassroots of England.

The pamphleteer, like the corantier, was usually a well-read person. While it is true that he often aimed his publication at the moderately learned reader, he also attracted a large popular audience. The anonymous tract, *An Answer to Mis-led Doctore Fearne, According to His Own Method,* which probably first appeared in 1643, no doubt drew readers from all social levels. The author defended Parliament's right to take up "defensive arms" against the king and insisted that punishing a tyrannical ruler was necessary. Such comments probably appealed to all anti-Royalists, of whatever class. However, many pamphlets, filled as they were with biblical references and allusions to such former literary figures as Shakespeare and Jonson, may have appealed more to the drawing-room reader than the ordinary man in London streets.

Because the pamphleteer was much less inhibited than the corantier,[3] newsbook compilers and authors also wrote pamphlets. One was John Birkenhead, who wrote *Two Centuries of Pauls Churchyard,* a witty satire on the Assembly of Divines which had been created by Parliament to work out church reforms, and *Assemblyman,* which was a violent attack on the same group. As has been noted, Birkenhead and his *Aulicus* were attacked in the first six months of that publication in at least a dozen pamphlets.

Marchamont Nedham was another corantier turned pamphleteer. In his *Britanicus,* he had become a kind of press agent for the Nathaniel Fiennes trial. Fiennes, the son of Lord Say, was tried in December 1643 for surrendering Bristol, where he was governor, to Prince Rupert. A pamphlet war erupted over Nedham's press agentry. William Prynne and Clement Walker coauthored a pamphlet, *A Check to Britanicus,* in which they attacked the newsbook compiler for supporting Fiennes. Nedham promptly answered with *A Check to the Checker of Britanicus.* John Taylor also answered with a pamphlet, *Crop-Eare Curried,* in which he took Prynne to task for his part in *A Check.*

There were other pamplet wars. John Cleveland, also a corantier at times, wrote *The Character of a London Diurnal,* which was a brilliant attack on London newsbooks. He was, in turn, answered by other corantiers in such pamphlets as *A Character of New Oxford Libellers.*

Henry Walker, who wrote such vigorous editorial asides

in *Perfect Occurences of Parliament,* probably was the most daring of these pamphleteers. His best-known anti-Royalist pamphlet was *To Your Tents, O Israel.* One day he hurled a copy of this publication into the King's coach. Needless to say, he went to pillory and his printer, Thomas Paine, went to prison.

Though it received little attention in 1644 when it was first printed, Milton's *Aeropagitica* was to become the most influential pamphlet of the time. His great plea for a free press was first a speech to Parliament; as were many other parliamentary speeches of that decade, it was preserved as a printed pamphlet. This, of course, was not the only pamphlet Milton wrote in the 1640's. There were his *Of Reformation in England* and his *Colasterion: A Reply to a Nameless Answer.* The latter was a response to a previously published anonymous tract, *A Book, Intitled, The Doctrine and Discipline of Divorce,* which, in turn, had been a criticism of an earlier Milton book.

During the newsbook blackouts and the periods when Parliament clamped down on newsbooks and seditious pamphlets, printers found a loophole for making money with news ballads. The pamphlet may have been the superior medium for invective, personal attack, and effective ridicule; but the ballad was favored by the common people for its expression of their own feelings and opinions. Royalists, particularly, considered this sheet verse an effective weapon against Parliament. London swarmed at the time with young men of wealth or aristocracy who, as holdovers from feudalism, still believed in the divine right of kings. They gave vent to their ideas in ballads of wine, women, money, power, injustice of fortune, and tyranny of the sword.

But by the 1640's, ballads had become more thoughtful, and political ballads abounded. Many were as vituperative as newsbooks and pamphlets. When the theaters were closed in 1642, many actors turned to ballad writing as a money-making device. They discovered the demand for the news and the satiric sentiments in their verse made their unlicensed printing and easy street sales a profitable undertaking. Posted at night on doors in streets and on trees by the wayside, these news-with-views rhymes could be bought for a penny in nearly every stationer's shop in London. Humble writers, such as John Cleveland, John Taylor, and Martin Parker, who has been credited with many base ballads against the Scots, at risk of pillory, jail, and even life, fought in rhyme for tolerance, liberty, and freedom—all modern editorial subjects.

If ballads were a criterion, popular sympathy was with the King. Ballads favoring royalty during the Bishops' wars were common. "The Soldiers' Delight in the North" described the loyalty of the King's Army and the joy of his men at an opportunity to serve their country. One told of a sea battle near Dover between Holland and Spain. It ended with a verse asking God to bless the King and Queen and bring them victories as he had "Elizabeth in the yeare 88." Others, rejoicing over the King's return to Parliament, reflected the seriousness of the political situation. These included "Glad Tidings of Great Joy," "The Happy Proceedings of This Hopeful Parliament," and "England's Cure after a Lingering Sickness."

Fewer ballads showed hostility to the King. "Judge Berkeley's Complaint" was written after Parliament had impeached that dignitary for agreeing with the King on the ship-money levy.

Of course, many, many ballads still celebrated, with pious sentimentality, such sensational news events as births of Siamese twins, murders, and hideous happenings. The latter were nearly always proclaimed as manifestations of God's wrath. "A Warning for Engrossers" told of what happened to a man who had hoarded corn to starve the poor. It ended:

> *So to Conclude and make an end,*
> *for Peace and Plenty, let us pray,*
> *That God may stand ye poore-mans friend,*
> *for ye Poore are now the rich-mans prey.*

Puritans did not approve of ballads; and when Parliament's army was successful, ballads favoring the Malignants increased. Several ridiculed the Assembly of Divines Committee. Parliament considered these verses scandalous and included them in its suppressive press measures. Still surreptitious ballad printing continued to flourish vigorously. However, as 1650 neared, the best ballad writers turned to pamphleteering, and the news ballad fell temporarily into decay after Parliament passed its most repressive ordinance against printing in 1649.

Meanwhile, on far away American shores, settlers must have looked forward in summer months to the arrival of ships from England with copies of corantos, diurnals, mercuries, pamphlets, and news ballads. And when the ships set sail for their return voyage, personal letters containing news and views of happenings in the colonies returned to friends and relatives in England. Some of these, as has been noted, found their way into newsbooks.

Particularly in the Massachusetts Bay Colony, which was destined to become the "cradle of American journalism," the first generation of settlers had little time for reading and less time for writing opinions. They were too busy hacking homes and livelihoods from the wilderness. The first press did not arrive until 1638, and it belonged to Harvard College, which had been founded only two years before. It took several months before this press could function for its stated purpose of producing "religious texts needed in schools and colleges."

The political-religious struggle in England was mirrored in the New England colonies. Idealistic ministers were the ruling and influential class. Those who emigrated to the Plymouth colonies in the 1620's (known as Independents) became embroiled with the Puritans, or Presbyterians, most of whom emigrated in the 1630's. The Independents believed in the right of self-government in the church; the Puritans believed in only one authoritative church and thought the desire for liberty in worshipping sinful. Inevitably a few of the more daring expressed their opinions in pamphlets.

The chief proponents for Puritan theocracy were John Cotton and John Winthrop, while the chief proponents for the Independents were Thomas Hooker and Roger Williams. What they wrote, though, had to be sent to England for printing because the Cambridge press was too busy printing textbooks. Besides its printing was inferior to that in London. Gregory Dexter, back in London, seemed to have been the chief printer for the colonial divines. In the 1620's and early 1640's he printed tracts by John Cotton, John Eliot, and Roger Williams, in which the authors set down their hellfire and brimstone ideas. In *Bloudy Tenant,* Roger Williams heaped invectives on John Cotton. But perhaps the most out-standing product of the times was Nathaniel Ward's *Simple Cobbler of Aggawam,* a mingling of satire and religious politics.

In reality there was very little demand in the colonies for printed material until the next decade. The colonials, for the most part being influenced by the pulpit, apparently were content to read month-old corantos from London, Royalist mercuries, and scurrilous pamphlets that filtered across the ocean. It was as if they were waiting for the years, not too far distant, when the colonial press would rival the pulpit as a vehicle for ideas.

6. Death of the Embryonic Editorial

The New England colonials in the 1650's must have cringed with pious horror at the commentary in English newsbooks that inevitably found their way to the American shores. So scurrilous were the pamphlets and so unorthodox the Quaker literature filtering across the Atlantic that a court ordered all such books confiscated and burned. New arrivals bringing such books with them were deported, and anyone found concealing such publications was heavily fined.[1]

Perhaps it was as well that Edward Winslow, the colony's agent, took such steps because the English press at mid-century was no example of purity for the colonials to follow. John Taylor, the Royalist printer, had not been too far wrong when he wrote in *Mercurius Pacificus* in July 1650 that one of the causes of the country's disorders was mercuries with "interwoven and mingled" truths and "falsities, jeers, mocks, frumps, flatteries, scoffs, and fooleries," which were the "spume, fume, scorn, froth of wit and the very dregs of folly." Such editorial utterances about news events as were not repressed during the Commonwealth era were completely obliterated in the early Restoration years. And the embryonic editorial, struggling for emergence in a free press during the 1640's, died aborning. It would not rear its struggling head for another fifty years.

However, the opinionated English press did not cease overnight with the death of Charles I and the enactment of the new licensing ordinance in 1649. The seven licensed weeklies in existence on September 28 of that year were soon replaced by two official licensed newsbooks—*A Briefe Relation* . . . , written by Council of State's own secretary, Walter Frost; and *Severall Proceedings of Parliament,* written by the Clerk to Parliament, Henry Scobell. These were augmented in December 1649 by a third newsbook, *Of Some Passages and Proceedings of and in Relation to Perfect Diurnal of the Armies,* written by John Rushworth, former licenser. The latter two would last until their final suppression in 1655.

In *A Briefe Relation,* Frost eliminated the introductory paragraphs of comment that had become almost commonplace in the 1640 newsbooks, used little or no discussion with his news accounts, which were again confined to foreign events, and devoted his few asides to praise of Cromwell and his activities.[2] It is small wonder that this publication, whose author thanked God for little news at home,[3] proved so unpopular that it was soon out of business.

Subauthor of *Severall Proceedings in Parliament* was Henry Walker, the pamphleteer who had flung his *O Israel* into the King's coach. Early in 1650, he became the newsbook's principal author.[4] Apparently, however, his trip to the pillory had taught him a lesson, for he abandoned almost all comment on controversial issues. Once (May 8, 1651) he criticized buyers and sellers of unlicensed newsbooks and warned them of their punishment. And five months later he printed a letter from the New England colonies telling of the pains and pleasures of converting Indians.

Walker opened each issue with a paragraph or two of innocuous, verbose statements favoring God, honesty, and wisdom. He even berated Quakers as disruptive and ungodly, and he insisted that the Lord stood with the Protectorate.[5] The newsbook author followed the same practices in his *Perfect Passages of Every Daies Intelligence,* a supplement to *Severall Proceedings.* Perhaps both newsbooks, which survived until the fall of 1655, lasted as long as they did because they never became important propaganda vehicles.

Rushworth, now secretary of the New Model, was assisted in conducting *A Perfect Diurnall of Some Passages* . . . by the ubiquitous Samuel Pecke. Evidently wishing to stay out of trouble, Pecke obeyed all laws and ordinances. He filled the publication with government "handouts." In his few comments, he restricted himself to praise of Protectorate policies and of Cromwell. Although he could write more clearly than many other newsbook authors of the era, he could not keep *A Perfect Diurnall* alive.[6]

When Cromwell returned from Ireland in 1650, the black curtain of newsbook suppression lifted slightly, and two long-run official weeklies were born. The first, and most important in its contributions to editorial development, was *Mercurius Politicus,* mouthpiece for Cromwell's administration. Its author was none other than Marchamont Nedham, who had been bribed to change sides again. But the director of this newsbook was the official licenser, Milton. As secretary of Foreign Tongues, Milton the year before had examined Nedham's *Mercurius Pragmaticus* for suspicious utterances, whereupon Nedham had gone to Newgate again. Soon after he emerged from there late in 1649, he had been paid fifty pounds for services rendered to the government, promised an annual stipend of one hundred pounds, and given the authorship of *Politicus.*[7] Possibly to show that he had changed sides as he promised, he wrote his powerful pamphlet, *The Case of the Common-wealth of England Stated.* This publication would prove useful in his contributions to *Politicus.*

As in his former newsbooks, Nedham not only used editorial asides but also began each issue with a page or two of editoriallike opinions. In the first fifteen issues, the breezy flippancy of his quasi editorials in the former *Pragmaticus* was apparent in his attacks on Royalists, Presbyterians, and Scots and in his "puffs" for the Commonwealth. He set a light, slangy tone in "lead" sentences. For example, in issue thirteen, he wrote: "Since my Satyrs are offensive (though hitherto they have been moderate enough) I shall make bold with one of the Prophets to jerk the Pharisees of times." And in the next issue, he wrote: "Alas, poore Tarquin [Charles II], whither wilt thou go! You know in Numb. 5 I told you, all my feare was, that He and His Jackies [Scots] would stand to it."

But with the sixteenth issue, the tone of these lead editorial utterances changed; and for the next forty-four numbers, Nedham began with serious editoriallike discussions in which he appealed to Royalists, Presbyterians, and Levellers to submit to the new government. Because of the swift change in tone and perhaps because Milton was licensing newsbooks, some authorities have claimed that the poet wrote these commentaries. In actuality, they were lifted, with a few additions and deletions, from *The Case of the Common-wealth*.[8]

The first of these serious lead disquisitions began: "CAN it in reason be expected that such refuse obedience to Authority, should receive the benefit of Protection—In answer to this Question, our first Politick maxime is set down in the negative, and grounded upon the following considerations."[9] Nedham followed this with thoughtful remarks on political theory. The reasoned logic of his arguments and their organization became more apparent as the weeks went by. True freedom, he wrote late in September 1651, did not consist in a license to do as you wish nor in exemption from taxes that were necessary for safety. Then he listed the "particulars" of true freedom as:

> First, In having wholesome Lawes suited to everymans taste and condition. Secondly, In a due and easie course of administration, as to Law and Justice, that remedies of evill may be cheap and easy. Thirdly, In a power of altering Governments and Governors upon occasion. Fourthly, in an uninterrupted course of Successive Parliaments. . . . Fifthly, In a free election of members to sit in every Parliament.[10]

Such discussions ceased early in October, but by the end of that month, Nedham was writing another series of forty-four serious discussions, each about four pages long. These he would publish five years later as a pamphlet, *The Excellence of a Free State*.[11] Again there was the question of whether Milton or Nedham wrote these quasi editorials. But Milton was only an associate. He may have added sentences, suggested topics, and supplied facts; but authorities now believe that Nedham was more likely the author.

Preaching the democratic principles of the right of people to have a voice in their government, Nedham was clearly and effectively defending the Cromwell regime. He pleaded for an enlightened public when he wrote that people should know what freedom was and enjoy it "in all its lovely Features" so that they could "grow zealous and jealous of it." Without question, he said, people should become "acquainted and thoroughly instructed in the means and rules" of freedom's "preservation against the adulterous wiles and rapes of any

projecting sophists." And he pointed out that "all incon-
veniences" had resulted from the ignorance of these "means
and rules that should have been communicated" to the people.[12]

Perhaps these lead discussions in *Politicus* were the
greatest single contribution to the evolution of the modern
editorial in that era. The device of printing a series of political
discussions first in newspapers and later as a pamphlet would
be used by English and American newspaper contributors in
the next century. And certainly Nedham's articles were forerunners of the English "leading article," counterpart of the
American editorial. Although too long for a modern editorial,
Nedham's utterances were designed to influence, as well as to
inform, the largest audience that *Politicus* could reach. Since
this newsbook became the most profitable and popular publication of its kind, Nedham probably reached a rather large
readership.[13]

Commentary in *Politicus,* however, was not confined to
lead discussions. Nedham used asides to praise Cromwell and
the Protectorate; and as was still customary, he impregnated
his news reports with opinions. In an account of a strike at
Newcastle (August 24, 1654), he wrote:

> We have had a great stop of trade by our own keel-
> mens pretence of too small wages from their masters;
> they all as one man stand together, and would neither
> work themselves, nor suffer others though our mayor used
> all possible means to satisfie them; whereupon he made a
> Proclamation but all was to no purpose. And now though
> a company of foot and a troop of horse be drawn into
> town, they continue their obstinacie.

In the meantime, Milton had been replaced as licenser
by John Thurloe, Cromwell's postmaster general and secretary of state; and Nedham, probably under Thurloe's tute-
lage, began writing an adjunct to *Politicus,* called the *Publick
Intelligencer.* The former was issued on Thursday, and the
latter on Mondays. Both were registered newsbooks. In his
new publication, Nedham gushed with praise for Cromwell
and with support for the government. He viciously attacked
opponents of the Protectorate—Quakers, Fifth Monarchists,
Royalists, and republicans.

But it was inevitable that Nedham, being the kind of

person he was, would eventually run afoul of authorities. In August 1655 Cromwell ordered enforcement of laws against the press and provided three new commissioners, one being the Lieutenant of the Tower, to carry out his directive. This action left Nedham with the only subsidized weekly for more than three years. He no longer printed lead discussions regularly. In the few that he did write, he was careful to return to his old breezy, jocular style. Apparently he was trying to toe the Cromwell line. But he must have displeased someone in power because in May 1659 he was removed as author of *Politicus*.[14]

Immediately he started his own weekly, the *Moderate Informer*; but when this proved impracticable, he wrote another long pamphlet, *Interest Will Not Lie*. Because he pointed out in this publication that all factions would benefit from an English republic, Rump Parliament was pleased and returned *Politicus* and *Intelligencer* to him. This time Nedham kept the two weeklies entirely inoffensive. However, after it became apparent that Charles II would be restored to power, the newsbook author made the mistake of criticizing Henry Muddiman [Gent], then the journalist darling of the Royalists. At this point, *Politicus* and *Intelligencer* were suppressed. And Nedham, who had done so much to refine early editorial attempts, fled to Holland with other Commonwealth personalities.[15]

The other officially licensed newsbook was printed in French and designed to explain Commonwealth policies to Continental readers. However, *Nouvelles Ordinaires de Londres* enjoyed a fair sale in London streets. Distributed by Nicholas Bourne, the courant printer of the 1622–49 era, it was written by William Dugard. He was probably aided by Milton, since the publication was sanctioned by the Council of State. Dugard relied heavily on government "handouts"; and although in his editoriallike expressions he was careful to be inoffensive, the newsbook died early in 1658.[16]

Despite restrictive licensing acts which grew even more repressive, Cromwell was not able to close down all newsbooks. His laws were resisted not only in London but also in provinces where printers were not above counterfeiting the licenser's imprimatur. After the Lord Protector dismissed

Rump, several unlicensed newsbooks suddenly appeared. Actually about twenty different newsbooks were being printed every week, although for the most part they contained no news about or comment on Parliament.[17] And it took more than two years, after the press act of 1649 was renewed in 1653, to ferret out and close down the underground Loyalist press. It was only after Cromwell enforced the press laws in 1655 that complete news darkness, except for Nedham's two publications, enveloped England.

Almost all newsbooks that had sprung up before this blackout were known to the reading public synonymously with their printers or undertakers because these were the men who set policies for their publications. Their hired authors were holdovers from the 1640's. However, their few editorial utterances never compared to Nedham's quasi editorials.

Among the returnees to the journalistic wars of the Commonwealth era was Richard Collings, who brought back his old *Weekly Intelligencer* for a few issues in the summer of 1651 and later for a five-year period. Though Collings was now writing in a "clear and disciplined" style, he restricted his comments to innocuous issues. If he thought he might have been outspoken, he was quick to apologize, as when he spoke against the "damned opinion of Predestination" and later said that an "unknown gentleman" had written the statement.[18] This excuse would be used much later by printer-publishers in America.

But Collings could still be logical in his deductions. "How black is the flower in my hand, and fairer than Beauty its self," he wrote in the September 7, 1652, issue. "Just so are cities which to Day are flourishing in all their glory, and tomorrow trembling at the voice of the Canon, and ugly as the face of ruine." Although his direct criticisms were rare, Collings occasionally showed compassion for Irish victims of famine and pestilence.[19] The press crackdown closed the *Weekly Intelligencer* in September 1655. Either Collings or Samuel Pecke revived it as the *Weekly Intelligencer of the Commonwealth* for thirty issues during the regime of Cromwell's son, "Tumbledown Dick." But, other than pious asides, there were few comments.

Another returnee was Daniel Border, who, like Walker, opened his various newsbooks with dull, trite statements against Presbyterianism and in favor of piety, honest government, and self-discipline. In June 1650 he revived the *Impartial Scout* for nine issues and resurrected the *Perfect Weekly Account* for four or five issues. The next year he tried the *Faithfull Scout,* and once he issued the *Armie Scout.* But these were off-again-on-again newsbooks. Border was frequently called in by authorities for questioning about offensive utterances in his opening paragraphs of commentary and his editoriallike asides.

Perhaps more than any other newsbook author, Border dared to criticize the government. When the nominated Parliament was dissolved, he wrote a two-page analysis of the reasons.[20] Although his opening paragraphs of commentary on current events were usually platitudinous, he could not keep his publication alive after 1655. Later he tried to revive the *Scout* under such various preceding adjectives as *Faithfull, National,* and *Royal.* Again he used opening paragraphs of trite comment. But this did not work either; and in 1660 the *Scout* breathed its last issue.[21]

Border was probably also the author of the *French Intelligencer,* a short-lived newsbook in the early 1650's. In this he was prone to his usual verbose, pro-Royalist, interwoven commentary. In an account of a solar eclipse, he inserted this remark: "I am sure no man more compassionates that Star-crossed gentleman [Charles II] than the author of this weekly sheet; and I desire that his condition may be a lively example to those . . . who rule over their Fellow-Commoners." [22]

Still another returnee was John Crouch, whose *Man in the Moon,* an unlicensed Royalist mercury, was addressed to a low-class audience. In unusually crude billingsgate, Crouch attacked Cromwell for granting an imprimatur to papistical and regicidal books and justified the divine right of kings with the theory that "all just power" was "derived from God to the King" and from "the King to the people." All other power came from "the Devil, usurped, wicked, false." [23] Even Royalists had rejected this theory.[24]

Of course, Crouch went to jail, but when he returned to the outside world, he began authoring *Mercurius Democritus.* Under various names this publication lasted until 1655. In it, Crouch avoided comment on politics. Instead he attacked rival newsbooks and offbeat religious sects, particularly the

Quakers, with smutty diatribes and caricatures. When *Democritus* was closed, Crouch tried *Laughing Mercury* and, after another sojourn in jail, *Mercurius Fumigosis,* which lasted until October 1655. Following Cromwell's death, he revived *Democritus* and *Fumigosis* for about eight issues each and *Man in the Moon* for one issue.[25] But by this time, comment even in his jocular, smutty vein was not allowed; and another newsbook author faded from the journalism scene.

Two newcomers made their appearance in the newsbook arena in the 1650's. One was George Horton, a printer-bookseller, whose *Moderate Occurrences* and *Faithful Post* contained a few personal asides. It is not known whether Horton wrote these newsbooks or whether he hired an author. At any rate, they did not last long; and later he tried variously *Great Britain's Post,* the *Political Post,* and the *Grand Politique Post.* Daniel Border may have written the latter, and he probably did write the aside comments in the *Weekly Post,* which superseded the *Grand Politique Post.* In the former, the author was extremely outspoken against the Quakers. Border also wrote the *Post* when Horton revived it for several months in 1659.[26] It was then that the two pleaded for peace and obedience in introductory quasi editorials.[27] Horton's real significance to the development of opinion writing lay in his relationship with Border as an early example of publisher-editorial writer relationship, one in which the two men agreed on what should be printed.

The other newcomer was known only as "B. D.," a printer who may have hired someone to write *A Perfect Account.* "B. D." omitted opening paragraphs of comment and was cautious and mild in his few anti-Quaker remarks. His asides tended more toward "editorial policy" than toward comment on issues. Once he apologized for using the English spelling of a French name.[28] Aside from being the printer behind the author, "B. D." contributed little to the fading practice of writing quasi editorials.

Though there would be other attempts to publish newsbooks, as will be seen, the use of introductory quasi editorials and asides for editoriallike utterances had come almost to a standstill by 1660. Those who wished to comment on news events and public affairs would find another medium for their arguments.

7. ENTER THE PAMPHLET

WITH THE RESTORATION and the continued newsbook black-out, writers turned more and more to the pamphlet for the dissemination of their views. As could have been expected, several newsbook authors, particularly those with Royalist leanings, tried a comeback when it became apparent that Charles II would ascend the throne. But only two of any importance emerged in the 1660–65 years. And they were instrumental in pushing editorial utterances into pamphlets.

One of these was Henry Muddiman. As the first newsbook author to climb aboard the Restoration bandwagon, he became the spokesman for the revived monarchy. Muddiman, who had never written for the press, came to London in 1659 at the behest of Sir Thomas Clarges, a Strand apothecary who was a brother-in-law of Lord General Monck. Sir Thomas had obtained permission from Rump Parliament to establish a bi-weekly newsbook; and he chose as his writer the son of a Strand tradesman, Henry Muddiman, a schoolmaster.[1]

In the *Kingdomes Intelligencer* and its adjunct, *Mercurius Publicus,* Muddiman had never been controversial. However, he had praised Monck and printed the general's manifestoes. In fact, it was his promotion of Monck and his vilification of the "good old cause" (as the Protectorate came to be called) that had rankled Nedham into attacking Muddiman, with the result that Nedham's newsbooks were suppressed for the final time.[2]

From his office at the Seven Stars in the Strand, Muddiman conducted his monopolistic newspapers until 1663. He gave little or no trouble to the official licenser, Sir John Birkenhead, the Royalists' vitriolic mercury writer of the 1640's. Neither did he contribute to the evolution of editorial writing. But his development of the writing of news events, as much as any other one factor, drove opinion writing for a time into pamphlets.

This is not to say that Muddiman did not comment on news events. He did. It was still the practice to clothe news accounts in an aura of comment, and Muddiman was as good at this as any other newsbook author. When he reported the coronation of Charles II, he wrote that the "sacred" ceremony "exceeded even the expectations of all beholders (whether foraines or natives) as well as the example of all his Glorious Ancestors." Heaven and earth had "conspired" to make "the occasion glorious," and "the weather itself (as once the Sun)" stood "still on purpose." Moreover, the "giddy brethren (who would all be Rulers and would have no other)" were "forced to confess that as we *never had such a King, so there never was* such a coronation." [3] But this was not separating the report of an event from his opinion. It was merely Muddiman's bias showing, much as does the bias of an interpretative reporter three hundred years later.

Known to his contemporaries as a good scholar and an arch rogue who wrote newsbooks for the money only,[4] Muddiman built up a rather good news-gathering organization of correspondents. When his publications were taken from him in 1663, he used this organization—a staff of clerks and a postal franking privilege, granted previously—to start a handwritten newsletter which he circulated biweekly for five pounds a year. In Parliament's press ordinances, no provision had been made to suppress handwritten newsletters. Thus, with freedom to write reports of Parliament's proceedings, Muddiman made news a more salable product than editoriallike commentary. And newsletters, which had never really disappeared, again became popular.

When the last great plague epidemic in London drove the King and his court to Oxford in 1665, Joseph Williamson, undersecretary of state, received permission to start a newssheet. Called the Oxford *Gazette,* it was moved after twenty-three issues to London and renamed the London *Gazette.* Issued twice weekly, it was written by Muddiman. But in its half-sheet folio form with its contents printed in two columns, Muddiman refrained from separate comment.[5] In reality, London *Gazette* was a long newsletter.

Roger L'Estrange was the other newsbook author. In 1663 he tried to bring comment back to newsbooks; but in this he was a failure. A rabid Royalist and a Cavalier pamphleteer, L'Estrange had spent four years in Newgate after a last-minute reprieve from a death sentence. During the weak, confused reign of Richard Cromwell, Cavaliers had used the press to gain ambitions, long held dormant under Oliver's rule. L'Estrange had entered the politico-press arena at this time. His pamphlets, often called libelous, were outspoken in their criticism of those who were trying to keep London quiet until Parliament could meet. By 1660, however, there was no further need to use the press to advance the Loyalist cause. L'Estrange, nevertheless, was one of the rash Loyalists who annoyed Charles II with incessant demands for revenge of the "good old cause" advocates. As a result, L'Estrange was not awarded the sole privilege of writing the two licensed newsbooks. Muddiman had received that pleasure.

Bitter at this rebuff, L'Estrange wrote a series of invective pamphlets in which he attacked the press. He also haunted the halls of Westminster to buttonhole members of Parliament and report instances of libel. Late in 1661, he issued *To the Earl of Clarendon, the Humble Apology of Roger L'Estrange,* a vituperative attack on Presbyterianism, in which he cleared himself of charges of disloyalty and attacked the illicit press. For this pamphlet and for his work as a self-appointed watchdog of the press, L'Estrange was awarded the Surveyorship of the Press.

With the legal power to search and seize, he then turned his amateur scouting into a nightmare for printers. He scoured the shops in Little Britain and St. Paul's Churchyard, confiscated libelous pamphlets (those which were concerned with the opposing side of any issue), and arrested printers. In April of the next year, he published *A Momento, directed to all that truly reverence the memory of King Charles the Martyr,* a pamphlet discussing the rise, fall, and remedies of the licentious press. He specifically attacked the Stationers' Company. Then in June, he issued *Considerations and Proposals of the Press,* a pamphlet in which he set down the penalties of death, mutilation, imprisonment, and abandonment for the offences of blasphemy, heresy, treason, scandal, and contempt of authority. This publication aided L'Estrange in realizing his ambition, the authorship of the monopolistic newsbooks. Muddiman was ousted; L'Estrange took over in August 1663.[6]

Almost his first act was to shorten the titles of the two newsbooks to *Intelligencer* and to *Newes*. He cut the size of the publications from sixteen to eight pages and used most of these to expose week by week the shortcomings of the press. In his first issue, August 31, he devoted almost all of the space to comment and included only six small items of news. In his first paragraph, he declared that even "supposing the Press [was] in order, the people in their right wits, and news or no news to be the question," he would never vote for a public mercury because he thought such publication would make "the multitude too familiar with the actions and counsels of their superiors, too pragmatical and censorious." It would give readers "not only an itch but a kind of colourable right and license to be meddling with the Government."

After three more long paragraphs in which he named newshawkers as guilty of seditious libel and treason and in which he promised with much circumlocution not to repeat stories, L'Estrange discussed his official duties. And he offered a reward to anyone who discovered a libel in printing, an unlicensed book in print, or a seditious books being sold by hawkers.

In his opening quasi editorials L'Estrange was vicious in his loyal support of the government and was abusive in his attacks on antigovernment factions. So intent was he in his opinion writing that he continued to ignore news, which readers by this time were demanding. He even failed to report the war with Holland. Inevitably his newsbooks which he had turned into political pamphlets, lost ground and were closed in 1666.

Perhaps L'Estrange tried too hard to make his publications a party organ. His efforts to revive quasi editorials that had flourished in the days of *Mercurius Politicus* probably failed because he ignored news. People would read opinion for opinion's sake in pamphlets which they knew were opinions, and they would read opinion mixed with news in newsbooks and newsletters. But primarily at this point they wanted reports of events. They wanted to know what was happening. L'Estrange did not tell them.

Actually, L'Estrange was a much better pamphleteer than he was a newsbook author. Between 1647 and 1666 he wrote at least eighteen pamphlets. He and writers like Milton helped popularize pamphlets as the forum for editorial comment on public affairs by leaders in national and civic life. In the Cromwellian era, pamphleteers had used gross language. In his reply to Salmasius's *Defense Regea,* Milton in Latin called his opponent a blockhead, ass, liar, idiot, dunce, vagabond, and Burgundian slave. Other serious-minded men used pamphlets to attack social and administrative abuses that had grown out of the civil wars and to take sides in controversies that had arisen from Puritan bigotry.[7] Others wrote of the need for legal and prison reforms. Addison and Steele were foreshadowed with lighter veined pamphlets that ridiculed incongruous fashions, inconstancies, vanity, and capriciousness of women. Some pamphlets, in the form of dialogues or letters, probably helped set a pattern for colonial pamphlets and opinion essay-letters of a later period.

During the Cromwellian period, many Royalist pamphlets had been printed in Holland and smuggled into England; after the Restoration, pamphleteers of the "good old cause" wrote their treatises on the continent and smuggled them into the country. On occasions, when one side deemed it necessary to answer a pamphlet blast from the other, a pamphleteer would be engaged to write an answer. And a pamphlet war would erupt.

Nedham and L'Estrange, of course, were prolific pamphleteers. Milton and John Hall were both asked to write pamphlets in answer to charges. John Streater was another political pamphleteer.

Although some pamphlets had to be smuggled into England, repressive press acts seemed to have had little effect on ballad printing. Ballad singing on the streets was stopped, but the rhyming and the printing continued. Political ballads littered London streets. One in 1653 began "have you the hungry bloodhounds seen?" The hounds symbolized a Parliament that killed a king and was looking for another. The next year Humphrey Crouch wrote "Lady Petunia's Journey," in which he spoke sanctimoniously of bloodhounds trampling on crowns and peasants advancing to the throne. By the 1660's, ballads tended to be news relations of sensational events of the "Listen-my-children-and-you-shall-hear" variety. Their influence on public opinion was waning. They were becoming mere entertainment and were passing into the field of literature.

Meanwhile, in the Massachusetts Bay Colony, leaders, struggling to keep alive the idea that only the godly had the right to police the state, kept a rigid hold on the little press at Harvard College. Colonials did not think people had a legal right to freedom of expression, which to them was a form of licentiousness. And they kept control of their press in order to maintain pure religious doctrines and worship, to guard public morality, to defend their charter rights, and to prevent the spread of dangerous ideas. By 1660, the one little press, now run by Samuel Green, patriarch of the famous Green printing family, was so overtaxed that another printing press was brought from England. With it came Marmaduke Johnson, a printer, to assist Green in printing Bibles and primers for Indians, almanacs, laws and other official documents, and a few sermons of approved orthodoxy.[8] Johnson, however, was soon deported for courting Green's daughter when he had a wife in England.

Nevertheless, colonials expressed their religious and political opinions in pamphlets that were printed in England. Inevitably there was trouble. In 1650 William Pynchon wrote a theological pamphlet, the *Meritorious Prince of our Redemption,* which was printed in the mother country. When it was circulated in the Massachusetts colony, the General Court declared the publication erroneous and heretical. All copies were burned publicly. The court also declared that God had called them to punish Pynchon, whereupon the author fled back to London. Furthermore, the court asked John Norton to answer the Pynchon pamphlet.

This was not the first attempt in the colony to stifle opinion. Previously, Richard Saltonstall and Samuel Gorton had been forced to acknowledge and bewail their offensive and blasphemous statements. Later John Eliot wrote the *Christian Commonwealth,* a pamphlet in which he gave his views on the proper form of government and advised that rulers be chosen by election. It appeared in England in 1659; but by this time Restoration was assured, and the General

Court in Massachusetts forced Eliot to acknowledge his error in scandalizing the English government and aristocracy.

The fact that Charles II had appointed a licenser of the press was incentive enough for the Massachusetts General Court to follow in Charles's footsteps. In October 1662, the first formal act of censorship in the American colonies was passed. Under it, nothing could be printed without the approval of Captain Daniel Godkin and Jonathan Mitchell. Although the court rescinded its licensing act after seven months, the appearance in the colony of another printing press sent the court back into session.

In May 1665, Marmaduke Johnson returned from England with a press of his own and petitioned the court for permission to set up a printing establishment in Boston. The court acted by putting teeth into another licensing act. No printing press would be allowed except at Cambridge, and anything printed there had to be passed by two of four censors: John Shearman, Jonathan Mitchell, Thomas Shepheard, or the president of Harvard College. The court was determined that nothing printed in the Massachusetts colony would express an opinion offensive to Charles II and his court party.

The policy of licensing printed opinion would prevail in the colonies for years. And the use of the pamphlet as the medium for disseminating opinion, as in England, would continue. Ideas set down by Milton, L'Estrange, and other English pamphleteers of later periods would influence not only the thought of colonial leaders but also the style and form of their opinion writing.

8. The Editorial Pamphlet

ALTHOUGH IN THE LAST THIRTY-FIVE YEARS of the seventeenth century, licensing acts limited the emerging daily press in England to brief accounts of news events, there were too many controversial social, political, and economic issues for news writers not to find a way to publish their views. It was during this period that the pamphlet, already a recognized opinion medium, came into its own; and serious-minded writers turned to it for commenting on public affairs.

In London, the political center of the country, members of such embryonic political organizations as the Green Ribbon Club did not long confine their activities to mere discussions. If they were to influence public opinion as they obviously desired, they needed a print medium to disseminate their views. With newssheets closed to them, they turned to the pamphlet. If they favored the current administration, it was not difficult to have their pamphlets licensed; if they were dissenters, it was hardly more difficult to find a "moonshine" press.

As it was emerging in the last years of the seventeenth century and as it would be refined in the next century by Jonathan Swift, Daniel Defoe, "Junius," and Thomas Paine, the pamphlet rightfully can be called a forerunner of the newspaper editorial and of the British equivalent: the leading article, or leader. For a very long period it would remain the most effective form for commenting on events and issues.

But unlike the modern editorial, the pamphlet was issued separately and apart from other news accounts, though, within the publication, there was often enough chronicle of a single event to "background" the views of the pamphleteer. Unlike the modern editorial, which, as a specific part of the newspaper, helps to sell the paper, the pamphlet of the seventeenth and eighteenth centuries was not written to make money, though "hack writers" were sometimes employed by political leaders to "ghost" their views. Unlike the modern editorial, the pamphlet was lengthy—sometimes as long as ten thousand words. Unlike the modern editorial which frequently expresses the views of an editorial board, the pamphlet was usually the opinion of one man, who was in a hurry to tell his views. Roger Palmer, Earl of Castlemaine, was in such a rush that he dictated his pamphlet, . . . *the Humble Apology of the English Catholics,* to the printer and then scurried out on the streets to distribute it.[1]

In this sense of immediacy, the pamphlet was similar to the twentieth-century newspaper editorial, and there are other similarities. Like many newspaper editorials, the pamphlet, unbound as were newsbooks, was aimed at a large public and designed to be read quickly and discarded. Usually with clear political implications, it provoked disagreement, as do many modern editorials. It argued a point of ethics or theology, or it was a protest for or against some unpopular movement; and, like the editorial, it tried to persuade the reader to agree. Its writer usually believed that the truth of an issue had been obscured from a public, which, when enlightened, would come to support his ideas.[2]

Press censorship of the late seventeenth and eighteenth centuries favored pamphleteers in England and in the American colonies, even though libelous and scurrilous utterances traditionally characterized their baroque style. In an atmosphere in which the power elite would not permit the oppositionists to speak, illegal pamphlets circulated with comparative ease because there was no adequate police force to confiscate all copies and presses. Pamphleteers probably flourished also because they believed in a kind of democracy, in liberty of opinion, and because honest and good men were on opposite sides of most issues.[3]

The great issue before the English people at that time, and therefore in a broad sense before the colonials, was Protestant succession to the throne. This issue involved Catholics versus Protestants and feudalism versus capitalism. In a way, England was living through a struggle similar to that in the United States three centuries later. Cromwellism had paved the way for capitalism, which would in the next centuries bring, first, revolutions and, then, destruction to one culture after another. Inner cities were turned into ghettoes, and civil wars did not bring either liberty of opinion nor social equality. Some pamphleteers argued progress or retrogression; others, consolidation of what had been achieved. Thus the pamphlet of that era served the purpose of the newspaper editorial and the underground press of a later century.

Midway in the seventeenth century, pamphlets generally lacked reasoned arguments and precise language. Many were satirical and often indecent. But toward the end of the century, the better pamphleteers, such as Andrew Marvell and George Savile, were writing well-organized, documented, and reasoned discourses. Some of these tracts, once considered politically significant, have been preserved as literary essays, their original purpose—to influence public opinion—long forgotten.

The first occurrence in England to touch off a flood of pamphlets in this era was the great fire of September 5, 1666, which destroyed all of London between the Tower and the Temple. Both business and residential districts were leveled. Commercial houses, where merchants and well-fed families lived and worked, met the same fate as houses of the poor. Eighty-nine churches, including St. Paul's, were burned. Bookselling shops and printing houses were destroyed. A half-million people crowded out of the city into the slum districts of the "Liberties." [4]

The fire, coming as it did on the heels of the last great London plague in which twenty thousand perished, affected the political atmosphere for twenty years, and it was the subject of many pamphlets. Rumors were rife. The lower and middle classes thought it was the result of God's anger at the ruling classes. Protestants believed Papists threw fireballs into houses. Even Roger L'Estrange was accused of throwing fireballs and was burned in effigy. [5] Court pamphleteers blamed the disaster on republicans. Typically pro-Protestant was the anti-Papist pamphlet, *London's Flames,* which hinted that the court was trying to suppress the truth. It was promptly banned. Roger Palmer's *Humble Apology of the English Catholics,* which raised a storm of indignation, was one of the numerous apologetic outbursts by Catholics. [6]

Other events inflamed mobs and sent pamphleteers scurrying to printers. Charles II, a secret Papist, favored religious toleration, partly because he hoped to include Catholics in an amnesty policy. His chief advisor, the Earl of Clarendon, Lord Chancellor, blamed all sides for the deterioration of affairs; later he was impeached by Parliament and banished from England. Prisons were then opened, and religious dissenters could assemble for a time; Charles's Declaration of Indulgence, which suspended ecclesiastical penal laws against dissenters, was denounced as a cloak for returning Popery to England and was struck down by Parliament. Then came the Conventicle Act, the Test Act, and the Non-Resisting Bill— all designed in one way or another to make the Anglican church dominant and suppress Catholicism, Presbyterianism, and Quakerism.

In the meantime, Charles had also signed the Triple Alliance, whereby England, Holland, and Sweden were aligned against France. He had hoped to force a secret agreement with France so that he and Louis XIV could divide Holland between England and France. Louis would then advance money for warfare. In return, Charles was to make England a Catholic state. Though this was a secret agreement, the Protestant masses scented war with Holland and papish schemes in every enemy act. By 1678, it was easy for them to believe that Titus Oates story of a Jesuit plot to assassinate Charles. In the ensuing frenzy of street fighting, Catholics were persecuted and imprisoned. When the secret agreement between Charles and Louis was ultimately revealed, Parliament was dissolved and chaos reigned on London streets.

The continuous pamphlet warfare between Protestants and Papists increased in tempo with each event and each rumor. Anything antigovernment was termed seditious. Roger L'Estrange, when forced to give up his newspaper, had lost much of his power as licenser, and libelous tracts flooded the country. Though he claimed to allow them because he was not paid regularly for his work,[7] it was more likely that the sheer number of pamphlets and broadsides made detection impossible. Not only did moonshine printers keep their presses busy, but broadsides and pamphlets poured in from Scotland and from Holland through Bristol, Newcastle, and Hull.[8]

L'Estrange himself found time to write twenty political

pamphlets between 1667 and 1680. Because his sympathies were with the Catholics, he devoted his abusive attacks to Presbyterians.[9] Some of his diatribes were answers to others. For example, in 1679 Ben Harris, who a few years later was to make journalism history in Boston, wrote a pamphlet, *Appeal from Country to the City,* in which he attacked the church and L'Estrange as instruments of Popery. Even though Harris was arrested, tried for libel, fined five hundred pounds, and sent to Newgate, L'Estrange answered the Harris pamphlet with *An Answer to the Appeal from the Country to the City.*[10]

The severe Conventicle Act also inspired many libelous pamphlets. Frank Smith's *Trap and Crucem* attacked the "bloody designs of all the Papists." Colonel John Streater wrote *The Character of a True and False Shepherd,* an anti-Episcopal phillipic, and *A Few Sober Queries on the Late Conventicle Act,* in which he claimed the Act was against the law of God and Magna Charta.[11] Charles Blount, a pamphleteer hired by the Green Ribbon Club, an organization of the developing Whig party, wrote as "Philopatus." One of Blount's better disquisitions was *Just Vindication of Learning and of Liberty of the Press.* His use of a Latin pseudonym to avoid detection, although used sparingly by writers in past eras, would become a common practice for the growing number of political commentators.

Many anonymous pamphlets were biased accounts of events, but these usually were introduced by the old "address to the reader." In purpose, content, and form these introductory remarks were pure editorial and not much different from many in modern newspapers. When William Penn, who was soon to bring Quakers to the North American shores, and William Mead were tried in 1670 on a charge of conspiracy, such an anonymous pamphlet appeared: *The People's Ancient and Just Liberties Asserted.* Its preface was a reasoned, but passioned plea for an end to religious intolerance and corrupt court practices. Except for the opening paragraph, which definitely belongs to the seventeenth century, and the quaintness of the language, it was an editorial in a very real sense.

"If ever it were time to speak or write," the author wrote,

" 'tis now" because "so many strange Occurances" required both. Using the second person, he told his readers that they could judge plainly "how much thou art concerned in this ensuing Tryal (where not only the Prisoners, but the Fundamental Laws of England) have been most Arbitrarily Arraigned." He pointed out that "Liberty of conscience" was counted "a Pretence for Rebellion, and Religious assemblies, Routs, and Riots." And to demand a right was "an Affront to the Court." The author also criticized the Recorder of London for discarding the Magna Charta. Proceedings of the court were called "monstrous and illegal." A man could not reasonably "call his coat his own," when property was made "subservient to the Will and Interest of the Judges." No man could call himself a freeman when all of his pleas for liberty were "esteemed Sedition, and the Laws, that give, and maintain them, so many insignificant pieces of formality." [12]

After several more short paragraphs in which the author related specific faults of London's Recorder and of the Canterbury Chaplain in their parts at the trial, he concluded that "we cannot choose but admonish all, as well as Persecutors, to relinquish their Heady, Partial and Inhuman Prosecutions" and "to reverence and obey, the Eternal just God, before whose great Tribunal, all must render their accounts, and where he will recompense to every Person according to his works."

Another issue often discussed by the pamphleteers was freedom of the press, a frequent editorial topic of modern times. An anonymous pamphleteer in 1696 in *A Letter to a Member of Parliament, shewing that a restraint on the Press is Inconsistent with the Protestant Religion . . .* wrote that there was "no medium between mens judging for themselves and giving up their Judgment to others." The press should not be restrained, "because it debars them from seeing those Allegations by which they are to inform their Judgments." Arguments for regulating the press, he said, only showed "the greatest necessity for the freedom of the Press." The more apt that men were to be mistaken and deceived by events, the more reason there was for them to examine carefully all sides of an issue and "for the Press being open to all Parties, one as well as the other."

He claimed that the Reformation was "wholly owing to the Press" and argued that "the Protestant Clergy," who were as ambitious as the Papists, had "by Persecution, [and] Restraint of the Press" given the Papists the opportunity to insult them. He saw no reason for biased and prejudiced clergymen to be the guardians of the press. If someone had to be a licenser, it should be a layman who had "no Powers, Prerogatives or Privileges to gain by the perverting of Scriptures." And he hoped that legislators "out of respect to the clergy, would not enact such a law as supposeth the greatest and most learned of them to be trusted with the printing of but a half-sheet in Religion without the consent of Lay Licenser." [13]

Such arguments about public affairs issues foreshadowed the pamphlets of Swift, Addison, Defoe, and Steele—all men who would have a decided influence on the form and content of opinion writing in the early colonial press of America. Although pamphlets were forerunners of editorial writing in their purpose and subject matter, they developed as separate entities from the newsletters and newssheets. But there was one brief period, before licensing was abolished in 1695, when another attempt was made to include editorial utterances in newssheets of the time.

In July 1679 the rigid press act had expired, and for several months the press was unrestricted. This was during the Titus Oates affair, and printers were quick to seize the opportunity to compete with the London *Gazette,* Muddiman's authorized news publication. Weekly newssheets devoted to one side or the other of the plot soon were being hawked on London streets. One of the first of these publications, the *Weekly Packet of Advice from Rome* later called the *Weekly Packet from Rome,* belonged to Harry Care. This publication looked like a typical newssheet of the time, with accounts of Continental Reformation events, but interestingly the Rome sheet was accompanied by a separate, single page of comment. Very popular with the masses, it was filled with venomous attacks on Roger L'Estrange who had fled into exile.[14] Although L'Estrange's pamphlets had brought him royal regard, his recriminatory discourses against Oates and others had sent him into exile again.[15] Care's *Weekly Packet* lasted until

July 13, 1683, and Defoe was later to say that it was the prototype for his *Review*.[16]

Other short-lived newsbooks of the period were John Smith's *Current Intelligence*; Ben Harris's *Domestick Intelligence or News From City and Country*; Nat Thompson's *True Domestick Intelligence* and his *Democritus Ridens,* which was probably an answer to John Flatman's *Heraclitus Ridens*; and Francis Smith's *Protestant Intelligence: Domestick and Forein.* Though the introductory paragraphs of most of these publications were comment, they explained editorial policy rather than the author's opinions on issues. John Smith began the first issue of his *Current Intelligence* on April 26, 1681, with:

> Amongst the several Intelligences none hath gained greater Reputation, than that which went formerly by the name *The Current Intelligence.* At the persuasion of some friends the Author does now again resolve to serve the Publick by the same title, with such passages of foreign and domestic affairs, as may be useful as well as pleasing to the reader, without any reflections upon either persons or things, giving only the bair matter of fact, as it shall from time to time occur to his knowledge.

But it was L'Estrange's publication, the *Observator,* which pointed the way to a division of newspapers into two kinds—those reporting news and those commenting on news. With what apparently had become a tradition with many news-sheet authors, L'Estrange returned from his self-imposed exile with an apologetic pamphlet in which he bitterly attacked dissenters. Once more in the good graces of Charles II, who by now was winning support of Parliament, L'Estrange founded the *Observator* as a political newspaper—a ministerial organ.[17]

The first issue appeared April 13, 1681. Though designed as a biweekly, the *Observator,* with two double-column folio pages, often appeared daily. L'Estrange wrote his publication in questions and answers, as a debate between a typical Whig and a typical Tory. He did not invent this form of opinion writing, but he was to make it popular.[18] Although he maintained that the *Observator* was not a newspaper, a term then coming into popular use, its regularity of publication and the use of events as "pegs" for discussions made it a "newspaper" to the masses.[19] And L'Estrange himself must have considered the publication more than a mere pamphlet because in 1685 he found it necessary to write a pamphlet to defend it.

His avowed aim for the *Observator* was "to encounter the faction and defend the government," and he used the publication to gain public acceptance for parliamentary petitions.[20] With vulgar but vivid English, L'Estrange viciously attacked Dissenters, Whigs, Trimmers, and Titus Oates. During the trial of the Earl of Shaftesbury, leader of the opposition to Charles, the *Observator* author was briefed almost daily by government officials for his diatribes against the accused. He defended other actions by the administration and argued for the right of the London mayor to choose a sheriff by the ancient tradition of drinking with him. He also encouraged all printing apprentices, exposed Whig revolt in the church, and attacked dissenting London ministers.[21]

With his return from exile, L'Estrange was granted increased powers as press licenser. Backed by a 1680 proclamation suppressing "the printing and publishing of unlicensed newsbooks and pamphlets of news," he succeeded within only a few months in closing down most of the Whig publications.[22] Although he was noted for his attacks on press freedom, L'Estrange wanted freedom for his own pen. When the printer of the *Observator*, Joanna Brome, was arrested for printing seditious libels, L'Estrange used the columns of his opinion publications to demand the reasons for the jury's verdict and to discuss his ideas of a jury's duties.[23]

But the *Observator* lasted only two years after James II, a Catholic, came to power. L'Estrange, finding he could not support the new king's declarations of tolerance, discontinued his publication early in 1687. The next year he was dismissed as licenser of the press.[24] Later he was accused of fomenting trouble and was twice imprisoned. Although he was intolerant and certainly an influential enemy of free discussion, L'Estrange can be credited with developing trends in opinion writing which would lead to further advancements toward the editorial. His political discussions in the *Observator* and his political pamphlets, although biased, became prototypes for newspaper opinion writers of the next century. Perhaps, even the greater press freedom which was only a few years away may be attributed in part to a reaction against L'Estrange's rigid censorship.

When James fled into exile and William and Mary ascended the throne in December 1688, peace suddenly began settling over England. In this new atmosphere, where in the furious partisanship of politics young children had learned to say Whigs and Tories, where everything new and interesting began to permeate even into the lowest classes, and where urbane manners were being acclaimed, Parliament voted not to renew the licensing act.[25]

During the last decade of the seventeenth century several newspapers were founded; but only one author, John Dunton, was to make any significant contribution to the development of news commentary. Other newspaper writers, apparently not sure of how free the press really was, confined themselves to newsletters or to cautious political comments in their news accounts. Scot George Ridpath in his news reports in the *Flying Post* favored the Whigs, while Abel Roper in the *Post Boy* favored the Tories; and both attacked the King.[26] But Dunton, already famous for his absurd political pamphlets, in 1689 began writing the *Athenian Gazette,* later called the *Athenian Mercury,* for readers "curious in philosophical and recondite" matters. This was a weekly publication devoted to answering queries sent in by readers. Questions covered love, marriage, manners, and clothes. In a few years, Daniel Defoe was to borrow from Dunton these topics as ideas for his own newspaper commentary.[27]

To John Dunton also belongs credit for resurrecting Birkenhead's idea of separating a newspaper into distinct parts. Dunton published another newsbook, *Pegasus,* so named for the woodcut of a postman on a flying horse. Published triweekly, it was more miscellany than newspaper and popularly was called a journal. Dunton wrote in the introductory paragraphs of the first number that "Our design is a TRI-PARTITE PAPER, NEWS, AN OBSERVATION, and a JACOBITE COURANT by three distinct hands." [28] This was to be the composition form in the next generation for such famous journals as *Payne's Universal Chronicler Weekly Gazette,* for which Samuel Johnson was to write his "Idler" papers. The "Observation" section of *Pegasus* contained comments on the passing scene. Dunton's publication was not purely a literary journal, as many such miscellanies came to be considered, nor a mere political discussion as could be found in the political pamphlets of the time. Rather it was a publication that chronicled as well as commented on the news, with a particular section for his comment. In this respect, Dunton was far ahead of his journalistic times. And he had laid the groundwork upon which authors of news publications in the next century could develop and refine their editorial utterances.

9. Early Colonial Tracts and Pamphlets

Although printers were operating in Massachusetts, Pennsylvania, and New York by 1700, news publications were nonexistent. But there were men who wrote their views of events and opinions about public affairs. Most prolific were the religious leaders, still the dominating personalities in the colonial power structure. Following the current practice in the mother country, they too used tracts and pamphlets to disseminate their ideas, though sometimes with unfortunate results.

Much of what was said in these publications was influenced by the same kind of political upheaval and religious reforms that plagued England in the last thirty-five years of the seventeenth century. In the colonies, power was slipping from a religious oligarchy to a royal governor who presided over a council. Property, not religion, was becoming the test for suffrage. With the passing of emigrant generations, literacy had declined. And in such an atmosphere, where every unfamiliar idea was likely to be acclaimed as evidence of the devil, it was easy for witchcraft fanaticism to reach a peak. Proponents of the old order among the clergy and the masses attempted to destroy ideas of a rising new order by accusations of witchcraft.

The New England Puritan, who had turned in early generations to fishing, shipbuilding, lumbering, and ocean trading to supplement his farm income, had bred sons and grandsons who were now becoming New England Yankees—a rising mercantile middle class. These were thrifty, parsimonious, intensely provincial people.[1] In fact, New Englanders had bred so fast that they had sent sons and grandsons into the middle colonies. There Puritan emigrants lived among

Dutch, Swedes, Finns, Huguenots, Palatines, Scots, and Quakers. And there toleration, rather than a particular religious citizenship, was more easily accepted as a basis for political rights than in the uptight Massachusetts colony. Farther down, in Maryland, Virginia, and the Carolinas, a population of varied creeds and races was doomed by soil and climate to remain longer under a Cavalier socio-political government.

The political unrest in England during this period had not been long in reaching New England shores, where it manifested itself against Sir Edmund Andros in a fight to retain old charters. Charles II had appointed Sir Edmund governor of New York in 1674; and James II, disliked by colonials even more than Charles had been, named him governor of the Dominion of New England in 1686. As such, he controlled most of the populated and prosperous sections of the seaboard. His highhanded methods were so detested by the colonials that outright rebellion almost developed. Connecticut even refused to surrender its charter to Andros and hid it in a hollow tree.

Colonial writers reflected this religious and political turmoil through their utterances in tracts and pamphlets. In those early days, when the few presses were tightly fettered by strict licensing acts, the pulpit was the medium for disseminating ideas. Ministers, as the respected leaders of settlements, had their sermons printed. These tracts were sold in the few bookseller shops. In Boston, the Mathers, whose influential writings would extend into the next century, were among the ministers whose sermons, tracts, and pamphlets contributed to religious controversies. They exhorted readers to severe living, denounced prevalent vices, and discussed political and economic development in the colonies. Except for a few sermons printed on colonial presses, pamphlets, for the most part, continued to be sent to England for printing. One reason for this action was that many of these discourses were designed to influence opinion in the mother country as much as, perhaps more than, that in the colonies.

The Mathers, like Roger L'Estrange, did not believe in the value of news and news comment for the masses because if people knew too much about the actions of their superiors, they would be prone to meddle in government and church affairs. But, also like L'Estrange, they appreciated the possibility of influencing public opinion through tracts and pamphlets. Increase Mather was a *status quo man.* An old Puritan Tory on theocratic lines, he was unread in politics. Conservative, dictatorial, and Presbyterian, he opposed Sir Edmund Andros and supported Sir William Phips, who in 1692 became the first royal governor of Massachusetts. Several pamphlets written before the turn of the century, such as *An Essay for the Recording of Illustrious Providences* and a *Vindication of New England,* showed a masterly slashing style, reminiscent of Marchamont Nedham's in his quasi editorials. In the latter pamphlet, Increase was trying to procure a new charter for Massachusetts. His persuasive power was evident in this passage:

> Poor New England! Thou hast always been the eyesore of squinting malignity; the butt of many envenomed arrows, which from time to time have been shot at thy tranquility; but none more wickedly designed than those late addresses which have (after their fashion) endeavored to alienate their Majesties affections from thee. However, let it be known, thou hast friends in England who sufficiently know thy circumstances to wipe off the dust now cast upon thee, and give thee better and more faithful character.[2]

Cotton Mather, as provincial and conservative as his father, Increase, had remarkable talent for "quick and sudden" writing of his opinionated pamphlets—certainly a modern editorial-writing qualification. Although early colonial pamphleteers had time between boat arrivals from England to write their disquisitions in a leisurely and dignified manner, Cotton may have written *The Declaration of the Gentlemen and Inhabitants of Boston and Country Adjacent* in this "hurry-fashion."

In *The Present State of the New-English Affairs,* he was as vituperative as the English journalists of a half-century earlier. He called the French "Gallic Bloodhounds" and blamed the invasion by "bloody Indians and Frenchmen" on the sins and abominations of New Englanders. He called for an awakening of public spirit and warned readers to "mind the business of your own station," to perform the duties they were commanded, and to leave the running of the government to "those that can have no other interest but what is yours." [3]

By 1700, a few tracts and pamphlets expressing views of colonials, were being printed on local presses, but this was not the result of press freedom. Long after the removal of the licensing act in England, the press output in the American colonies was still being censored. The prevailing view toward printing was expressed by Sir William Berkeley, governor of Virginia, who in 1671 thanked God that "we have not free schools nor printing," and he hoped that "we shall not have these hundred years; for learning has brought disobedience and heresy and sects into the world, and printing has divulged them and libels against the government. God keep us from both." [4]

In Massachusetts, both Samuel Green and Marmaduke Johnson, who were finding it difficult to make a living from their printing presses in Cambridge, petitioned the council for the right to print in Boston, but it was not until 1674 that Marmaduke was allowed to move his press to the port city. In the meantime, he had become impatient and printed without license a pamphlet, the *Isle of Pine*. For this he was fined five pounds. The next year the General Court learned that another pamphlet, the *Imitation of Christ,* by Thomas à Kempis, a German monk of the fourteenth century, was in the press. They directed licensers to revise the work more fully and stop the distribution of what had already been printed.[5]

When Marmaduke moved his press to Boston, everything he printed had to be licensed. To insure observance of this licensing order, the Reverend Mr. Thomas Thatcher and Increase Mather were added to the other licensers.

Even such pamphlets as *Narrative of the Troubles with the Indians* were published "by authority." When Johnson died a few months later, his press passed into the possession of John Foster. By 1681, when Foster also died, his Boston press had become such a convenience to the community that it was deemed a necessity; and Samuel Sewall, a liberal-minded pamphleteer, was granted authority to operate the Foster press. Because no other press was permitted in Boston unless its owner first petitioned the council, Sewall had a printing monopoly. When he retired in 1684, his printers were allowed to continue under the supervision of licensers.[6] It was not until

June 1693 that another printer, Bartholomew Green, was granted a license to print in Boston.

Parliamentary instructions to all royal colonial governors gave legality to licensing. They were told "to provide all necessary orders that noe person keep any press for printing, nor that any book, pamphlet, or other matters whatsoever be printed without your special leave and license first obtained" because great inconvenience could arise from the liberty of printing.[7] Before John Buckner could use a press that he took to Virginia, he was called before the governor and council and ordered not to print "anything hereafter until his majestie's pleasure shall be known." Buckner never used his press.[8] Governor Andros required a printer to pay a five hundred pound security as well as have all his papers, books, and pamphlets licensed. This, of course, was prohibitive to poor printers who were scarcely eking out a living as it was. Richard Pierce, who had learned his trade under Sewall and Green, was appointed official printer, but even he could not publish the ever popular almanacs without first having them licensed.[9]

Printing, however, was in the colonies to stay, and censorship could not keep a few brave souls from having their opinions printed nor a few starving printers from making a few shillings. When William Penn in 1682 brought his first Quaker settlers to Pennsylvania, one William Bradford was among them. One of the first items off the Bradford press was an almanac by Samuel Atkins. Both Bradford and Atkins were called before the provincial council for printing after one date "the beginning of the government here by the Lord Penn." The council took offense to the terms "Lord Penn" as being contrary to Quaker thinking and ordered Bradford to delete the phrase and "not to print anything but what shall have lycence from the Council."

Quaker colonial authorities, who seemed to think printing a black art and an unhallowed mystery, reprimanded Bradford on another occasion for printing and selling copies of the Pennsylvania Charter.[10] Later his press was confiscated and he was imprisoned for printing *An Appeal from the Twenty-eight Judges to the Spirit of Truth,* a pamphlet by George Keith. This publication apparently had been instrumental in creating a schism among Philadelphia Quakers.[11]

The next year Bradford was released from prison and his

press restored. He moved to New York, where he had been
offered the position of public printer. There, one of the first
items he printed was his own pamphlet, *New-England's Spirit
of Persecution Transmitted to Pennsylvania.* A quarto pamphlet of thirty-eight text pages, it was an account of his persecution and trial.[12]

In referring to New England's persecution, Bradford may
have had in mind the fate of what has been called the first
colonial newspaper. In 1686 Benjamin Harris, who, it will be
recalled, had been imprisoned in England for a seditious pamphlet, had escaped to Boston before he could be arrested for
another libelous pamphlet. There he had opened a bookshop
in conjunction with a coffeehouse. When Governor Andros
left, Harris, who may have longed wistfully for his London
newspaper days, must have decided the time had come for the
colonies to have a newssheet. Familiar as he was with the perils
of writing such a publication, he, nevertheless, took the calculated risk, probably with the hope that his venture might
prove financially rewarding and perhaps with a perverse delight at the prospect of jolting Bostonians. Whatever his reasons, he hired Richard Pierce to print *Publick Occurrences,
Both Forreign and Domestick* on September 25, 1690.

There had been other news publications printed in Massachusetts, notably the "authorized" *The Present State of
New-English Affairs,* the Cotton Mather broadsheet which had
included a report from Increase Mather. But *Publick Occurrences* was the first such publication that in form, size, and intent resembled a typical English newssheet of the time. It was
printed on a folded sheet, the fourth page being left blank,
presumably, one historian has said, for readers to add items by
hand and forward the paper to distant friends.[13] There were
two columns on the 6-by-9½-inch pages, and "Numb. 1" appeared in the top left corner of the first page—typical procedure of English papers.

Not only did this indicate that the publication was intended
for regular issue, but in the introductory paragraphs, also
typical of many English news publications, Harris called himself a publisher. He declared that he intended to print monthly
"A Faithful Relation" of occurrences so that "memorable oc-
currents of Divine Providence" would not be forgotten, "as

they so often are"; so that people would understand "the Circumstances of Public Affairs"; and so that "False Reports, maliciously made and spread among us" could be corrected. He even proposed to expose the names of malicious raisers of false reports and supposed that no one would dislike "this Proposal, but such as intend to be guilty of so villainous a crime." [14]

Taken as a whole, these paragraphs were a comment on the character and actions of Bostonians. As such, they must have been upsetting, coming as they did in the midst of the witchcraft issue. Strangely, though, it was not this commentary that most bothered authorities. It was Harris's audacity in printing without a license his "Reflections of a very high nature" and his "sundry doubtful and uncertain" news reports that disturbed the governor and the council.

One of the items which apparently dismayed the authorities was a report of recent events in the French and Indian War. Harris was injudicious enough to call the Indians "barbarous," particularly those who were allies of the English, and "miserable Savages, in whom we have too much confided." Because colonials were concerned at this time with trying to win the friendship of neighboring Indians, this item was probably considered a criticism of colonial policy. Another item that caused consternation was a gossipy account of the French King's taking immoral liberties with the Prince's wife and causing the Prince to revolt. The Puritan clergy of Boston were understandably horrified that such news could be read by their parishioners.

Harris also used the old coranto device of attaching a moralistic sentence at the end of each news item. He noted that "Christianized Indians in some parts of Plymouth" had set aside a day of Thanksgiving "to God for his Mercy in supplying their extreme and pinching necessities under the late want of corn" and for the prospects of a good harvest. To this, he commented: "Their example may be worth mentioning."

Publick Occurrences was suppressed by a general court, which called the publication a pamphlet. The governor and the council defended their action in a broadside, which proclaimed their "resentment and disallowance" and forbade anyone "for the future to set forth anything in print without license first obtained from those appointed by the Government to grant the same." [15] It would be naïve to suppose that Harris was not well-aware that by his "editing" process—choosing which items to include—and by his "editorial" comment—bias through adjectives and phrases—he would offend the authorities just as he had earlier in England. And it is doubtful that *Publick Occurrences* had much influence on the evolution of the newspaper editorial. When colonial newspapers did begin to publish regularly, their authors and publishers would find additional ways of commenting.

In the meantime, Thomas Maule, a Quaker pamphleteer, attempted to circumvent the rigid licensing act of the Massachusetts colony. Knowing it would be impossible to have his booklet licensed in Massachusetts, he traveled to New York. There he was able to get the governor of that province to license it and William Goddard to print it. But when Maule imported copies of *Truth held forth and maintained . . .* and circulated them in Massachusetts, he was no luckier than Harris had been. A New York license was not permitted in Massachusetts. The council declared that the pamphlet contained "many notorious, and Wicked Lies, and Slanders not only on private persons but upon Government, and also divers Corrupt, and pernicious Doctrines, utterly Subversive of the True Christian and professed Faith." [16] The Massachusetts House of Representatives declared the pamphlet was "stuffed with many notorious and pernicious Lies and Scandals" against certain "private citizens, Government, Churches, and Ministry." All copies were seized and publicly burned. Maule was required to post bond and ordered to appear before the "next Court of Assize & General Goale Delivery." [17]

He was later acquitted, but his experience did not deter later pamphleteers. In fact, a controversy arising from the establishment of a new church in Boston in 1699 brought a rash of pamphlets and more unpleasant experiences for printers and writers. The next twenty-five years, however, would see the continued use of the pamphlet as the medium for editorial expression, just as it had been and was in the mother country.

10. Experimental Era

In the seventeenth century, precursors of the newspaper editorial had appeared in several forms. Addresses to the reader, sporadic quasi-editorial comments, side sheets of commentary, and opinionated news accounts—all had been forms for early deliberate attempts at disseminating views about news events. They appeared in newsletters, newsbooks, newssheets, and the first English newspapers. These, it may be said, logically represented one geneological line of the newspaper editorial. Another was the polemical pamphlet. Often vicious, scurrilous, abusive, and seditious, pamphlets had come to be the accepted form for political observations by leading thinkers, who wrote them for the intellectually elite few. In that these, too, served the purpose of the editorial, they also may be regarded as editorial progenitors.

As newspapers increased in number, both in England and in the colonies, pamphlets, as they were known in the seventeenth century, would slowly recede into the background because they would not have the distributional advantages of the newspaper. They would continue, even in the mid-twentieth century, but they were destined to become the expression of views of an organized movement, a group, or a committee. Often they would be written through a cooperative effort of several people.[1]

The eighteenth century, however, ushered in two other kinds of editorial utterances. One was the opinion newspapers known today as "essay papers." The *Tatler* and the *Spectator* were the leaders. Opinions expressed in these publications and the style of writing used in them profoundly influenced opinion writing in the emerging colonial press. Then there were the highly regarded letter-type commentaries, in which the writer would address his political and social ideas to his readers. Sometimes these were published first in newspapers and later as pamphlets. Sometimes they appeared first as broadsides or pamphlets and later were reprinted in newspapers. Whereas the essay type would eventually pass into magazine literature and lose some of its journalistic image, the letter type would emerge as a manifest progenitor of the modern newspaper editorial.

Indeed, the first quarter of the eighteenth century can be called fairly an experimental era in news opinion writing. Besides new types of publications, new forms appeared in daily newspapers, by then becoming more popular and more numerous. The old "address to the reader" and other quasi-editorial forms took on new dimensions. The letter-introductory, as it was called in England, was something of a wedding between the essay and the quasi editorial.

When Queen Anne came to the English throne in 1702, England was already involved in a transformation from the old order of ostentatious social life of the aristocracy to a new order of more genteel manners and morals of a rising commercial middle class. Outbursts of city mobs began to diminish. "Gulls" and "roarers" no longer roamed at will to outrage and assault their victims. These trends toward order would intensify during the reigns of Anne and George I. Where the ruling order had been a pretentious class of ornately-dressed periwinkled men and of beauty-patched, false-eyebrowed women, now political and social importance was passing into the hands of the plainly-dressed middle class emerging in the aftermath of the civil wars.

And in this era of international trading, the older class still delighted in quips and raillery, and atheists took pleasure in jeering at sacred things. But the new order, with a Puritanical background, were serious-minded, progressive citizens, who worked at upgrading their standards of culture, honor, and religion. They were instrumental in reforming debt laws, improving prison conditions, and outlawing witchcraft. With more leisure that came from financial strength, they were interested in new ideas and attitudes, tolerance, and consideration for others.[2] Thoughtful intellectuals, politicians, and businessmen met in the increasingly popular coffeehouses to discuss news and views of wars, of Whigs and Tories, and of the first real cabinet.[3]

Pamphlets enjoyed their greatest vogue in the Queen Anne period. The appearance of any such important publication was a great event, to be talked about and discussed for weeks.[4] Many of the most prolific and better pamphleteers of the time were already well known to English and colonial readers. These men were not only literary authors, but also contributors to the popular essay papers and to daily newspapers. Among them were Jonathan Swift, Daniel Defoe, Richard Steele, and Joseph Addison.

Swift, born in 1667 of Irish Catholic parents, has been considered, perhaps rightfully, nearly without rival as a polemical pamphleteer. His discourses have been called a harbinger of the newspaper editorial.[5] As early as 1691, he had contributed literary essays to the *Athenian Mercury*, the aforementioned Dunton publication. But Swift's pamphlets ranged over a wide variety of subjects: foreign affairs, church issues, peace, controversial political figures, education, and Ireland. Indeed his political pamphlets became the terror of the Whigs. His early religious pamphlets argued for the church interest of the Tories. Later he changed sides and attacked the extremism of Tories.

His promotion of Irish trade and educational reforms revealed his interests in subjects typical of those used by the modern editorial writer. The arguments Swift advanced in a broadside, *The Conduct of the Allies and of the late Ministry in beginning and carrying on the present War* would appear in many American newspaper editorials during the Vietnam War three hundred years later. In his usual clear, pointed, and precise style, he attacked the war on the grounds that it lay too great a burden on the nation. Only a little longer than a leading article, this publication had such a great effect on public opinion that the Duke of Marlborough was shortly relieved of his army command.[6]

Daniel Defoe, slightly older than Swift, was born of London Presbyterian parents and was in London when Roger L'Estrange was at the height of his popularity. By the turn of the century Defoe was already well known, though perhaps not well liked, for his pamphlets. He had written satiric tracts on church and political issues,[7] and in his *Essay on Projects* he had revealed his liberal views on education, insurance, and treatment of sailors.

A political propagandist in the new century, he defended the policies of the Whigs in scores of anonymous pamphlets.[8] He supported William's plan for partition of Spain and pleaded for return to a parliament not controlled by financial interests. He discussed foreign affairs, inevitability of war with France, misdeeds of stockjobbers, and rights of people as opposed to highhanded independence of the Tory Parliament. And he contributed his share of tracts advocating reformation of manners.[9]

In his *The Shortest Way with Dissenters,* an ironic attack on the church, Defoe argued that it was important for dissenters to conform occasionally. Unwisely, he also wrote that dissenters should be repressed at all costs. The pamphlet was ordered burned, and Defoe was tried for seditious writing, pilloried, and sent to Newgate.[10] But his contributions to the evolving newspaper editorial through his writings for the journals of that day and through his stream of pamphlets (in 1715 alone, he wrote at least thirty) on such subjects as economics, commerce, social problems, servants, and political issues made him a popular and influential journalist, whose tracts set precedents for colonial pamphleteers.[11]

Joseph Addison and Richard Steele, like Swift and Defoe, were already writing at the turn of the century. Both wrote anonymous pamphlets. Although their contributions to periodical journalism far overshadowed their pamphleteering efforts, their persuasive discourses on morals and politics could be found in colonial bookseller and print shops.

Contributions of Addison and Steele to the periodical, or essay paper, however, had a remarkable influence on shaping public opinion and on the subject and style of editorial comment in the developing newspaper. Essay papers, which grew in popularity (more than three hundred had been published by 1718),[12] were outgrowths of Roger L'Estrange's *Observator* and John Dunton's *Athenian Mercury* and *Pegasus.* Although popularly called newspapers, these publications were neither newspapers nor magazines in the modern sense.[13] But discourses published in them appear to parallel closely syndicated columns often found on modern editorial pages in that they interpreted current news and gossip or commented on the passing scene of manners and morals. Frequently comment in essay papers affected public opinion.[14]

The first of the essay papers to appear in the new century was authored by John Tutchin, who revived Roger L'Estrange's title, the *Observator,* for his publication. Tutchin, who for seditious pamphlets in 1685 had been sentenced to serve seven years in prison and to be whipped once a year through all market towns of Dorset, used for his comment on political affairs L'Estrange's dialogue form—a conversation between an outspoken Whig and a countryman. As a weekly Whig political organ, the *Observator* was more pamphlet than newspaper. Soon, however, Tutchin was again in trouble with the authorities. The House of Commons considered that at least five issues contained "matters scurrilous and malicious" that reflected on its proceedings and tended to promote sedition in the kingdom. When Tutchin and his printer were tried for libel, the *Observator* author was accused of being "a seditious person, and a daily inventor and publisher of false news, and horrible and false lies and seditious libel." [15] Even though he was found guilty, Tutchin continued to attack the Jacks (Jacobites) and the admiralty in his publication until 1712, when a newspaper tax killed this paper along with many others.

Longest lived and perhaps one of the most influential of the essay papers was Defoe's *Review,* which revolutionized journalism, according to one historian.[16] Called a *Weekly Review of the Affairs of France, purged from Errors and Partiality of News-writers and Petty Statesmen of All Sides,* it soon became known as the *Review.* Defoe probably conceived the idea for this triweekly publication while imprisoned at Newgate for his indiscreet pamphlet, *The Shortest Way with Dissenters.*[17] In his *Review,* Defoe improved on Tutchin's *Observator* by discarding, for a time, the dialogue form of comment, and writing pungent and persuasive political criticism as an adjunct to mere news writing. In his concern in these essays with the social scene, impending legislation, projected treaties, and national debt, he was moving much closer to the modern concept of the newspaper editorial as a means of interpreting news and influencing public opinion.

As were many of these early journals, the *Review* was subsidized, probably by Robert Harley, secretary of state. And Defoe was able to keep the journal alive for nine years, a full year after the newspaper tax had killed almost all other such publications. His pertinacity and assiduity in writing every word of each issue—and he used advertising only when he did not need the space for his comments—must have played an important role in the *Review*'s longevity.[18] But much acclaim must also be given to Defoe's utterances.

The principal feature of each issue was a single essay, in which Defoe interpreted current events and gossip and commented on manners and morals. The *Review* was not very old when he added the Scandinavian Club, an idea he probably borrowed from John Dunton's *Athenian Mercury*. Here Defoe answered questions from readers whom he himself invented. They were concerned with such domestic problems as love and marriage, educability of the deaf and dumb, money lending, and ministers who used sermons for political discussions. Defoe may have seen himself as a kind of counselor and guide in his essaylike answers. From even the "easiest, lightest questions," he tried "to draw some useful inferences, and if possible to introduce something solid and something solemn in applying it." He was resolved "to exalt virtues, expose vice, promote truth, and help men in serious reflection."[19] Sometimes this feature was issued as an extra under the title the *Little Review*. Later Defoe changed this name to *Miscellanea* and issued it only occasionally. By this time, his answers were running sometimes to one-thousand-word essays. Addison and Steele would borrow this idea for their club of commentators.[20]

Defoe wrote in language that appealed to freeholders and electors (property owners). Though he tended to make his essays rather lengthy, usually twelve hundred to two thousand words, many came within the accepted length of the modern longer newspaper editorial. Frequently he wrote "on the subject of peace," and on one occasion he invited "all parties to put their helping hands to this necessary work, and principally to choose such gentlemen to represent them in the approaching Parliament as are blessed with those healing principles which seem particularly *and* absolutely necessary at this extraordinary junction." This he did by telling his readers "whom they should *not* choose, by way of direction to the affirmative, whom they *should*."[21] American editorial writers have used this same method.

Through the years quite a few of them have also advanced Defoe's argument for the need of a balance of power. "We do not fight against France as a kingdom" or against the French king as a king or as "a tyrant insulting the liberties of his own subjects," he once wrote. Instead "we fight against France as a Kingdom grown too great for her neighbors" and against the French king as "an invader of our nation's rights" and as "an oppressor of the common liberties of Europe." By fighting, he said, "we . . . reduce him to a condition that he may be no more dangerous to his neighbours." This would "reduce his exorbitant power" and "that little understood but very popular and extensive word, *a balance of power*." [22]

Like most newsmen, Defoe was concerned with freedom of the press—a subject for many of his essays. He thought it "was the right of Englishmen to speak freely in things relating to their general interest," but only with the restraint "that they spoke the TRUTH." He did not believe, however, that this "liberty extended to a general latitude of forging what stories they thought fit" or of speaking "whatever they pleased without respect to fact." Justice in England was eminent "for correcting the manners of the age, and though there may be a deficiency in our law, that a man cannot be punished for lying, yet he may certainly be punished for printing lies." [23]

Defoe examined in detail (March 29, 1711) the proposed tax of one halfpenny sterling on each printed half-sheet and of twelvepence sterling on every advertisement. This was an attempt by Anne's administration to raise revenue and curb the press. The tax would lead, Defoe wrote, to "filling the world with written newsletters," in which men would be free to write about what they please." Laws could be made "to refrain circumstances" and "to silence such or such subjects." They could be made to "prohibit printing anything relating to government and parties" or "to politics and national affairs." But if they prohibited in general and without exception, they were an indication that the government had "something to do they dare not let the people hear of."

A year later (April 29, 1712) Defoe again discussed the proposed act which was then being debated in Parliament. This time he attacked the tax from the economic point of view. He surveyed the printing trade in England and declared that three thousand poor families would be out of work immediately. He hoped Parliament would think of some method to prevent this. He did not think the tax was "calculated to raise money so much as to suppress" the output of the press. "To tax any trade so that it cannot subsist under the payment is not a means to raise the money but to destroy the trade." Then he proposed two ways of making the laws effectual: first, "by introducing and proportioning" the tax on each article so that it could be paid and the taxed object still exist; and second, "by limitations and exceptions" in order that what was "thought needful to suppress" could be suppressed and what deserved to be preserved could be preserved. Under a moderate tax the trade could exist. His "limitations and exceptions" were "instructive" writings, which he hoped Parliament would not take away from the poor.

Economics and trade were frequent subjects of the leading essay in the *Review*. Again and again in simple terms Defoe explained consumer credit as the ruination of trade, which he called the life of England's wealth. And he said that the conduct of lawyers in insolvent debtor cases was disgraceful. He wrote on the labor market, inflation, deflation, monopolies, increased wages, ceiling prices on coal, and a guaranteed wage scale for laborers.[24]

The last issue of the *Review* was dated June 11, 1713. Several incidents may have contributed to Defoe's decision to abandon the publication. Undoubtedly the tax eventually caught up with him; but Defoe was again imprisoned in that year for three pamphlets he had written on the succession question.[25] It may have been, too, that Defoe believed the *Review* had served its purpose. More than any other single influence, his articles had caused a split in the Tory party and brought the Whigs to power.[26]

Unquestionably, Defoe had advanced the development of editorial comment. He would make further advancements in the next few years, as will be seen shortly. But in the meantime, the *Review* would remain for many years an influence on English and colonial thought and journalism. Defoe wrote a preface for each of the nine volumes and bound each volume as a book. These were stocked by colonial booksellers and printers; and a few years later when weekly publications began in the New England colonies, some of his journalistic devices as well as his ideas would be used.

Among other influential weekly journals of the first quarter of the eighteenth century were the *Examiner,* the *Tatler,* and the *Spectator*—all apparently capitalizing on and perhaps improving on Defoe's commentary in the *Review.* The *Tatler* was Sir Richard Steele's journal, although the author assumed the name of Isaac Bickerstaff, Esquire. A triweekly, two-page publication, it was the first of the journals to appeal directly to the new polite society. The first issue, April 12, 1709, began with a preface that stated the publication's purpose was "to offer something, whereby such worthy and well-affected Members of the Commonwealth may be instructed after their Reading, what to think." [27] The remainder of the paper was devoted to seven short articles or news features. At first these articles were strictly political, but subsequent issues began with an essay of light commentary on modes, manners, and intellectual interests of coffeehouse habitués. These revealed disgust at frivolity and incompetence and exposed the vagaries of prominent socialites by satirizing such practices as gambling, duelling, swindling, and by ridiculing snuffboxes, canes, cursing, fops, and dandies.[28]

With the eighteenth issue of the *Tatler,* Joseph Addison began contributing an occasional essay. He brought to the commentary in the essay paper a classical clearness and a critical taste that made these essays and later those in the *Spectator* very close to the present-day editorial on social, moral, literary, and some political subjects.

The *Tatler* lasted only until January 2, 1711, and probably was dropped because Steele and Addison were planning to start the daily *Spectator.* In the meantime, however, another weekly political journal had made its appearance—the *Examiner: or, Remarks upon Papers and Occurences.* Started on August 3, 1710, by Dr. William King and subsidized by Tory Viscount Bolingbroke who was intriguing to end the unpopular war of the Spanish Succession, the publication was filled with bitterly controversial essays and letters. King was probably one of the first modern genre of "daily" editors. Apparently he was a compiler only. He seemed to have assigned subjects to a stable of essay writers. And he insisted that all contributors keep their essays and letters short. In their length, arrangement, and number of paragraphs, these editorial utterances were the same as those that editorial boards would demand two hundred years later.

Among King's stable of writers was Jonathan Swift, whose short but venomous political letter essays were more influential than his pamphlets. In direct, terse, simple, forceful English, he commented on affairs of Church and State. He seemed to have understood that a newspaper could advance a man's ambitions or a governmental policy. He compared policy acts with principles of statesmanship and arrived at conclusions that justified Tory acts and blamed Whigs. His intense bitterness against Whig statesmen was manifested in his attacks on Walpole whom he called "Sir Bluestring." [29]

Addison and Steele's *Spectator* was not the first daily publication to hit the London streets. That honor belonged to the *Daily Courant* born March 11, 1702. But this paper purported to give "no comments or conjectures" of its publisher. As did other such newspapers which were soon to be founded, it contained a few items of shipping news, a half-column or more of advertisements, and new items translated from Continental newspapers. These latter, of course, still combined the chronicle of events with commentary. But by the time the *Spectator* was first published on March 1, 1711, the English were thinking in terms of two kinds of newspapers: those of opinion and those of information. The *Spectator* was the former. It would be another ten years before the two would be combined into one publication.

Steele wrote the more original *Spectator* letter essays; and Addison, the more effective. In order to maintain their anonymity, they created the lovable Sir Roger de Coverly, whose letters are now known as the Roger de Coverly papers. Each issue, one page printed on both sides, contained only one essay on one subject. Sometimes Swift contributed an essay.[30]

The publication proved popular, and by the tenth issue, Addison could claim three thousand copies were being sold daily. In an age when every copy had many readers, this was probably an unusually large acceptance of the casual, charming, and amusing commentary on the passing scene. The *Spectator* was also widely read in the country, on the Continent, and in the colonies. Although Addison and Steele avoided anything didactic, their essays were influential in modifying dress and in making morals more healthful.

July 31, 1712, would be the day "on which many eminent authors would probably publish their last work," Addison wrote in the *Spectator* of that date. On that day the newspaper stamp tax went into effect. Few weekly historians would "be able to exist under the weight of a stamp act." If a "sheet of blank paper" had "this new imprimatur" clapped upon it before it was qualified "to communicate anything to the public," it would not last long. Addison's prediction was true. He and Steele raised the price of their publication, but the *Spectator* folded six months later.

The essay papers were widely imitated by a number of short-lived publications and paved the way for a new crop of six-page weekly journals. These followed a pattern. They started with an essay of the *Tatler* type, which was followed in order by news of foreign events, of state affairs, and of London happenings. The last page was filled with late paragraphs and advertisements.[31]

Defoe, Addison, Steele, and Swift all wrote for various of these publications. But to Defoe belonged the honor of the next step toward the developing editorial. He began writing the leading essay for these new journals in a new shorter form, the "letter introductory," an essay addressed to the owner or the publisher of the publication. In that these were in a language that even the underaverage reader could understand, in that they were usually on only one subject, and in that they appeared in the same place in each issue, these were very close to the modern editorial. Historians have recorded that Defoe, a Whig, undertook to moderate Tory commentary by attaching himself to Tory journals. To the latter he pretended to be a Tory, while he was reporting Tory actions to Whigs. But Defoe was first and foremost a committed journalist, and he may have worked for the publication which he thought would give him the opportunity to influence the largest readership.

The first Tory journal for which Defoe wrote was *Mist's Weekly Journal,* which was established toward the end of 1715 and which by 1717 had become quite popular. He wrote the leading essay in this every week from August 1717 to November 1718, again from January 1719 to July 1720, and occasionally thereafter until October 1724.[32] These were the first of his letters introductory, and they were much nearer to the modern newspaper editorial than were his *Review* essays or the *Tatler* or *Spectator* commentaries.

They took the form of letters ostensibly from interested

readers. They were addressed to Mr. Mist, the publisher. Actually Defoe wrote them under a fictitious name. Sometimes, in one letter he would raise a question which he would answer in the letter of the next issue.[33] His subjects covered a wide range: obscene literature, religious toleration, political issues, journalistic independence, tyranny of absolute monarchs, education for children, and treatment of prisoners—all modern editorial subjects. On many of these issues, such as principles of good government, essentials of true justice, primary conditions of social welfare, he was in advance of his contemporaries. In the delightfully humorous and imaginative letters in which he commented on the passing scene, he frequently showed improvement over the *Tatler* and *Spectator* essays.[34]

In one of his first letters introductory in *Mist's,* he described in detail conditions in prisons. He started with an address which led into his description.

> Good Mr. Mist—Something of charity, not always of Lucifer! I hope you have some room to speak for God's sake, and to give a lift to those that apply to you for help *in forma pauperis.*
> The Votes (Mr. Mist) if you give yourself the Trouble to read them, will shew you every day the Addresses or Petitions of the Miserable, representing to Parliament the deplorable conditions of the poor insolvent Debtors, *lying in prison,* nay I had almost said, Flying to Prison, from the harassing violence of inexorable Creditors.[35]

Defoe also showed (October 31, 1719) concern for inconsistent practices in journalism. He criticized the use of charlatanic political essays in the same issue in which deceptive medical advertising was printed. As "Philygia," he proposed that Mr. Mist start a crusade against "quack" doctors. "You generally begin," he told the publisher, "with disabusing the publick, pointing out lies, and reflecting Errors of your Brother newsmongers," and yet "you never fail to send" your reader "to ten or a dozen Places where he is sure of being abused and imposed on in the grossest Manner." The advertising on the last page never failed to have "as many Lies in it as all the rest have Truths." In this way, Defoe wrote, "your Paper, which was designed for a receptacle of Truth is become a Refuge of Lies and the Reputation you have acquired" only "serves to recommend the grossest impostures."

Defoe was known as the author of *Mist's*. In those days, a journal author was responsible for "editing" and was under the orders of the publisher, who guided the paper's policy.[36] Defoe's duties at *Mists's* also included translating foreign news for the section of the paper headed "Foreign Affairs." Here he attempted to be factual, but occasionally he expressed his own strong views. Once in an account of the Russian Northern War then in progress, he denounced at great length and with indignant eloquence the cruelties and oppressions which the Russians were inflicting on the Swedes. Apparently even Defoe could not get away from the practice of infiltrating factual news accounts with comment when he felt strongly on an issue.

But his letters introductory drew readers. They were especially appealing to middle-class women who were becoming avid journal readers. Perhaps for this reason, Defoe's services were sought by other journals.[37] At any rate, in June 1720, while Mist and his printers were in Newgate for printing "false, malicious, scandalous, infamous, and traitorous libel" in reports of proceedings of the House of Commons, Defoe began writing for *Applebee's Original Weekly Journal,* a Tory organ then six years old.[38] John Applebee, publisher, arranged for Defoe to write letters introductory and to help manage the publication.[39] His first Applebee letter was signed "Oliver Oldway," and as "Oliver," Defoe discussed a bill before Parliament that was aimed at suppressing any further South Sea Bubble schemes to defraud the government. He graphically described London the day after the Bubble burst. As he sometimes did, Defoe varied his format by launching first into the event and addressing Mr. Applebee at the end.[40] In other letters he once more urged improvement of conditions for insolvent businessmen and for unemployed weavers who were turned out in the streets because women had started wearing dresses made of calico from India. He attacked the stockjobbers in Exchange-Alley and urged suppression of practices detrimental to honest business and to the general financial equilibrium of the country.[41]

Defoe, as "A. B.," referred to such pieces as letters introductory in *Applebee's,* July 23, 1720. He recommended that "the front of journals" should contain something "Solid and Instructive": such subjects as "Treaties and Negocia-tions," conquests, princes, and governmental acts in which the world was involved. In his letter of the next issue, he ridiculed this idea, but seemingly that was Defoe's method of presenting various aspects of a subject.

In his letter of June 10, 1721, as "Caution," Defoe dis-cussed duties of a journalist. It was the duty of a newspaper author "to collect daily the best Intelligence of publick affairs." And "Caution" advised writers of letters introductory not to provoke or give offense, but to make people laugh instead of cry. For that reason, letter writers should comment on news items. He used an example of an old woman committing suicide by throwing herself out the window and said that the subjects for comment on this event might be the "Effect of Love . . . 'pon Fancy" in old age. There was room for comment in these letters on "Public Credit, Commerce, State of our Morals, Decrease in Virtue, Increase in Crime, Assaults made by mad Men upon Religion, Growth of Atheism, ill Habits, ill Man-ners, and ill Customs of the AGE."

If these utterances were not enough to show Defoe as the prototype of the modern newspaper editorial writer, his *Applebee's* letter of August 25, 1722, gave additional proof. After his "address to Mr. Applebee," in which he again dis-cussed the duties of a journalist, Defoe used the editorial "we" to present his advice or admonitions. He explained that when he spoke in the "Language of the Newspaper," he was speaking in the first person plural as the publisher and his assistants. In this letter, too, he counseled journalists not to countenance "plots," and said that "duty to the government we live under dictates to us not to blow the Coals of Disorder and Tumult. While we enjoy our own Peace, we ought not to disturb the Peace of the Community."

Interestingly, in his letter of April 28, 1722, Defoe came out against smallpox inoculation. This was a year after James Franklin started his anti-inoculation campaign in the *New-Eng-land Courant*.

Accident though Defoe's letters introductory may have been, many English newspapers soon were adopting the device. And it was to remain for many years as a precursor of the leading article in numerous British journals and newspapers.

Defoe also wrote letters introductory for other publications, among them *Whitehall's Evening Post* and the *Daily Post*.

Another set of letters, written about this time, were to prove quite influential on colonial thought and journalism. John Trenchard and Thomas Gordon, under the pseudonym of "Cato," wrote a series of opinionated articles in the form of letters for the London *Journal*, which had started in 1719 as a rival to *Mist's* and *Applebee's,* and for the *British Journal*. John Trenchard, known to his contemporaries as "a man of severe principles with regard to Liberty," [42] called on Thomas Gordon, another author with libertarian principles, to help write the letters. Previously the two men had written for the *Independent Whig* a series of letters in 1720 that were concerned with religious liberty; but their Cato letters, printed in the London *Journal* from November 1720 to December 1723, were the most influential.

The first Cato letter called "for public justice upon the wicked managers of the South Sea Scheme." In other letters Cato discussed the responsibilities of the government in protecting citizens, liberty and rights of citizens, representative government, and freedom of expression. This series of 144 letters was collected in 1724 and published in four volumes. Widely read in the colonies, the letters were reprinted whole or in part in the New York *Gazette,* the *New-England Courant,* and the New York *Weekly Journal*. Still later other Colonial newspapers would use them. They would prove especially useful in helping to crystallize political ideas that would lead to the American Revolution.

11. Colonial Imitations
of English Polemics

In 1700, there were about 250,000 Europeans in the American colonies. Of these, about 45,000 lived in Massachusetts with nearly 8000 living in Boston, the cradle of American journalism. Four years later Boston, still the largest town in America, had grown to nearly 10,000 people. Every small community was a closed enclave where unwelcome dissenters were banished and extralegally punished. In areas even more remote, settlers, still busy hacking their meager homes from the woods, were, for the most part, uneducated, lonely, and distrustful of leading magistrates and of government. Indentured servants—English nondescripts, German peasants, and after 1718, Scotch-Irish—were slowly pushing back the frontier. Religious sense, common sense, a taste for work and for simplicity were instilled in children of these hardy frontiersmen. They had little reading matter other than the Bible.

Twenty-five years later, five news publications had been founded. Printers of at least three of these folio-sized newssheets imitated their English counterparts by using essays and letters filled with editorial utterances about news events and public affairs. The true pamphlet remained, and would remain for a long time, the prestige form for printing such opinion. And in it, too, the English influence, direct and strong, was manifested.

These publications were born into a world whose inhabitants everywhere were stalked by common enemies—the long, bone-chilling winters, the French, the Indians, and the Devil. In growing Boston, English-type coffeehouses and taverns provided places for men to discuss their views of events and issues evolving from these foes.

In long Sunday sermons and Thursday lectures, devoted

pastors, who were usually erudite men with access to English newspapers and newsletters, discussed happenings of the world. News of catastrophes, of public or royal anniversaries, of public executions were announced with appropriate comment. The sins of the people had called down the wrath of God who had unloosed the French and the Indians as punishment for the infidelity of New Englanders. The smallpox epidemics in 1703 and 1714; the severe winters of 1706 and 1717, when men and animals froze on roads, in barns, and even in houses; the fire of 1711 that destroyed a hundred houses and deprived 110 families of shelter; and the hot dry summer of 1714 with its wheat crop failures—all were the results of the sins of the people. Furthermore, strict and pious ministers hurled invectives against the detested Louis XIV and the pagan pomp of Catholic civilization. These were the long, dull sermons that were printed in pamphlet form and sold by the ten booksellers and print shops in Boston by 1717.

The clergy during the first quarter of the eighteenth century, although they would not always be the dominating figures in New England, still maintained social preeminence. However the king had changed the charter, and a prospective citizen no longer had to prove that he was a member of the Calvinist church. And already government influence was passing from the clergy into the hands of businessmen, godly and ungodly. Increase and Cotton Mather were still the leading opinion makers in New England, but their dominance would be challenged by other clergymen and soon by a young and vigorous journalist.

In 1700 Bartholomew Green printed a pamphlet for Increase, *The Order of the Gospel Professed and Practiced by the Churches of Christ in New England*. This was answered by sundry ministers of the gospel in New England in a pamphlet, *Gospel Order Revisited*, which was printed in New York because "the press in Boston" was "so much in awe" of the Reverend Mather that no printer there could be obtained. Green answered this charge in a tract with a preface by Cotton Mather, and a pamphlet war was in progress. Another ecclesiastical opinion writer of the era was John Wise, who opposed the Mather idea. His two pamphlets, *Churches Quarrel Espoused* and *Vindication of the New England Churches*, were democratic counterblasts at Presbyterian propaganda. Toward the end of the period, the Reverend Jonathan Edwards, greatly influenced by Milton and Locke, was beginning to wield influence with his printed sermons and religious tracts.

Meanwhile the ministers, apparently aware that their political influence was slipping, began to speak and write on civic and governmental issues. Cotton Mather published a number of his lectures in which he advised his readers and listeners on their duties in town government, on their conduct of business, and on their general behavior. In this respect he was concerned with the same subjects as Defoe, Swift, Addison, and Steele. In fact, one historian has called Cotton Mather a "kind of seventeenth century William Allen White" in that the forthright utterances of both were concerned with community affairs.[1]

In another pamphlet, Cotton Mather pleaded for the godly administration of civic affairs. In 1719 he and a group of ministers, acting as a kind of ecclesiastical editorial board, produced a pamphlet, *A Testimony Against Evil Customs*. In this they spoke out emphatically on the conduct of New Englanders. They advised against "riotous or immodest irregularities" at wedding ceremonies and the wasting of time and money at frivolous dancing schools. Though their style was different and not nearly so effective, their subjects were the same as those of English journal writers of the era.

Colonial pamphleteers of this period were interested in business and financial affairs also. In 1719, a pamphlet recommending the building of marketplaces in Boston was printed. Cotton Mather, in a pamphlet, *Fair Dealing between Debtor and Creditor,* admonished against the dishonesty of going into debt. And down in Philadelphia, Andrew Bradford printed an anonymous pamphlet, *Some Remedies Proposed, for the Sunk Credit of Pennsylvania*. Among other pamphlets Andrew had printed was an antislavery tract.

The coming of newsletters and newspapers to Boston would slowly rob the pulpit of its news media value, but the pamphlet would long be used by thoughtful opinion leaders for the dissemination of their ideas. Even Benjamin Franklin would write a pamphlet when he wanted to discuss his plan for the reform of currency. Moreover, there was no space in the small colonial newspapers for the lengthy discussion that pamphleteers liked to write.

Establishment in 1692 of an intercolonial postal system with postmasters, who "knew all" and had access to incoming mail as well as franking privileges, hastened the birth of colonial newspapers. The postmaster at Boston in 1704 founded the first continuously printed newspaper in the colonies, the Boston *News-Letter*. John Campbell for at least a year had sent handwritten newsletters to the governors of other colonies. But copying the letter was a time-consuming burden, and Campbell decided printing was the answer to his problem.

Only slightly larger than Ben Harris's paper of 1690, it looked like the English newspaper of the time. "Published by Authority" adorned the masthead, and sometimes "Undertaker" Campbell had to wait "on His Excellency for Approbation" of the news he had collected.[2] His news items were clipped from London newspapers that were weeks old. Because he regarded news as recent history, he printed his items chronologically rather than the latest happening first.

The only editorial utterances appearing in this tiny newsletter were moralistic comments, the type that had been common for years in English news publications. When a woman committed suicide, Campbell hoped that "inserting such an awful Providence" would not be offensive "but rather a warning to watch against the wiles of our Grand Adversary."[3] He once regretted having to insert an account of a man being severely whipped for selling tar mixed with dirt, but he hoped such news would "be a *caveat* to others, of doing the like, least a worse thing befal them."[4]

The Boston *News-Letter* was not a lively paper, and in spite of franking privileges, Campbell probably never sold as many as three hundred copies of one issue. Still the paper was the only news publication in the colonies for fifteen years. By this time, people had come to regard the newspaper as an adjunct to the post office. But when a new postmaster was appointed in 1718, Campbell refused to relinquish his *News-Letter*. The new postmaster, William Brooker founded another, the Boston *Gazette*; and he hired as its printer, young James Franklin, who had recently returned from England with a new press. Shortly Brooker was replaced as postmaster and publisher of the *Gazette* by a new man, who promptly took his printing away from the audacious Franklin.

The first issue of the *Gazette* was dated December 21, 1719. Like the *News-Letter,* the *Gazette* was "published by authority" and was patterned on English newspapers, with foreign news first, then home news, usually sparse, and finally an advertisement or two. Sometimes the publisher used a preface in which he promised that his publication would be beneficial and entertaining.[5]

The *Gazette* was livelier and better printed than the *News-Letter.* But John Campbell, probably rankled at having a competitor, foreshadowed the "personal journalism" of the next century by hurling invectives at his rival. He pitied *Gazette* readers. The new publication smelled "stronger of beer than of midnight oil," although Campbell was later to maintain that "no opinions, ideas, or arguments" ever appeared in his own paper.[6]

One day after the *Gazette* had made its first appearance in Boston, Andrew Bradford down in Philadelphia began publishing that city's first news publication, the *American Weekly Mercury.* It was the first newspaper outside of Boston and the first one, other than Ben Harris's abortive production, to be under direction of a printer. Much like its two Boston predecessors, it was tiny, it looked like English newssheets, and it reprinted stale news from months-old English papers. English authorities at this time usually did not exert "direct influence" on the newssheets, but colonial governments were extremely sensitive about printed criticism, as Andrew Bradford was soon to discover. Colonials did not always understand that freedom of thought and expression meant equal freedom for the other person, especially if that person held hated opposition ideas.

As a typical colonial printer-editor, Andrew did not differentiate between reporting an event and commenting on it. Because almost all of his items were copied from British newspapers, they were infused, of course, with the comments of the original author. But on rare occasions when he wrote local news, he, too, interpolated editorial comment. In one story, Andrew cloaked a vigorous attack on the British policy of banishing felons to the colonies in a news account of the latest shipload of "malefactors" to arrive in Maryland.

"These criminals," he wrote, were "cunningly" eluding their "punishment of hard service" on plantations to which they had been sentenced. If they could "muster a small parcel of money as a gratuity" to the merchant for their trouble and passage, they were "set at liberty as soon as they set their Feet on this Shore" and were "equal with Freeman in these Parts, to settle and traffick," and might "in a small time claim a Liberty above" the freemen.[7]

When Andrew printed a portion of a pamphlet on the remedies for restoring credit, he unwisely added this comment: "Our General Assembly are now sitting, and we have great expectations from them at this Juncture, that they will find some effectual Remedy, to remove the dying Credit of this Province and restore us to our former happy Circumstances." [8]

This was twentieth-century editorializing and not to be condoned by eighteenth-century colonial authorities. Andrew was called before the Provincial Council, reprimanded, and ordered not to print anything relating to the affairs of any governmental agency without permission of the governor or secretary of the province.

In the meantime, another Boston publication was founded. It would bring life to American journalism and take a giant stride in the evolution of the American newspaper editorial. James Franklin, disappointed in not being retained as printer for the postmaster's *Gazette,* founded the *New-England Courant.* While in England learning the printer's trade, James had been exposed to new ideas and philosophies. He had seen and probably had met Defoe, Swift, Addison, and Steele. He had witnessed the success of Defoe's *Review,* the *Examiner,* the *Tatler,* and the *Spectator.* He knew that to be a success, a newspaper had to contain more than stale news copied from other journals. It must be amusing. He also knew that a newssheet could be a power for the dissatisfied and could agitate the rich and the clergy who controlled Boston.

Since returning to Boston, James had met in Richard Hall's Coffee House several others dissatisfied with the city's stultifying atmosphere. Among them were John Checkley, writer, librarian, and apothecary, whom Cotton Mather considered a servant of the Devil, a traitor to the king, and an infamous blasphemer; Dr. Douglass, an avowed radical who opposed the clergy in colorful language; Jeremy Gridley; and the Reverend Henry Harris, a Church of England adherent. James had discussed with these men and their followers political events and local issues. They formed the Hell Fire Club and became a stable of writers for James Franklin's new publication. When the first issue of the *New-England Courant* appeared April 7, 1721, it looked like an issue of the *Spectator*. For the new publication, club members wrote short formal essays and letters signed with odd and humorous fictitious names. The opening essays discussed such general topics as zeal, hypocrisy, and learning. They were signed with such names as Timothy Touchstone and Abigail Afterwit.

In the first issue James criticized the content of the Boston *News-Letter* by calling it "a dull vehicle." John Campbell answered by saying that James gave "a very, very fulsome account of himself, reflecting, too, too much that my Performances are now and then very, very Dull." [9] Also letters in the first issue vituperatively opposed clerical domination and attacked smallpox inoculation, which the Mathers advocated. This developed into a kind of editorial campaign. Articles and letters in later issues protested with argument and ridicule against inoculation on the ground that it was a doubtful and dangerous practice. All but one Boston physician wrote letters opposing inoculation for James Franklin's newssheet.

The Mathers were obviously nettled. Increase wrote a pamphlet, *Address to the Public,* in which he called the *Courant* "a wicked libel." He also used the *Gazette* to warn people against Franklin's *Courant*. He wrote in a letter to that publication that he could "well remember when the Civil Government would have taken an effective Course to suppress such Cursed Libel," and if some action was not taken, he was afraid "some Awful Judgment" would "come upon this Land and the wrath of God" would arise and there would be no remedy.[10] Also, the Reverend Thomas Walter, Increase's grandson, wrote a broadside, *The Little Compton Scourge: or The Anti-Courant*. In the form of a letter addressed to the *Courant,* it was signed Zechariah Touchstone. James Franklin printed it. The third issue of the *Courant* had two replies to the Walter broadside—one by Dr. John Gibbins and one by Checkley, who was choosing the material for the *Courant*. The latter charged Walter with immorality and drunkenness. For months Bostonians were entertained by the journalistic battle between the Mathers and the *Gazette* on one side and Franklin and the *Courant* on the other.

The Hell Fire Club attacked the government of the province, its principal agents, the clergy, and private individuals in a freehanded manner. Each issue of the *Courant* began with an essay. In this practice James Franklin was following in the footsteps of Defoe and his letter introductory. With the use of Benjamin Franklin's "Silence Dogood" letters, it was more apparent that English journals were serving as models. Like Defoe, Ben addressed these letters to the author and printer. Like Defoe, he introduced the subject in the opening paragraphs and then discussed the issue and offered advice. But like Addison and Steele, Ben Franklin wrote in a flippant, ironic style. They were satire of the *Spectator* type. The first Dogood letter appeared in March 1722. Filled with genial humor and surprising urbanity, Dogood letters introductory spoke of human foibles, such as drunkenness, and urged the wealthy to help struggling young yeomen in business.

In June 1722 James Franklin grew bold enough to print a letter that criticized the government. The writer of a letter purportedly from Rhode Island suggested that the government had not been effective enough in suppressing pirates off the New England coast.[11] For this, James was imprisoned a month, but he continued printing criticism. In January of the next year he printed in one issue three letters offensive to the authorities. One was an essay which mockingly denounced religious hypocrites and intimated that New England had its share of these detestable beings. A letter writer deprecated the political contentions of the day and regretted the departure of Governor Shute. Another letter writer took the opposing view and suggested that the Governor would probably work against the interests of the province when he returned to the mother country.

As might have been expected, the paper was censured for its mockery of religion and its affront to the government.

Furthermore the General Court forbade James to print anything without its first being supervised. When he ignored this order, he was arrested. But James circumvented this action by using brother Benjamin's name as publisher. The attempt to indict James failed, and he was discharged from his bonds in May.

Down in Philadelphia, Andrew Bradford watched the Boston developments with interest. In his *Mercury* of February 19, he commented on the Franklin case.

My Lord Coke observes, that *to punish first and then enquire,* the Law abhors; but here Mr. Franklin has a severe Sentence pass'd upon him, even to taking away Part of his Livelihood, without being called to make Answer. An Indifferent Person would judge by this Vote against *Couranto,* that the Assembly of the Province of Massachusetts Bay are made up of Oppressors and Bigots, who make Religion the only Engine of Destruction of the People; and rather because the first letter in the *Courant* of the 14th of January (which the Assembly censures) so naturally represents and explodes the *Hypocritical Pretenders to Religion.* Indeed, the most famous Politicians in that Government (as the infamous Gov. D - - y and his family) have ever been remarkable for hypocrisy: And it is the general Opinion that some of their Rules are rais'd up and continued as a scourge in the Hands of the Almighty for the sins of the People.

Thus much we could not forbear saying, out of compassion to the distressed People of the Province, who must now resign all Pretences to Sense and Reason, and submit to the Tyranny of Priestcraft and Hypocricy.

In November 1725 William Bradford founded the New York *Gazette.* The father of young Andrew in Philadelphia, he was past sixty when, observing the success of the Boston papers and of his son's publication, he gave the third largest city in the colonies its first newssheet. It was a small two-page paper and contained foreign news copied from English newspapers from three to six months old, lists of arrivals and departures of ships, and a few advertisements. He was not too old to start a new business venture, but he was too old and ingrained with Loyalist ideas to risk, as he had in his younger days in Philadelphia, incurring the wrath of authorities by printing comment.

However, James Franklin's sheet had broken ground for colonial newspapers that would be founded in the next quarter of a century. By imitating the editoriallike essays and letters of the popular English journalists of the time, he had opened the way to a prototype of the newspaper editorial, just as Defoe, Addison, Steele, and Swift had provided models for the English leading article. Even as early as 1723, the Boston *News-Letter* adopted James Franklin's use of letters and essays. In that year Campbell turned his publication over to Bartholomew Green, his printer, who proposed that "all inglorious gentlemen" send him accounts of philosophical transactions and political history. It had taken almost one hundred years for colonials to have their own newssheets, but it took only another twenty years for comment on controversial social, political, and economic issues to be initiated. Modern type editorials were still years away; but once started, comment and criticism would grow and develop.

12. POLITICAL EDITORIALIZING AND BIASED NEWS STORIES

PARTY PRESS, with its letters introductory and its essays that attacked or defended policies of the "in" governments, came to England in the second quarter of the eighteenth century. Newsbooks had been subsidized a hundred years earlier, but now political writers were paid large salaries by the government.[1] Party lines were drawn tight, and the fight to report and to comment on governmental actions developed into open warfare between newspapers. Not even the American personal journalists of the next century would be more venal in their attacks on each other than were the letter and essay writers for the English press in this period. Across the Atlantic, where weekly newspapers were springing up in nearly every colony, printers read English newspapers and followed in their footsteps.

London had about eighteen newspapers in 1726, and that number would grow in the next twenty-five years. Several would last only a few months, several only a few years; but a few, such as the *Daily Gazetteer,* would become institutions. Furthermore, the developing provincial newspapers, which, like those in the American colonies, filled their columns with essays and letters reprinted from London publications, were growing in stature and importance.[2] The economic recovery of Britain after the South Sea Bubble crisis and the reorganization of the postal service in 1741 gave impetus to the developing press with its political commentary.

In the first quarter of the century, as has been seen, there were two kinds of newspapers—the journals, which for the most part were essay papers, and the daily and triweekly newssheets, which mainly contained news accounts, biased though they might be, and advertisements. As 1750 neared, it became apparent that the press had entered a crossover period. A few journals were decreasing the number of essays and letters and were printing news items of the kind found in the dailies. Sometimes a journal issued its news items as a supplement—a reverse of the practice used by Harry Care, who fifty years earlier had used a side sheet of commentary to accompany his *Weekly Packet from Rome*. At the same time, a few dailies and triweeklies began printing a letter introductory or a short essay on their front pages. By mid-century, use of opinion elements on the front page had become rather generalized, even in the provincial press. Perhaps as much because this commentary occupied the first or lead position in the newspaper as that it discussed important issues of the day, it would come to be called in England the leading article.

Letters introductory also underwent developments. In the first place, they were shorter, as were the essays. In this sense, they came a bit closer to the modern conception of the newspaper editorial. As early as 1707, Lord Halifax had predicted that well-conceived and concise observations would replace labored and lengthy discussions of timely subjects and that length of newspaper commentary would be proportionate to the importance of an issue.[3] He foresaw these being written while news was still "fresh." In other words, he had predicted a development in editorial writing that was occurring a quarter of a century later. By 1750, even publishers of provincial newspapers were demanding that contributions be kept short and to the point.[4]

In the second place, instead of addressing the publisher, as did Defoe, a few letter writers were addressing their remarks to a fictitious person. This, of course was in addition to writing under a pseudonym. A front page letter in the *Champion*, for example, was addressed to "Capt. Hercules Vinegar" of Pall Mall, who was in reality Henry Fielding.[5] In the *Daily Gazetteer* a series of letters introductory was addressed simply "To the Fool" and was signed "Your most affectionate Kinsmen."[6] Undoubtedly the purpose of both fictitious names was to retain anonymity. Even then, both printer and publisher were held responsible by the public and by law for the contents of their publication, and many newspapermen were still being arrested for defamation.[7]

Late in the 1740's, two literary figures, with their polemical essays and letters, contributed better form and greater importance to the slowly developing editorial. Tobias Smollett and Henry Fielding,[8] better known today for their novels, were particularly outspoken in their political commentaries. Fielding, who heaped contempt on Tory leaders and proponents of Hanoverian succession in the *Champion* and the *True Patriot,* introduced the use of italics, of asterisks for names, and of dashes between the first and last letters of words—an affectation that would prove popular in the coming years both in England and in the colonies. When he started the *Jacobite Journal* in December 1747, Fielding announced:

> In this dress I intend to abuse the *** and the ***; I intend to lash not only the m - - - stry, but *every man* who *hath* any p - - - ce or p - - no - - n from g - vernm - nt, or who is entrusted with *any degree of power or trust* under it, let his r - nk be ever so *high* or his ch - r - cter never so good. For this purpose I have provided myself with a vast quantity of *Italian* letters, and asterisks of all sorts, and so for all the words which I *embowel,* or rather envowel, I shall never mangle them but they shall be well known. . . . This I promise.[9]

Issues discussed in letters and essays during this period included the excise crisis of 1733, the bank contract of 1735, the continuing Spanish monopoly of colonial trade and the depredations of English seamen by the Spanish Navy, the resulting war with Spain, the War of Austrian Succession, and always the fight for press freedom, particularly the right to print reports of parliamentary proceedings. The Broad Wheel Tax, bad habits, bad roads, lotteries, cruelty to animals, education of the poor, Tithe Bill, depopulation through emigration to the colonies, hospitals, and postal routes were topics of more local interest.

Among the ministerial organs were the *Free Briton,* the *Daily Gazetteer,* the London *Journal,* and the *Champion.* They defended Sir Robert Walpole's policies of encouraging trade, of reducing taxes, of retaining friendship with France, and of avoiding war with Spain. It was Walpole's practice to supply his highly paid scribes with arguments to be used in essays and letters, with anticipated questions from the opposition, and with answers to these.[10] Francis Walsingham was a generously subsidized writer for the *Free Briton* and the *Daily Gazetteer.* James Pit, another government writer, contributed essays to the London *Journal* under the pen name, "Francis Osborne." Henry Fielding used the pseudonym of "Captain Hercules Vinegar" in the *Champion.*

The leading opposition newspaper was the *Craftsman.* It was founded in 1726 by Nicholas Amhurst, who conducted the publication under the name of "Caleb D'Anvers." Its most eminent contributions of letters and essays were Bolingbroke, who wrote as "Humphrey Oldcastle," and Daniel and William Pulteney. The Amhurst-Bolingbroke-Pulteney publication also used letters and short essays sent in by readers. William Pulteney later took over management of the *Craftsman* and held editoriallike conferences where subjects and writers of the publication's commentaries were discussed—one of the earliest known instances of an editorial writers' conference. Pulteney was insistent that printed discussion be kept short.[11] Other opposition newspapers were *Mist's Weekly Journal* and the *Evening Post,* but it was the daring attacks upon Walpole and his Whig party in the *Craftsman* that finally forced the prime minister to enter the political press picture.

From the first appearance of the *Gazetteer,* Amhurst of the *Craftsman* wasted no time in calling names. He alluded to the conductor of that newspaper as "a contemptible fellow" who was "retained on purpose to assert falsehoods" and who would "disavow or persist in them as long as Walpole would pay him." [12] This evoked an immediate answer. The "authors" of the *Craftsman* were denounced as "grovelling, abandoned, and despicable implements of slander." [13] Personal journalism was under way.

Week after week, essays and letters in the *Craftsman* in sonorous billingsgate attacked with vigor the "influence," placemen, sinecures, and corruption in government. Its authors took the side of the British merchants who were determined to break the Spanish monopoly on colonial trade. They demanded war. The ministerial newspapers defended Walpole's peace policy, or settlement by treaty. Letters and essays in the opposition newspapers were more influential in swaying public opinion, and war was declared. But, then, writers in the *Craftsman* denounced Walpole's war tactics. Again propaganda in the opposition publications helped swing the public against Walpole, and he was forced to resign in 1742.

What was considered fair comment in the *Daily Gazetteer* became seditious libel in the *Craftsman,* whose printer, as many another, was fined, pilloried, and imprisoned. Several times this publication and *Mist's Journal* were barred from the mails in an attempt to shackle them, and printers of provincial newspapers were arrested for daring to print letters from these two Tory newspapers.[14] Nevertheless, letters and essays in these opposition organs accomplished what today's editorial writer hopes to do—influence public opinion.

With Walpole's departure, the viciousness of personal journalism began to tone down somewhat. By this time, too, men of formal education no longer disdained writing for newspapers, and essays and letters became more literary. As the halfway mark of the century neared, many letters introductory and lead essays contained moral, philosophical, and religious, rather than political, commentary.

But news accounts had not changed much from the days of the early corantos. They were still impregnated with indirect comment or had attached paragraphs of vigorous editorial assertions. Publisher-editors in the provinces peppered letters and essays from contributors with editorial notices in which they chastised or rebuked or propagandized. Moreover, a few, who printed a column of local news, were beginning to insert here and there a paragraph of pure editorial.[15]

Biased adjectives and name-calling were favorite ways of indicating opinion. In the *Leedes Intelligencer,* an account of a violent demonstration against the new Holbrook curate, the Reverend Mr. Fawcett, was more defense of the minister than news report. The editor said that the curate had been "deservedly" nominated by the Leedes vicar, a "legal" and "duly licensed patron." Holbrook demonstrators were called a "furious, frantic, lawless Rabble," who assaulted Fawcett with "dirt, stones, and brickbats" and "whatever instruments of violence their Fury could furnish." The curate was treated in an "insolent, unheard of manner."[16] And the same publisher-editor ended a highly biased account of some "loose, idle Fellows" playing Shake Cap, a gambling game, by saying that he was publicizing this "notorious" game, "at the request of some well-disposed People" in the hopes that "methods can be taken" to "put a Stop to this infamous Practice." [17]

Of particular importance to the developing editorial, however, were the paragraphs of editorial opinion placed between items in the local or regional news columns. In such a paragraph, the publisher-editor of the Glouster *Journal* once complained of town and county people "bred to Labour" who left their trade and became beggars "under Pretence of Want of Work" when everyone knew employment was available. The editor said that this was a grievance that needed redress and the "attention of those Persons whose Duty" it was to remove such "causes of Complaint." Otherwise, this "growing evil" would produce "consequences very pernicious to Society." [18]

Such vigorous editorial comment in separate paragraphs within the local or regional news columns were few and far between before 1750, but it was a significant advance. As will be seen, it would slowly develop into a kind of editorial column.

13. News Commentary Grows
in the Colonial Press

As ACCEPTANCE in England of letter and essay commentary in newspapers increased, the importance of the political and religious pamphlet as a medium for dissemination of opinion slowly decreased. Politicians and journalists were coming to understand that pamphlets and tracts were not as effective an instrument for guiding public opinion as they had been in earlier periods. Collection into volumes of letters introductory, such as those that had appeared in *Mist's* and as the "Fool" letters, probably proved more profitable than, and as influential as, pamphlets.

But in the American colonies, where newssheets were few and space in them limited, the pamphlet for a long time would remain the favorite form for expressing views on important issues of the day. Apparently the most learned colonial opinion writers still believed with Defoe and L'Estrange that "convenient hints and touches" in the shape and air of a pamphlet could turn the "affections" of the common people.

Although theological treatises predominated in the pamphlet output during the second quarter of the eighteenth century, the tendency of pamphleteers to tell colonial readers that God was punishing sinners with thunder, lightning, earthquakes, and inundations was lessening.[1] Utterances in the *New-England Courant* against the tyranny of Puritan divines was causing a swift decay in secular authority. Many people no longer attended church regularly. But such ministers as Jonathan Edwards, Charles Chauncey, Samuel Johnson, who would become the first president of what is now Columbia University, Jonathan Mahew, controversial George Whitefield, and Gilbert Tennent played leading roles through printed sermons and religious tracts in the Great Religious

Awakening. Their discussions, which aroused the conscience of people and the indignation of the Puritan Clergy, led to missionary work among Indians. Their philosophies swayed social and political thought and created a democratic spirit in religion. In 1735 Benjamin Franklin contributed to this "Awakening" by writing three pamphlets in defense of the Reverend Mr. Whitefield.

But humanitarian and political pamphleteering increased. John Woolman, also a minister, wrote pamphlets on the evils of war, of lotteries, of Negro slavery, of rum, and of cruelty to animals. Both Anthony Benezet and Ralph Sandiford wrote tracts on slavery. Political pamphlets foreshadowed the political newspaper propaganda of a later period. Samuel Sewall joined with Edward Rowson in the writing of *The Revolution in New England Justified*. They argued against "the doctrine of passive obedience and non-resistance," which was then the practice.

Jeremiah Drummer in 1728 wrote *A Defense of the New England Charter*. At a time when the House of Commons was considering annulling the charters of New England colonies, Drummer argued that people had "a good and undoubted Right to their respective charters," that it was "not the interest of the Crown to resume the charters if forfeited," and that it seemed "inconsistent with justice to disenfranchise the charter colonies by act of parliament." [2]

Benjamin Franklin wrote *Plain Truth: or, Serious Considerations on the Present State of . . . Pennsylvania,* in which he begged readers "if not as Friends at least as Legislators" to consider military protection as a part of the government's duty to the people. He also proposed the formation of an English-type school in a pamphlet which proved influential in spurring foundation of the University of Pennsylvania.

Freedom of expression and economics were other subjects of colonial pamphlets. Charles Chauncey wrote a sermon, published in 1739, *The Only Compulsion proper to be made Use of in the Affairs of Conscience and Religions*. He argued for liberty of conscience, but maintained the orthodox view, that abuses of liberty and licentiousness should be banned. Later, Elisha Williams, under the pseudonym, "Philalethes," wrote *A seasonable Plea for the Liberty of Conscience, . . .*

without any control from human authority. He spoke openly about matters that affected "the good as a whole"; however, he excluded Papists—a typical Protestant view of that time. Benjamin Franklin and an anonymous pamphleteer in South Carolina discussed the monetary issue of currency in pamphlets.

Colonial printers must have been happy that more and more people were writing commentaries for publication because pamphlet printing was one of a printer's most lucrative jobs. Even with a variety of printing jobs, such as money, government statutes, letterhead stationery, almanacs, broadsides, and pamphlets, these early colonial printers needed other means of income to feed their large families who lived upstairs over their shops. On the ground floor along with their seven-foot English Common Presses, composing stones, "horse" and "bank" tables, and wetting trough, they kept a supply of books, almanacs, English newspapers, and pamphlets for sale. Some also ran apothecary shops and post offices.

Printers by this time were spreading into nearly all of the colonies; and where the printer went after 1726, there soon followed a newspaper as an additional means of livelihood. The five newspapers in three colonies in 1725 had grown by 1750 to fourteen in six colonies. A printer usually migrated to a colony at the invitation of its government which needed its edicts and statutes printed. Such printers founded newspapers not only for the financial rewards but also later for their usefulness to them as political instruments.

Though the colonial printer himself might not write often for his publication, he spoke of himself sometimes as an "undertaker" or "author," after the current fashion in England. The names, forms, and makeup of their papers were patterned after English publications. And printers depended on English newspapers not only for their foreign news items but also for their editorial commentary in the form of letters and essays addressed to the printer. Such original opinion elements as did appear in these early colonial newspapers were written in a form and style closely imitating similar contributions in English newspapers.

In March 1727, shortly after the death of James Franklin's *Courant,* Samuel Kneeland, who had printed the Boston *News-Letter* since 1722, founded the *New-England Weekly*

Journal. Like James Franklin, Kneeland, who used a publisher's name of "Proteus Echo, Esq.," had a stable of writers. Among them were the Reverend Thomas Prince and the Reverend Mather Byles, modified ecclesiastics, who wrote essays and letters that closely followed the style of Addison and Steele. In fact, their commentaries were more imitative of *Spectator* essays than were Franklin's "Dogood" letters.

By this time, a milder theological tone had prevailed in New England, and the essay commentary in Kneeland's publication was more ethical in quality than dogmatic or religious. Such subjects as covetousness, idleness, merit, loose living, solitude, and immoderate laughter were common. After 1734 discussions on contemporary issues of political, economic, and scientific importance increased; and a few essays and letters on beauties of knowledge and women's education were printed. Governor William Burnett was said to have written a series of eighteen essays for the *New-England Weekly Journal.* As other colonial newspaper printers were doing, Kneeland printed letters and essays not only from English journals but also from other colonial newspapers.[3]

Another Boston publication was not as cautious as Kneeland in printing "offensive and hurtful" commentary. When Thomas Fleet took over the Boston *Weekly Rehearsal,* founded in 1731 as a political organ, he solicited opinion writers by inviting "all Gentlemen of Leisure and Capacity . . . to write anything of a political nature, that tends to enlighten and serve the Publick, to communicate their productions, provided they are not overlong."[4] In the Boston *Evening-Post,* also founded by Fleet, contributed essays and letters provoked ministers to denounce the publication as "a dangerous engine, a sink of sedition, an error and a heresy."[5] To this, Fleet replied that he printed sermons because he thought people wanted to read them.

"Of all the books of Controversy" that he had read, and he had read some, Fleet wrote, "I never met one that blamed the Printers." Even the "great Dr. Edwards, who, for his knack of finding fault, might have claimed the office of Accuser-General of All Europe," never "meddled with printers." It was only of late "that some weak men have thought it the safest and easiest way to answer books, and prejudice people against authors and printers." [6] Thus, when his freedom to print was attacked, Fleet did not fear to comment.

On another occasion, he wrote that it seemed a bold stroke for ministers to advise against reading pamphlets and newspapers. To him, the Divines wanted people to be ignorant, and the "next stroke" probably might be "the *Liberty of the Press.*" [7]

In 1748, the Boston *Independent Advertiser* was founded as a Whig Organ. Its vicious and sarcastic essays and letters, like those in the English political newspapers, were chiefly political. It was an opposition organ, whose contributors, including Samuel Adams, advocated the rights of people against domination by the British. In the first issue, the author wrote the customary address to the readers, in which he said that "our present political state" afforded "matter for a variety of thoughts of peculiar importance to the good People of New England." He proposed to print whatever was pertinent and decent. And he promised to publish whatever would tend to "defend the rights and liberties of mankind, to advertise useful knowledge" and "to improve trade, the manufactures, and husbandry of the Country." This, then, openly portended the political opinion writing which would dominate colonial newspapers in the next half-century.

Meanwhile down in Philadelphia, where utterances in Andrew Bradford's *American Weekly Mercury* had occasionally conflicted with Pennsylvania Quaker authorities, the publisher-author of that newssheet began using letters introductory and essays on the front page. These were either copied from English journals, such as were the Cato letters, or were imitations of such writings. Furthermore, Bradford would become embroiled in a newspaper war with charismatic Benjamin Franklin.

Even before Franklin became the owner of a newspaper, however, Bradford was occasionally inserting a paragraph of editorial comment, either as a kind of preface to a letter or essay or as an ending to a news story. Particularly in the winter when the colonies were locked in by the weather and when even months-old English newspapers were hard to come by, Bradford would use apologetic prefaces, such as: "In this scarcity of news, I here present to my readers a small essay on Entertainments." [8] Or "Having but few remarkable occurrences to fill up our paper at present, we believe it will not be unacceptable to our Readers, to incert the following letter from a Gentleman to his Friend upon the loss of his only Daughter." [9]

In 1726 Benjamin Franklin returned from his two years in London where he had read the London *Journal* and the *Craftsman*. He believed that Philadelphia was large enough for two newspapers. He formed the Junto Club, an organization of men who managed to squeeze time from their reveling to write essays. Among them was Joseph Breitnall, a Quaker who wanted Quaker material printed. The Junto planned to start a newspaper. But Samuel Keimer, the grotesque printer for whom Franklin had once worked, forestalled their plans. On December 24, 1728, he founded *The Universal Instructor in All Arts and Science and Pennsylvania Gazette*.

Then Franklin went to Andrew Bradford and offered his cooperation in killing the Keimer newspaper. Bradford agreed to print the "Busy-Body" essays in his *Mercury* because he was feeling the pinch of competition with Keimer, who had succeeded in taking from him the government printing contract. The *Mercury* publisher must have been delighted to feature, on his front pages, essays not copied from months-old English publications.

The Philadelphia public, perhaps tired of reading stale news from the continent, found the Busy-Body essays delightful. Franklin wrote the first six and Breitnall wrote almost all the others. The first Busy-Body essay was in the form of a letter addressed to Mr. William Bradford and was signed "The Busy-Body." Here Franklin gave the design for the series and observed that, the *Mercury* being "frequently very Dull," he "out of zeal for the Public Good," would make "Nobody's Business" his business and discuss and censor "Vices and Follies" of his countrymen, books, morality, or philosophy, and sometimes politics. He hoped he would be entertaining and instructive.[10] Other Busy-Body papers that Franklin wrote were in the form of essays, although in one, he included a letter from a purported reader who signed herself "Patience." This he introduced with a preface and ended with commentary. Patience, a single woman who kept a shop, made a complaint familiar to the modern supermarket manager—women with small children who "run about and do petty Mischief" by pulling items off the lower shelves, mixing up items, and even "making water" on the floor.[11]

Quite Addisonian in form, style, and content, the Busy-Body essays were not very malicious, nor did they have the youthful flavor and bold political views of the Dogood letters. Instead Franklin and Breitnall joked about the craze for treasure hunting or about importunate friends. And they censored bad morals of the day by eulogizing virtue and by alluding to local morals. Breitnall, who had read Gordon and Trenchard's Cato letters, not only wrote social satires on illness, tea drinking, and ladies but also discussed, in a serious vein, manners of the poor and the rich, the young and the old. In that he often must have written these in haste to meet the newspapers' deadline,[12] he was writing as the modern editorial writer.

In the next to last Busy-Body essay, its author, under the signature of "Brutus," discussed liberty versus tyranny and quoted liberally from a Cato letter. He ended with a plea to readers to "exact" themselves "for liberty" and not "tamely sit by and allow any part of it to be wrested" from them "by any man, or combination of men, whatsoever." Instead, they should "take care to transmit it to Posterity, rather improved than in the least diminished; one day, one hour of virtuous liberty" was "worth a whole eternity in bondage." [13] This essay appeared a few days before an election; and although the author of the next Busy-Body urged readers to study records of all candidates, he favored the reelection of the city sheriff.[14] In purpose and intent these two essays were similar to editorials.

Authorities considered the "Brutus" comments a reflection on the king and the government of Britain that tended to incite Pennsylvanians to overthrow their colonial government. Bradford, as the publisher, was arrested. But he took his case to the people in the columns of his *Mercury*. Subsequently, his trial was dropped.

When Benjamin Franklin acquired his own newspaper, the Busy-Body essays disappeared. Bradford, however, continued to print letters introductory and essays in his newspaper. After 1730, English journals and newspapers arrived in the colonies more regularly and more frequently, and newspaper printer-publishers had a greater choice of British publications from which to reprint essays and letters. But Bradford continued to use the Cato letters. An introductory essay in 1732 defended freedom of speech, but expressed abhorrence of those who published attacks on religion. This essay ended with a Cato letter on liberty. Again two years later a letter in the *Mercury* explained that freedom of press meant "Liberty, within the bounds of Law" or the liberty to examine "the great Article of our Faith." [15] Bradford also printed the Cato, Junior letters.

Religious controversies, fashions, education, hypocrisy, parents who made marriage matches for their children, personal liberty, fidelity, temperance, duties of a good magistrate, public justice, economic issues—all were discussed on the front pages of the *Mercury*. Nor was Bradford above the commentary of personal journalism. Not only did he become involved in a controversy with Franklin's friend, Andrew Hamilton, the famous lawyer; but twice he prefaced a selection from Addison with editoriallike comments aimed at Benjamin Franklin, then a rival newspaper publisher. One letter, addressed to "Mr. Franklin," used Franklin's own deistic comments in reverse.

But Franklin's competition hurt the *Mercury*. When Bradford died in 1742, his wife soon had to abandon its publication. However, his nephew, William Bradford III, shortly after Andrew's death, founded the *Pennsylvania Journal,* which was destined, as a Patriot organ, to contribute still further to the evolution of the newspaper editorial.

With the aid of Hugh Meredith, a fellow printer, Franklin had bought the Keimer newspaper, which had lasted only thirty-nine issues, and changed its name to the *Pennsylvania Gazette*. Their control dated from October 3, 1729. At first they published a half-sheet twice a week, but soon they resumed weekly publication. Less than a year later, Franklin became the sole owner. He was to make it the best newspaper in the colonies—a newspaper with influence.

Franklin filled the front page of the *Gazette* with European news and the second page with local news and letters from readers. This was his entire newspaper in the winter months. But in the summer and autumn when publications from the mother country were plentiful, he added a third and fourth page. Here he printed Assembly proceedings, advertisements, ship arrivals and departures, and rates of money exchange.

However, it was his letters on the second page which are interesting to the history of the evolving editorial. They were, to be sure, more like "letters to the editor" found on today's editorial pages than like the modern editorial. But they appeared on the left-hand page, typical location for future editorials, and they were on the same page with local news, the location of the first editorial paragraphs in American newspapers.

Franklin was aided in writing these letters by members of the Junto Club. As were most satirical essays of the time, the letters in the *Gazette* were filled with moral platitudes. A letter in one issue would often refute the arguments of a letter in the preceding issue—an interest-sustaining device used earlier by Daniel Defoe.[16] Following current practice, Franklin reprinted *Tatler* and *Spectator* essays, which he pretended were sent in by readers. Sometimes he introduced these with paragraphs of opinion, as when he reprinted *Spectator* No. 451 on slander.

As the purported contributor, Franklin, in this preface, complained to the printer that the *Gazette* was "sometimes as empty" as other newssheets. For the most part, he wrote, the printer had "the modesty to keep it clear of Scandal, a subject that others delight to wallow in." Because so much scandal had been printed, people "seem to think everything around them tainted." And he advised the printer to let his newspaper act as a looking glass, in which readers could see "their own Picture, and learn to know" what they were "doing weekly." If they liked what they saw, they could "proceed for the future." In this way, the printer would duplicate the "performance of the immortal Mr. Addison, who to his own and lasting honour of the English Nation" had laboured hard and "sometimes with success, to reform the follies and vices of his Country." [17]

Generally, Franklin, not inclined to risk his growing prestige and wealth by incurring the wrath of the government, steered clear of criticizing the administration. Once he printed a letter, signed "N. N.," that complained of icy streets in Philadelphia and that commended an old woman for sprinkling ashes before her doorsteps. Other such letters suggested the need for city watchmen, city firemen, and clean, lighted streets. But Franklin kept these commentaries light and humorous, as when, in reporting the rumor that a bolt of lightning had melted the pewter buttons on a farmer's breeches, he commented: " 'Tis well nothing else thereabouts was made of pewter." [18]

His serious letters were more philosophical and scientific in nature, and thus more literary than journalistic. Perhaps Franklin's most influential statement on freedom of the press appeared in an essay, "An Apology for Printers." [19] Probably it was an accurate statement of popular opinion in a time when people did not differentiate between freedom of speech and freedom of the press. In this essay, Franklin recognized the importance of the opinion element in newspapers when he wrote that printing was concerned chiefly with men's opinions and that most things that were printed promoted or opposed a viewpoint. When men differed in opinion, the press ought to give both sides "the advantage of being heard by the Publick."

When the Zenger Case erupted in New York, Franklin printed a four-part essay, purportedly written by James Alexander.[20] The final sentence may have presented Franklin's view of the right to criticize in print: "Upon the whole: To suppress enquiries into the Administration is good policy in an arbitrary government: But a Free Constitution and Freedom of Speech have such a reciprocal dependency on each other that they cannot subsist without consisting together."

Personal journalistic comments began between Franklin and Bradford when each stole letters from the other's publication. This developed into a political quarrel in 1733. Franklin's letters tended to show the viewpoints of the people, while Bradford's showed those of the administration. Franklin chided Bradford for inaccurate reporting, for spreading perfidious rumors, and for making false accusations. Other points of contention between the two Philadelphia printers were Masonry (which Franklin defended), papism, heredity, and

the controversial Reverend George Whitefield. Colonial newspapers from Boston to Charlestown chose sides in the Masonic
and religious controversies and copied letters from either the
Mercury or the *Gazette*.

But Franklin's political influence was wielded more
through personal contacts than through his newspaper. The
Gazette went blithely on through the diphtheria epidemic of
1746 and the invasion of French privateers without any comment on these events. Instead, in letters, Franklin, as "Plain
Truth" emphasized the need for reading books, for toleration, for freethinking, for education, and for military prepar-
edness. In 1748, he began turning the *Gazette* over to David
Hall, a printer who earlier had become Franklin's partner.
Under Hall, the publication printed scarcely anything but
letters and essays from English journals and other colonial
newspapers.

In 1742 New York, then the third colonial city in size,
was the scene of the biggest newspaper controversy since
James Franklin's trouble with the *Courant*. It will be remembered that William Bradford established the New York
Gazette seventeen years earlier. Bradford had given New York
authorities no trouble, having contented himself with printing
stale news and a few essays and letters that moralized on such
subjects as disciplining children. The city, however, had become embroiled in a political struggle between the governors
and the aristocrats on one side and the popular movement on
the other. Although Bradford in his *Gazette* tried to remain
neutral, he favored the administration. Leaders of the popular
movement resorted to pamphlets and broadsides to charge the
government with bribery and suppression.

However, when the new governor, William Cosby, and
Rip Van Dam, who had been acting governor for more than a
year, started squabbling, William Smith and James Alexander,
leaders of the popular faction decided they needed a publication to present their views. They persuaded John Peter Zenger,
a former William Bradford apprentice who now owned his
own print shop, to establish the New York *Weekly Journal*.
It was soon the focal point of the Cosby controversies. In the
first issue on November 5, 1733, and again on December 3,
essays on freedom of the press were filled with allusions to

Cosby and his conduct. A month later, a letter writer attacked Cosby for allowing French warships to enter the harbor and spy on the city's fortifications.[21] From then through February, Zenger reprinted Cato letters on the absurdity of the divine right of kings and governors, on the privilege of the individual to criticize government, and on other ideals of a democratic state.

To counteract these, Bradford printed *Spectator* essays on scandal and lying to criticize Zenger. In turn, Zenger denounced the *Gazette* as "a paper known to be under the direction of the government, in which the Printer of it is not suffered to insert anything but what his Superiors approve of." [22] But this was not the first attack on Bradford. Earlier Zenger had used a device that would later be a popular medium for political criticism in colonial newspapers—an advertisement. This particular one read, in part: "A large Spaniel, of about Five Feet Five Inches High, has lately stray'd from his Kennel, with his Mouth full of fulsom Panegyricks, and in his Ramble dropt them in the New York *Gazette*." [23] Once again personal journalism had grown from political controversies.

Letters, seemingly from readers but probably written by Smith or Alexander, kept the Cosby issue before the public. One commended Zenger for bringing the controversy into the open and not hiding "behind retrenchments made of the supposed laws against libeling." Such retrenchments soon would show all men "to be weak, and to have neither law nor reason for their foundation." The writer warned Zenger that he should concern himself with the precarious liberties and properties of New York's people because "slavery is like to be entailed on them and their posterity if some past things be not amended." [24]

Another letter writer said that he could not be persuaded to move to New Jersey because that "would be like leaping out of the frying-pan into the fire," since "both are under that same governor." He predicted that men's deeds would be destroyed, judges would be arbitrarily displaced, and new courts erected without the consent of the legislature. "Who, then," he asked, "can call anything his own?" [25]

A few months later, a letter to Mr. Zenger commented on the definitions of freedom of the press that had appeared in Andrew Bradford's *American Weekly Mercury*. The letter writer ended with this vigorous comment: "Glorious Liberty of the Press! We may write what we please, but then we must take care that what pleases us pleases our Masters too.—We may write! but if we do not write as they think fit, they'll make us smart for it! O Glorious Liberty!" [26]

Inevitably the continued publication of such letters resulted in Zenger's arrest on a charge of printing "Scandalous, Virulent, and Seditious Reflections." Zenger conducted his newspaper for nine months from jail. He was defended at his trial by the famous Philadelphia lawyer, Andrew Hamilton, whose eloquent argument, which cleared Zenger, helped to establish truth as a defense in seditious libel cases and right of a jury to determine the fact in such cases. After this, colonial newspaper writers seemed to agree that they could criticize government. Authorities would file informations, but usually no further action would be taken against printer-publishers.

The fifteen years following Zenger's trial in 1735 made a great difference in the comment elements in colonial newspapers. Political and economic discussions became more absorbing, and more accessible intercommunication between colonies made exchange of newspapers easier. Although these newspapers continued to imitate English publications in treating political news-commentary as literary events, disputes between colonial newspapers developed. In 1746 colonial news readers were entertained by an exchange between the New York *Weekly Post* and the *Maryland Gazette*. Thomas Type in a letter to the *Post* accused Maryland of Catholic sympathies because the colony did not contribute to the Cape Breton expedition. Timothy Antitype answered in the *Gazette* that Maryland's poverty kept the colony from contributing. Thomas Type retorted that Maryland's poverty was the result of improper regulation of tobacco trade.[27]

All Southern colonial newspapers were more literary than their Northern counterparts. When William Parks founded the *Maryland Gazette* in 1727, he, too, followed the English custom of printing opinionated letters and essays. He even instituted the practice of giving his opinion essays titles, such as "Plain Dealer," "Free-thinker," and "Censor." This practice was soon adopted by other colonial newspapers. But when Parks printed letters concerned with the political and economic controversies of the colony, he incurred the wrath of Lord Baltimore, founder of the colony. And after a few months, Parks refrained from printing utterances about these controversies. Instead he used fables, allegories, legends, and fairy tales, which, like Defoe's *Aesop Fables,* cloaked sermons that warned against sin and vice. Sometimes he prefaced his reprints from English journals with such comments as: "In the hopes it may prove diverting, if not useful to some of our readers, we give them the following letter from an English Journal." [28]

Thomas Whitemarsh, printer-publisher of the *South-Carolina Gazette,* produced a typical Southern colonial newspaper. In an Addisonian-like essay, he invited communications from readers for the purpose of "interspersing the Dulse with the Utile." But he advised contributors to "avoid giving offense, either publick or private," and particularly to forbear all controversies, both in Church and State.[29] English influence was further apparent in an occasional letter introductory. Once, "Honestus" contributed a *Spectator* on tradesmen's reputations and prefaced it with a diatribe. In this he said that since he was not "so expert a Scribbler as those" who usually contributed to the *Gazette,* he was not pretending to send "efforts of my own pen." Yet he expected the printer to insert the *Spectator* essay because it was from "a writer whom I would advise your good Friends to endeavour (if they can) to imitate." [30]

Whitemarsh also used editoriallike postscripts. Following a letter from "Mary Meanwell," who had complained of giggling young girls and fellows at church services, Whitemarsh wrote that he feared "we may be looked upon as meddlers in other Men's business." And he modestly disclaimed the abilities of Addison.[31]

Addison and Steele imitations and reprints and the Cato letters became the most popular, quotable, esteemed sources of colonial social ideas in this period. But printed political opinion and criticism of local customs and mores had taken a giant step forward in the evolution of the editorial. Fomenting opinion, stirred by utterances in letters, essays, prefaces, and postscripts, would take on a national character in the next twenty-five years, when political propaganda would lead even closer to the emergence of the true editorial.

14. FIGHTING PROGENITORS, 1750–1765

THE GENERATION OF PRESS COMMENTARY that began in the mid-eighteenth century and ended with the Stamp Act crisis produced the immediate forefathers of the newspaper editorial. It was the generation that could not be skipped if newspaper authors were to have the right to comment on governmental affairs. Without this freedom to criticize affairs of state obtained through legal battles in this period, newspaper editorial writing probably would not have evolved as rapidly as it did in the upcoming generations. In its raucous fight for freedom, the English press, always strides ahead of the colonial press, may have helped give colonial letter writers of the Stamp Act period the impetus for their successful campaign to win public opinion.

As noted earlier, newspapers in London, the press center of the British Empire, could be divided roughly into daily newspapers, an outgrowth of the old news letters and corantos, and into the weekly or semiweekly journals of comment, an offspring of the pamphlet and the news commentaries of Roger L'Estrange and Daniel Defoe. And the trend toward cross-breeding between the dailies and the journals of opinion continued in this fifteen-year period.

One of the pacesetters for such developments was the *Gazetteer*. In its columns, letters to the printer on political and topical subjects were still the main form for disseminating opinions. Either unsigned, or signed with fictitious names, they were sometimes written by its printer, sometimes by paid correspondents, and often by its readers—merchants, lawyers, moral reformers, and military strategists.[1]

In that the printer was receiving a large volume of these letters, he was forced into performing the editorial function of choosing which contributions to print and, in particular, the most significant. The latter, often more than a column in length, was featured each day on page one, usually in column two following a column or more of the theatrical advertisements. As the first of a number of such letters, its initial paragraph was adorned with a factotum block, a typographical device to draw attention to the opinion of the day. Letters of lesser significance filled the remainder of page one and that portion of page four that was not devoted to advertisements. Other dailies and weeklies bunched their letters to the printer on inside pages.

By 1762, page-four letters to the *Gazetteer* were being summarized by the author or compiler in a column headed "Observations." Such summaries were infused with frequent editoriallike utterances that explained, enforced, or refuted statements in the letters.[2]

But this was not the only place in the *Gazetteer* where the compiler interjected his comment on news events. On page two, the opening paragraph of the news column was sometimes used by the printer for his comments to the public and for brief editoriallike utterances on the most striking news events of the day—foreign or domestic.[3] As yet, this was not a daily practice, but it was a format that would be used more frequently with the passing years and that newspaper editors of the youthful United States would use.

In the 1750's, over such signatures as "Probus," "Pro-Patria," "Philo-Britannicus," "Gallicus," "True-Whig," and "A Moderate Whig," newspaper letter writers discussed high prices, peace, commercial problems, domestic economy, improved health facilities, educational reform, regulation of liquor, foreign policies, manners of the age, and dozens of other subjects which today would be considered proper and timely editorial topics. Frequently, a literary figure was employed to write a series of these essay-type letters.

One of these was Samuel Johnson, whose prose style would influence sentence length and paragraph arrangement of a new generation of letter writers and of a later generation of editorial writers.[4] In his subject matter and satire, Johnson followed in the footsteps of Defoe, Swift, Addison, and Steele. His essay letters in the *Rambler*, 1750–52, were more pompous of diction and moralistic of tone than his shorter "Idler" essay letters printed in the *Universal Chronicle and Weekly Gazette* from 1758 to 1760. Six years had made a difference in the evident ease and simplicity with which he wrote his commentaries. In his apparent ability to write quickly under the pressure of a deadline and to turn to fresh subjects, he was displaying the diversity considered desirable in the modern editorial writer.[5]

After 1760 each newly organized newspaper printed a column or two of Johnsonian-type commentary; and newspapers, now usually four-page, full-folio publications, more and more were taking over the commentary function of essay sheets and pamphlets.[6] These latter type publications, however, had not yet yielded their influence as disseminators of commentary and molders of opinion. And in the 1760's an unusually prolific use of them by political figures helped precipitate the legal battle for press freedom. The accepted definition of a journalist at this time leaves little doubt that the intent of these publications and of the letters to the editor was very close to the purpose of the twentieth-century editorial writer. A journalist, according to one letter writer, was "an Historian," who "distributes for a time Reputation or Infamy, regulates the opinion of the week, raises hopes and terrors, inflames or allays the violence of the People." [7]

Moreover, in view of the rapid political changes, it is easy to understand how newspaper authors with this understanding of their duties could run afoul of authorities. When George III came to power in October 1760, England had been involved for four years in the Seven Years War, of which French-English colonial rivalry was only one issue. The new King, with definite ideas of his regal duties, disliked William Pitt, the Great Commoner, who had headed a coalition government since 1757. Under the influence of John Stuart Bute, his Scot mentor, George III required less than two years to gain control of the House of Commons from the Whigs and to force Pitt's resignation so that he could appoint Bute prime minister. But it took the press less than a year to force Bute's resignation. George Grenville then became prime minister, but press criticism of his prosecution of the Wilkes Case and his ill-advised Stamp Act were influential in unseating him two years later.

Political figures involved in the various ministerial changes employed professional pamphleteers and writers of letters to the printer to help them mold public opinion. Bute was no exception, and the attack upon Pitt's war policy produced the most numerous pamphlets and letter essays of the era.[8] Israel Mauduit's pamphlet, *Consideration on the Present German War,* the first influential press attack against Pitt's policy, argued against the high cost of the war. This publication evoked an opposition pamphlet, *Vindications of the Conduct of the Present War,* which, in turn, was answered with *Seasonable Hints from an Honest Man.* When Pitt resigned, he accepted a small pension for himself and a title for his wife; and Bute's hired writers derided this action in columns of letters to the printer and a flood of anti-Pitt pamphlets.[9] In turn, John Wilkes and John Almon defended Pitt and attacked the Bute ministry. Two other events which evoked a rash of pamphlets and letter essays were the Wilkes Case and the stamp tax imposed on the American colonies.

The real political battles, however, were fought in the columns of the weeklies, and it was their authors and printers who led the fight for the right to criticize the government. Bute, unaccustomed to press abuse of successful politicians, had used the *Universal Chronicle or Weekly Gazette* for planted announcements and anti-Pitt letters.[10] After he became prime minister, he used the press even more lavishly in an effort to create a favorable public image. Particularly, he was interested in combating the *Monitor,* which had been outspoken in its criticism of him.

The *Monitor,* a Whig publication founded in 1755 by four political writers, was the spokesman for Pitt's brother-in-law, Earl Temple. It was written mostly by Arthur Beardman; but John Wilkes, a member of Parliament who wrote pro-Pitt pamphlets, frequently contributed letters. As a rival to this publication, Bute hired Tobias Smollett to write the ministerial *Briton.*[11] Smollett, who later gained fame as a novelist, was a master of invective. Although he was heavy-handed and slow in writing,[12] the opposition apparently thought him dangerous enough to found within a week the *North Briton.* Supported by Temple and written largely by Wilkes, it was to become the "greatest propagandistic" publication during the reign of George III.[13] Not to be outdone, the administration a few days later replied to this publication with the *Auditor,* a weekly directed by Arthur Murphy, the dramatist.[14] These four organs, popularly called pamphlets, became the vitriolic spokesmen for the warring political parties and factions within parties. Leading London newspapers and colonial newssheets reprinted wholly or in part their utterances. Such reprints often were accompanied by editorial remarks about the weekly from which the letters were taken.[15]

On the one hand, the *Briton* and the *Auditor* defended the ministry and its actions and abused Pitt, war contractors, and West Indian planters.[16] Their authors discredited rival weekly writers with the previously often-used device of name-calling. Smollett invented ridiculous names for his opponents. Wilkes was Captain "Iago Aniseed" and "Jack Dandy." Charles Churchill, who, while Wilkes was serving with his army regiment, wrote much of the *North Briton,* was "Bruin" and "Lloyd." Arthur Murray labeled Wilkes "Colonel Squintum" in his grotesque descriptions of the cross-eyed man.[17]

On the other hand, the *Monitor* and *North Briton* attacked Bute's foreign policy, heaped odium on Scots, and advocated stripping Spain and France of their colonial possessions.[18] Wilkes, a master propagandist, not only used name-calling, but he also employed innuendo, repetition, ridicule of the Royal family, emphasis on administration ideas abhorrent to the Whigs, hints of a Stuart restoration, and the hoax.[19] For example, in the early part of 1762, Wilkes wrote a letter signed "Viator" and sent it to the *Auditor.* In it he made the ridiculous statement that the great peat bog in Florida could furnish heat for the West Indies. Murphy not only printed the letter in the *Auditor* on December 8, but he also attached editorial comment in which he accepted the letter as pro-Bute sentiment. The *Evening Post* and *St. James Chronicle* joined the *North Briton* in editorial ridicule of the facts in the letter.[20]

The *North Briton* seldom missed an opportunity to print comment on freedom of the press. Wilkes set the tone for this in the opening paragraphs of the first issue when he said that liberty of the press was "the birth-right of a Briton" and "the finest bulwark of the country." Furthermore, "weaknesses, inability, and duplicity" of "all bad ministers" should be revealed to the public.[21]

Later when the authors and printers of the *Monitor* had been arrested for libelous statements, Churchill, probably at the instigations of Wilkes, told *North Briton* readers that "the liberty of the press, that bulwark of the liberties of the people" was "so deservedly esteemed that every attack made on it" was "productive of danger." When punishments for speaking out in the press had been inflicted, "disagreeable consequences" had resulted. No "candid man," then, could imagine that "at this juncture any step should be taken, which might be deemed a wanton, vexatious, and oppressive infringement of that glorious privilege." [22]

After the *North Briton* had attained great popularity and extended its influence into the grass roots, Wilkes became even more daring in his criticism of George III. In a letter, supposedly from the pretender to the throne, Wilkes was particularly vicious, and the King wanted libel action brought against the publication's author.[23] But before the general warrants could be issued and arrests made, Wilkes was criticizing graft in Bute's government and the cider tax. He explained that the "*odious* and *partial* manner" in which the law was to be enforced would repeal "the favorite law of our constitution, which has ever been considered the birth-right of an Englishman; I mean the trial by JURY." [24] The trials which grew out of Wilkes's editorial utterances in the *North Briton* did much eventually to bring about jury trials in cases of seditious libel.[25]

In the next to last issue of his journal, Wilkes predicted that when Henry Fox, paymaster general and Bute's spokesman in the House of Commons, resigned and was awarded a peerage, a change in government would be near. He also warned that "the liberty of communicating our sentiments to the public freely and honestly" would not be easily relinquished.[26] Bute resigned six days later.

The last issue of the *North Briton*, the famous No. 45, was in proof and ready to be printed April 9, 1763. In it Wilkes criticized governmental interference in the business of the East India Company. But when Bute resigned, publication was held up. On April 13, Wilkes explained his reason for this action in a broadside. The paper had been "steady in its opposition to a single, insolent, incapable, despotic minister," Wilkes wrote, but he was reserving opinion on George Grenville, Bute's replacement, until it could be determined that

Bute was not dictating policy to the new minister. By April 23, Wilkes had decided to publish No. 45. He made a few changes in the original proof and included an attack on the King's April 19 speech to Parliament. His statement that "every friend of his country must lament" the sanction given by a reverend King to "odious measures" and to "unjustifiable, public declarations" so irritated George III that messengers were sent with general warrants to arrest the authors, printers, publishers, and booksellers of the "seditious and treasonable" publication.[27]

Forty-eight arrests were made, forty-four before Wilkes himself was apprehended. Those arrested eventually sued the messengers for false arrest. Wilkes, however, was expelled from Parliament as it was judged that libel privileges did not extend to members of the House of Commons. No. 45 was burned publicly, but not before a sympathetic mob almost tore it from the hands of the hangman. Wilkes, who would later reprint the *North Briton* in volume form, and his No. 45 became the rallying cry for those in England and in the American colonies who were to fight for the liberties of the people.

Legal cases evolving from *North Briton* No. 45 caused a transfer of political authority "from government and the law to the people and the law." Decisions handed down evoked a "new interpretation of the powers of government and of the liberty of the press." [28] But if Wilkes helped to bring about a realization of the need for jury trials, he was also instrumental in advancing the development of the editorial. As the most influential writer in the four propaganda weeklies, his writings in the *North Briton* set the pattern for the transition of news opinion writing from the pamphlet to the newspaper leader, or editorial. As one historian has observed, "As a literary composition and as an instrument of political attack or defense, the leader (or editorial) gained appreciably in form and in importance" [29] from Johnson, Smollett, and Wilkes.

After the death of these four political weeklies, there was a noticeable increase in the number and kind of letter essays in the London dailies and triweeklies. They followed patterns in form and in substance of those in the deceased publications.

Though there would be sporadic new political organs, by 1765 London newspapers were being recognized as the mouthpieces for particular political factions. The London *Evening Post*, for example, was known as the communication organ for Temple.[30]

And there was a decided decrease in the number of prosecutions for libel. Printers of *St. James Chronicle* were not prosecuted when letters in their publication signed "Civicus" and "X" were declared by government officials to be "derogatory to the Crown and Parliament." The attorney general did not think that in the temper of the times he could prosecute successfully.[31] It would be another half-century before the Congress of the young United States would arrive at a similar conclusion.

15. Colonial Printers Discover Propaganda

In the same fifteen years that had seen the English press fight for freedom to comment, the press in the American colonies was struggling along at about the same pace of the English newsletters of a half-century earlier. It could develop only as population increased and as communications improved between the colonies. In 1750 there were fewer weeklies in all the colonies than there were dailies and triweeklies in London alone. Six colonies had no newspaper. But by 1765, twenty-three colonial news publications were serving a population of fewer than two million people. Only Delaware and New Jersey had no publications.

Literacy in the colonies was even lower than that in England. Both pamphlets and newspapers were written for an upper-class, or wealthy, reading public. A majority of colonial adults still depended on hearing news and views read to them in coffeehouses and taverns. At mid-century, pamphlets were still the favorite medium for communicating ideas about serious public issues. But in a fifteen-year time span, events and the spread of newspapers through the colonies would change the small colonial newssheets into propaganda publications.

Printer-publishers of the era were sometimes barely able to read themselves. With one press and two or three fonts of worn type, they spent at least three days of each week printing pamphlets, broadsides, almanacs, and business stationery. They used the other days to print their folio-sized newspapers. One page of these was filled with standing advertisements; but the first page, after the English fashion, usually contained an address to the public, or a letter essay addressed to the printer. It was in these that the colonial printer-editor expressed his feeble and timid editorial opinions.

Publication of blatant criticism of the Crown's actions was studiously avoided because suppression of the newspaper, confiscation of press, imprisonment, and fines could, and did, follow. Even the printing of a pamphlet could incur the wrath of the administration. One of the most noted incidents of this type occurred in 1754 in Boston, where two brothers, Zechariah and Daniel Fowle, had separate printing establishments. Zechariah printed the *Monster of Monsters,* a pamphlet that satirized the General Court and an excise tax then being debated before the Massachusetts Assembly. Signed "Thomas Thumb, Esq.," but with no imprint, the publication was called a false, scurrilous libel that reflected on the proceedings of the House in general and on many of its worthy members in particular.[1] The House assumed Daniel Fowle had printed the pamphlet, and he was arrested. The hangman was ordered to burn it; and Fowle was tried, reprimanded, jailed, and ordered to pay costs. A year later the printer wrote and published *A Total Eclipse of Liberty* and two years later *An Appendix to a Total Eclipse of Liberty*—pamphlets that gave an account of his trial.

Two years later, printer-publishers of the New York *Gazette: or, the Weekly Post-Boy* escaped with much less severe treatment. James Parker and William Weyman, joint owners of the publication, had printed in their March 15, 1756, issue a commentary essay, "Observations on the Circumstances and Conduct of the People in the Counties Ulster and sions. When the two men revealed the name of the author and Orange, in the Province of New York," which had been written by the Reverend Hezekiah under an assumed name. The two printers were arrested and brought before the Bar of the House because the piece was said to contain "sundry, insolent, false, and malicious Expressions, calculated to misrepresent the conduct of the Representatives of the People of the Colony." Weyman said that he thought he was printing news, and Parker revealed that he deleted indecent expresapologized, they were discharged. When Watkins was called before the Bar of the House, he apologized, too, saying that he had been carried away by his zeal for the welfare of the people. He was reprimanded and also discharged.[2]

As long as pamphlets and letter essays in the newspaper were confined to comments on manners and morals—after the fashion of Addison, Steele, and Johnson—or to commentary on community needs, such as better roads, wandering cattle, or higher wages, the printer-publisher was on a safe course. Benjamin Franklin's pamphlet, *Observations concerning the Increase of Mankind,* which argued for higher wages in a free land, was not considered objectionable. Neither were such letters to the printer as that from a housewife in Boston who complained that giving fees "to the nurses of lying in of women" was "a needless expense." [3]

In reality, many colonial printer-publishers around the mid-eighteenth century had only a slight conception of their ability to use editorial commentary for influencing public opinion even on municipal issues. On June 19, 1754, an American Congress met at Albany, New York, to make a treaty with the Six Nations of Indians in order to prevent the Indians from uniting with the French. Members of the Congress were chosen on the principle of representation. One delegate was Benjamin Franklin, who presented a plan for uniting the colonies. But the Albany Congress received little attention in the colonial press.

Six weeks earlier, the famous "Join or Die" snake cartoon had appeared in Franklin's *Pennsylvania Gazette,*[4] and had been reprinted in four other colonial newssheets. In Franklin's paper, it was printed at the end of an article detailing the French capture of Captain Trent's party, who were erecting a fort on the Ohio River. The author, very likely Franklin, had urged, toward the end of the account, a union of colonies to resist French aggression.

And months after the conference, a letter writer in Samuel Kneeland's Boston *Gazette* hoped and prayed to "the Almighty" that the British colonies would cease their "impolitically" and "narrow, separate and independent views" so that they could secure "the inestimable blessings of civil and religious liberty." And he called on "the God of heaven" to "grant success to the plan for a union of the British Colonies on the continent of America." [5] No other letter essay writers apparently commented on this conference.

At this time printer-editors probably believed with the authors of the *Independent Reflector,* a short-lived New York essay newspaper, that a printer should not "publish everything that is offered to him." Rather he should print what was "conducive of general utility" whether the author was "a Christian, Jew, Turk, or Infidel." A refusal to print would not be an "immediate abridgement of Freedom of the Press." But it would be a criminal act if the printer prostituted "his art by the publication of anything injurious to his Country." [6]

Even the stamp tax of one halfpenny imposed by the colonial governments on Massachusetts newspapers in 1755 and on New York newspapers in 1756 did not seem to upset printer-publishers. Possibly they believed that this act was necessary since the revenues would be used in their own colonies. Modeled on such acts in the mother country, these taxes were in effect until 1760.

But by that time the idea of Americanism was growing. Colonists, restive under restraints being imposed on them by the Crown, were becoming more outspoken. Printer-publishers were bolder in printing expressions of resentment. And passage of the Sugar Act, the Navigation Act, and other restrictive trade laws did little to allay growing dissatisfaction. Establishment of permanent garrisons of British troops in the colonies and taxing of the colonists for maintenance of these garrisons further increased resentment.

Understandably, then, the Stamp Act of 1765 brought colonial opposition openly into print. In spite of the constant call for payment of overdue subscriptions, printer-editors were beginning to make money from their newspapers. And the Stamp Act, which required that the printer pay one halfpenny to a penny to have his sheets stamped and two shillings for every advertisement, would have meant financial ruin. It would have been almost as effective as the old licensing acts in silencing the press if the new feeling of Americanism had not invaded the ranks of the printer-publishers. As it happened, they discovered the secret of propaganda, and colonial newspapers took the first great stride toward editorial activity.

Samuel Adams, who had filled up the pages of the short-lived Boston *Independent Observer* with anti-Tory comments, became the leading agitator for the Radical or Patriot groups. In 1775, he was again agitating in Benjamin Edes and John Gill's Boston *Gazette and Country Journal*. Under such fictitious names as "An American," "Popululos," and "A Religious Politician," he did much to foment opposition to every proclamation or act handed down by the British government.

In letters to the printers, he used each new law as an argument for uniting the colonies in a revolution against the parent country. He examined the act, reviewed it, and then reprobated and condemned it in strong language.

Although Boston has long been acknowledged as the center of the revolutionary movement, there were indications in other newspapers that the seeds of revolution were springing up in other colonies too. In 1754–55, the "Watch-Tower" letters on the first page of Gaine's New York *Mercury* were written by William Livingston, who two years before had written moral and political essays for the *Independent Reflector*. Purpose of the "Watch-Tower" letters was to stir colonial patriotism against the French and Indians. In these, Livingston used the term "natural rights," [7] a phrase that would become popular in the next few years.

Like the Livingston letters, another series of letter essays, now known as the "Virginia-Centinal Papers," were widely copied. Printed first in the *Virginia Gazette,* they, too, were written to arouse patriotism against the French army.[8] In both sets of letters the language and tenor of coming revolutionary diatribes were apparent.

Some controversial opinion writers of the 1750–65 years still preferred the pamphlet as a medium for communicating their views of events and actions. In these longer publications, authors could be more detailed, comprehensive, and coherent in the presentation of their arguments than in a letter to the printer. A few pamphleteers showed their concern for humanity. For example, Anthony Benezet is believed to have been the author of *A Short Account of that Part of Africa Inhabited by Negroes,* printed in 1762. In it he showed the iniquities of slave trade and the fallacies of the arguments for it.

But the majority of pamphleteers were concerned with political and economic arguments.[9] Pamphleteers on the tax issue flooded shops of booksellers with their writings. Francis Bernard and Governor Stephen Hopkins of Rhode Island wrote from the British viewpoint. James Otis and Daniel Dulaney, with the idea of no taxation without representation, wrote the more influential Patriot tracts.[10]

Newspaper letter writers took up the arguments of Otis and Dulaney. The colonies were in the midst of a depression, and people were in no mood for additional taxes. When news reached the American shores that the stamp tax had been tentatively proposed in March and that Parliament had actually adopted the Sugar Act on April 5, letters to the editors of newspapers, particularly those in the northern and middle colonies, began to reflect a concern with how the tax would be paid. At first, there was a tendency by some printer-publishers to use letters from contributors of both sides.

But by August and September, the *Pennsylvania Journal* and the *Massachusetts Gazette and Boston News-Letter* were printing letters urging ladies to wear "decent plain dresses made in their own country" rather than expensive English gowns.[11] The Boston *Post-Boy and Advertiser,* and the Newport *Mercury* printed letters suggesting the use of less costly mourning clothes.[12] Letters in the *Massachusetts Gazette and Boston News-Letter,* the Boston *Post-Boy and Advertiser,* and the Newport *Mercury* advised replacement of British manufactures with those in the colonies.[13]

The printer-publisher of the Newport *Mercury* began printing in August, 1764, a series of letters signed "O. Z. &tc &tc," which encouraged local industries, manufactures, growth of flax, hemp, and wool, but which favored British rule. Typical of O. Z.'s editoriallike utterances was this remark:

> We cannot repress our filial Gratitude when we consider that at the same Time Molasses is reduced to Three Pence per Gallon Duty, a Bounty of £8 Sterling per ton is granted for Hemp raised in the Colonies. The Benefits the Colonies receive, we think, overbalance the Impositions supposed to be laid upon them.[14]

In his letter of November 19, 1764, "O. Z." praised the Pennsylvania legislature for seeking a royal government. An answer to O. Z.'s letter appeared in the Providence *Gazette.*[15] Reminiscent in style of Henry Fielding in the *Jacobite Journal* of nearly twenty years earlier, it was signed "I***" and accused "O. Z." of conspiring against "the liberties of the Colony." Showing the influence of Fielding even more, printer Thomas Green wrote in the "Prospectus" issue of his *Connecticut Courant*:

> It is now confidently affirmed by some, which however may not be true in fact, that the severity of the news of

the a - t of P - - - - - - - - t is to be imputed to letters, representatives, NARRATIVES, &c., transmitted to the m - - - - - - y about two years ago by persons of eminence this side of the water. . . . To whatever cause these severities are owing, it behooves the colonies to represent their grievances in the strongest point of light, and to write in such measures as *will be effectual* to obtain redress. The northern colonies have sense enough, at least, the sense of *feeling;* and can tell where the *shoe pinches.*[16]

By early 1765, rumors of the impending passage of the Stamp Act were so strong that Benjamin Franklin, as colonial agent, was in London to lobby against it. But he was unsuccessful. News of its passage reached the colonies in April. The tax was to be imposed as of November 1, and the small colonial newspapers had seven months to whip public opinion "to a fever pitch" and galvanize people into action.

On May 11, William Goddard, printer-publisher of the Providence *Gazette,* printed a fifteen-hundred-word letter in his publication that was widely reprinted in other colonial newspapers. Written by "Plain Yeoman" to a great personage in Old England, the letter hinted at violence. The writer said that the mother country was being presumptious to tax the colonies and abridge "such privilege as we have long enjoyed." He warned that if tax measures and restrictive practices continued, "the people of Britain may begin to tremble for their own liberties."

Such letters traveled up and down the communication chain of newspapers. The argument that Parliament had no right to tax the colonies without representation was a common theme. The New York *Gazette, Pennsylvania Journal,* and *Maryland Gazette* printed a letter from "Freeman," who said that the prime minister had grounded "his Pretence of the Parliament's Right to tax the Colonies" on the fact that the colonists were *"virtually represented in Parliament."* If, therefore, he failed to prove "their being so Represented, he must, by his own Argument, give up the Point," and admit that Parliament had "no Manner of Right to tax the Colonies." [17]

But it remained for the author of a front-page essay in the New York *Mercury* to become almost lyrical in his irony.

It is enough to melt a stone, or even the harder heart of a villain, when he views this wretched land, sinking under the merciless and ill-timed persecution of those who should have been its upholders and protectors.

It is enough to break the heart of the Patriot, who would joyfully pour out his blood, to extricate his beloved country from destruction, to find her fainting and despairing, hourly expecting to be utterly crushed from the iron rod of power.[18]

Printer-publishers, if indeed they did not write many of these letters, were expressing their editorial opinions by printing them. Their views also infiltrated notices to readers, when they pleaded for payment of overdue subscriptions. Daniel Fowle told readers of his *New-Hampshire Gazette* that the stamp tax would "oblige the Printers of this Continent to Raise more Money every Year, than was ever raised at year's end." [19]

As early as August, when the British government began preparing for enforcing the act by appointing stamp distributors, newspaper letter and essay writers had become abusive, scurrilous, and even vulgar in their utterances. In New York, John Holt, printer-publisher of the New York *Gazette: or, Weekly Post-Boy,* was the only newspaper owner in the city daring enough to put out the one issue of the *Constitutional Courant.* Filled with virulent diatribes against the Stamp Act, it was said to have been written by one Andrew Marvell. Such phrases as "vile minions of tyranny" and "chains of abject slavery" were used for perhaps the first time. Later they would be common in Revolutionary propaganda. A form of Franklin's snake device was used as an adornment, and people were urged not to "pay one farthing of tax." This publication was reprinted in Boston and Philadelphia.[20]

In the *Connecticut Courant,* Cato denounced those who would accept the positions of tax distributors as "base defectors" and warned that such people would inherit the "Curses of Widows and Orphans" and would be treated "as the Authors of their Misery." History would treat them "with the most terrible Imprecations." [21]

In Boston, Benjamin Edes and John Gill in their *Gazette* published a continuous stream of letters to arouse feelings against the Stamp Act. Samuel and John Adams and their friends sat up late into the night writing letters that would be reprinted in newspapers up and down the coast. They made the *Gazette* the mouthpiece of the Loyal Nine, the organization that was soon to be known as the Sons of Liberty.[22]

So virulent had the letters become and so effective had they been in molding public opinion that only a few opposing writers dared to comment on their scurrility. "Civis" wrote in the *Connecticut Gazette* that "a perfect Frenzy seems to have seized the Mind of the People and renders them deaf to all Reason and Consideration." [23] Jared Ingersoll, who personally opposed the tax but who through high-minded consideration accepted the position of Connecticut tax distributor, wrote in an open letter to the publisher that newspapers were handing out "personal abuses in the most unrestrained way and would not publish anything that would tend" to abate the prejudices of the people.[24] Less than ten days later, Ingersoll was seized by a number of Patriots and forced to resign publicly.[25]

John Adams in a letter to the printers of the Boston *Gazette* in August urged the editor-publishers not to be intimidated "by any terrors, from publishing with utmost freedom" or be "wheedled" out of their "liberty by any pretence of politeness, delicacy, or decency . . . three names for hypocricy, chicanery, and cowardice." Though later Adams would criticize the Tory press, now he wrote: "The stale impudent insinuations of slander and sedition, with which the gormandizers of power have endeavored to discredit your paper, are so much the more to your honor; for the jaws of power are always stretched out, if possible to destroy the freedom of thinking, speaking, and writing." [26]

Colonial governors complained to British officials of inflammatory utterances and malicious falsehoods in the newssheets, but no action was taken.[27] Riots, mobs, and roaming bands of the Sons of Liberty intimidated the British officials and kept them in their houses. Colonial delegates to the Stamp Act Congress, which met in New York in October, attacked the laws as unconstitutional because colonists were not represented in Parliament. This conference did not go unnoticed in the press. Hugh Gaine in his *Mercury* called it the most important meeting that "ever came under consideration in America." [28]

In the last issue before the act went into effect on November 1, many printer-editors used graphic-type editorials. Some used mottoes as subtitles for their publication. "The United Voice of All His Majesty's *free* and *loyal* Subjects in America —LIBERTY, PROPERTY, and *no* STAMPS" was used by the New York *Gazette: or, Weekly Post-Boy.* "Those who would give up *Essential Liberty,* to purchase a little *Temporary Safety,* deserve neither *Liberty* nor *Safety*" was printed across the front page of the *Connecticut Gazette.*

Several newspapers used a form of Franklin's snake-device cartoon or skull-and-crossbones cartoons. Some, particularly those in the southern colonies, announced their demise, and several used funereal themes, the most noted of these being William Bradford's *Pennsylvania Journal and Weekly Advertiser.* His famous tombstone edition of October 31, 1765, was a typographical masterpiece as a graphic editorial. His marginal comment, "Adieu, Adieu to the LIBERTY of the Press" and his use of skull and crossbones, surrounded by the phrase "An Emblem of the Effects of the STAMP O' the fatal STAMP" were as much an editorial as his introductory essay in this issue.

After the "fatal day," many papers continued to print, but without imprimaturs and titles and with no stamps. Mobs in some cities had destroyed the stamped paper; in other cities no one would jeopardize his life by collecting the tax. By the end of 1765, almost all of the newspapers were still being printed. They continued to be filled with letters expressing resentment against the act.

Printer-publishers must have been exhilarated by their feeling of importance to their communities. The opinion makers in the colonies had come to realize the importance of the newspaper as a weapon. Though there would still be pamphleteers, the newspapers were becoming the approved medium for making and molding political opinion because they could supply circulation. Letters, essays, snake devices, and other graphic editoriallike devices may not have been the biggest factors contributing to the repeal of the Stamp Act in 1766, but they made activists of printer-publishers. No longer would most of these men hesitate to print criticism of the government if they wanted to further the growing Americanism. In the fateful years ahead, these men, through printing letters, would develop appositiveness, a necessary requirement of editorials.[29]

16. Arrival of "Leaders"

As the cold winter months of early 1766 slowly dragged by, the question of the colonial Stamp Act plagued the commercial interests of England. Across the Atlantic, colonists had agreed on a nonimportation policy; and English merchants, shippers, manufacturers, and country gentlemen-farmers suddenly found themselves in financial difficulties. Overextended credit to the Americans and an overstock of goods that colonials would not accept, if shipped, forced more than a few English businessmen into bankruptcy.[1] Sailors walked the streets or gulped ale to pass the time. Weavers and iron mongers rioted when their shops were closed. Hunger stalked the farm workers, and prices soared.

Merchants and shippers were hardest hit because lucrative markets outside the American colonies had not been established. And it was the merchants who probably were more influential than any other group in securing the repeal of the Stamp Act.[2] They not only manned a writing campaign of appeals and petitions to their parliamentary representatives and the King, but they also bombarded such commercial newspapers as Lloyd's *Evening Post and British Chronicle* with pseudononymous letters to the printer. Filled with complaints of hard times, almost all of them advocated repeal of the act.[3] When their pocketbooks were hit, English businessmen were more interested in expediency of repeal than in independent claims of colonial legislators.

The English press at this time was comparatively free from governmental influence. Although the majority of London weeklies and dailies were decidedly opposition newspapers, on the Stamp Act issue such publications as the *Public Advertiser* and the *Daily Advertiser* opened their columns to both sides.[4]

One outspoken government writer, as "Anti-Sejanus," answered with spirit and resolution procolonial "Sejanus" by advocating enforcement of the act. He labeled actions of Americans as ingratitude and said the mother country could no longer be imposed on by "frivolous pretences." He predicted that if Parliament repealed the act, ungrateful Americans would find another way to assert their freedom. The only way to subdue this spirit of rebellion was by a strong show of authority.[5]

As was to be expected, another pamphlet war erupted over 'this issue. Much of this writing resorted to personal abuse. Charles Lloyd and Thomas Whateley, pamphleteers for the deposed Lord Grenville, were on one side; and Edmund Burke, secretary to the new minister, and Grey Cooper, a young lawyer who hoped to gain a government position, as he did, expounded for the administration.[6] But these men and many others, such as William Knox, John Almon, Samuel Johnson, and William Dowdeswell, at the same time were writing letter essays for newspapers.

On the same day that Parliament had repealed the Stamp Act, King George had officially approved the Declaratory Act. This bill declared that Parliament had the right to exercize control over the colonies.[7] But "Anti-Sejanus" had been right. The colonists were not satisfied. Crisis followed crisis. And British business interests became as insistent as the government that Parliament should rule the colonies.[8] Comment by political letter writers and printer-editors began to reveal this attitude.

"Veritas" and "Mercator Americanus" in letters to the printer of the *Gazetteer* sympathized with American grievances and advocated conciliation to preserve commercial advantages. But "A Boston Saint" favored current government policies.[9] In an italicized notice on April 29, 1775, Edward Benson, the *Gazetteer* printer, told his readers that there was no longer any basis for compromise. Only submission or war was left.

The provincial press from the beginning was more sympathetic to the government position than were the London newspapers. Typical was the *Stamford Mercury*. Its September 5, 1776, issue carried a letter reportedly from Philadelphia

to a gentleman in Dublin. It contained this irreverent explanation of the Declaration of Independence:

The 4th of July the Americans appointed a day of fast-
ing and prayer, preparatory to their dedicating their country to God, which was done in the following manner: The
Congress being assembled, after having declared Americans independent, they had a Crown placed on a Bible,
which by prayer and solemn devotion they offered to God.
This religious ceremony being ended, they divided the
Crown into thirteen parts, each of the United Nations
taking a part.

Following the repeal of the Stamp Act, newspapers had
only a brief period of relative tranquillity before they were
embroiled in their own battle with Parliament. Though the
controversy was more concerned with reporting news than
with writing opinions, it evoked a rash of opinionated letter
essays and pamphlets. Colonial newspaper editors and letter
writers watched developments with more than a little interest.

This issue involved the right to print parliamentary proceedings and, thus, freedom of the press. For several years,
leading London newspapers had grown bold enough to print
proceedings as a type of fairy tale. For example, proceedings
were reported in the *Gazetteer* as if they occurred at meetings
of the Robin Hood Society.[10] The old device of dashes between
first and last letters of names was used. But this was only a thin
veil for readers. Printer-editors now had parliamentary reporters, and they wanted flexibility. By the late 1760's, agitation for the right to report proceedings began to appear in
letters to the printer and in occasional paragraphs of comment
by newspaper conductors. "The liberty of the press," according
to one writer, had "ever been the scourge and terror of pride
and tyranny." And when "this sacred right" was "invaded"
as it was with the denial of the right to print proceedings, "we
may be sure that the political Lent of forty days tyranny is
not far removed." [11]

Charles Say, publisher-editor of the *Gazetteer*, preceded
a letter by "Serious," who had discussed liberty of the press,
with an editorial paragraph. "If the liberty of the press ever
becomes licentiousness," he wrote, "there are sufficient laws in
being to curb and punish it; but the whole house need not be
destroyed because a chimney smokes sometimes;—though in-

deed it is much to be desired that a proper line was fixed to divide the one from the other" in order to ascertain the legal and constitutional liberty of the press.[12] In a later issue, Say told his readers that Parliament "ought never to be considered as objects of satyrical raillery," but that acts and laws were "almost always ample field for remarks, in which the greatest talents of wit and humor may be exercised" with advantage to the public.[13]

In one of his pamphlets, David Hume indicated the confusion that must have plagued printer-editors of the time. "The unbounded liberty of the press," he wrote in his final sentence, was an evil for which it was difficult to find a remedy.[14]

In 1771 the House of Commons, apparently tired of reading about its actions in print, decided to invoke a fifty-year-old resolution that declared giving accounts of proceedings to newspapers a breach of privilege. It ordered printers of offending newspapers arrested and brought before the Bar of the House.[15] But by this time, John Wilkes, back from exile and prison, was an official of the city of London. Acting under his guidance, the printers hid from the messengers who carried summonses for arrest. A dispute then developed between the House on the one hand and the city authorities, who believed making arrests was their prerogative, on the other. Consequently, they granted a kind of asylum to the printers until Wilkes considered the time propitious. Then the printers were arrested by their own men and brought before Wilkes sitting as a justice. As such, he dismissed the printers because they had committed no crime. House members were placed in a ridiculous position. After this, Parliament made no consistent effort to limit the political press by claiming parliamentary privilege, though it would be another twenty years before juries could decide the law and fact in libel cases.[16]

As was to be expected, British newspaper letter writers had in this affair a *cause cèlébre*. Nearly all were critical of the actions by the Commons. And when Wilkes dismissed the printers, one editor headed his London column with a letter addressed to the city aldermen, whom he extolled for their heroic actions in "defending the rights and privileges" of the printers.[17]

The "Junius" letters, begun even before the eruption of the newspaper fight with the House of Commons, were the most outstanding and influential pseudonymous commentaries contributed to English newspapers in this pre-Revolutionary period. A master of invective, "Junius" addressed his utterances to a limited upper-class reading public in an effort to impress them.[18] Identity of Junius has remained a secret, although pamphleteers then and historians later have written reams of speculation about him. More recent historians have leaned toward the theory that he was Sir Philip Francis.[19]

The first Junius letter, addressed to the printer of the *Public Advertiser,* appeared on January 21, 1769. In it, the author attacked the Grafton ministry for the large national debt, the country's wasted revenues, the alienation of the colonies, and the odious administration of justice. Sir William Draper answered this letter for the administration, and Junius replied on February 7. Exchanges between Junius and Draper continued in the *Public Advertiser* through February. Then Junius dropped Draper and began addressing his remarks to other members of the administration on whom he wished to animadvert. For a year, the politically daring Junius letters with their barbed insults directed at public figures and at corruption, contumacy, and immorality in public and private life, became one of the most absorbing topics at the popular coffeehouses.

In journalese of the period, Junius with his venomous pen "kindled fury in political circles." [20] He used Latin-patterned sentences interspersed with carefully placed short ones. His adroit paragraphing must have been pleasing to the eyes of his readers. Certainly he impressed newspaperdom. His letters were reprinted by nearly every London newspaper and periodical, often the day after they appeared in the *Public Advertiser.* They were picked up by the provincial press and reprinted by colonial newspapers. An unauthorized collection of his early letters was bound and sold by rival newspapers and printers even while Junius was still writing. And by 1774, Henry Woodfall, printer-editor of the *Public Advertiser,* was in the midst of plans with Junius to publish the letters in two volumes, for which the author was to write the preface.

One of the most sarcastic of the Junius letters was addressed to the Duke of Grafton, May 30, 1769. The author attacked the Duke's administration, his ancestry, and even his mistress. He accused the Duke of indolence, inconsistency, and betrayal of his friends. Furthermore, the Duke had vacillated in handling the colonial issue to such an extent that Junius declared his "conduct comprehends every thing that a wise minister should avoid."

But the Junius letter of October 5, 1771, has been called the most valuable of the sixty-nine letters. In it, the author pleaded for unification of various political factions and for leaders to give up their personal ambitions. The people of England either "must stand or fall together"—a phrase much used then and later. He blamed the Lord Mansfield for attacking the liberty of the press and said he himself would defend "the legal liberty of the meanest man in Britain" as he would his own.

Two of the most elaborate of the Junius letters were concerned with the Wilkes's affair. The first, and most famous, included an address to the King. "It is the misfortune of your life," Junius told the monarch, "that you should never have been acquainted with the language of truth, until you heard it in the complaints of your people." It was not too late for him to change his ways, however, and Junius reminded the King that he had been well received by the people when he first ascended the throne, but that he had trusted the wrong advice, particularly about his treatment of Wilkes, of Ireland, and of the American colonies.

It has been said by one English critic that Junius rehabilitated "intellectually the newspaper commentator" and that he was the "first to show the perfection to which the leader-writer's art could be brought." [21] In the light of the cutting sarcasm and invectives that Junius used, this evaluation may have been more an Englishman's prideful boast than a true statement. But there seems little doubt that Junius exerted a tremendous influence on his readers in England and in the American colonies. In those critical years, his letters were effective in bringing English citizens and American colonists to a clearer understanding of their constitutional rights and in infusing in them a determination to retain those rights. His form and style, widely imitated, was a marked improvement over political commentaries in English newspapers of a quarter of a century earlier.

But there were other signs that English newspapers were maturing and that the leader (editorial) and leader paragraph had arrived to stay. In the first place, by 1770 the printer was losing his identity with the newspapers he published. Prominent London newspapers were passing into the hands of several proprietors, who employed someone to manage the publication for them. This might be a printer or one of the owners or another man. He was known as the publisher. Because advertising had come to be a good source of income, much space heretofore devoted to long political harangues was now being used for printing advertisements.[22] Fewer long political letters were used, and comments of the publisher began to appear elsewhere in the newspaper.

The *Morning Post and Daily Advertising Pamphlet,* founded in late 1772, profoundly influenced the London newspaper world. It was owned by three men, one of whom was the Reverend George Bate. Its publisher was John Wheble, and its printers were Edward Cox and George Bigg. This was the first English newspaper since *Spectator* days not to devote its major utterances to politics.[23] Parliamentary debates were summarized instead of being printed verbatim, and only portions of speeches were printed. Instead of lengthy political letter essays, Wheble and Bate commented on sports, theaters, and criminal trials in a gossipy, witty, scandalous manner. It did not take long for this trend to spread to other newspapers or for the Reverend Bate to become involved in a few fist fights.[24]

With the *Morning Post* to point the way, all prominent dailies were soon reporting news more fully and using literary elements as regular features. Letter essays to the printer, although still predominantly political in theme and still signed pseudonymously, were, for the most part, shorter. (Some of the Junius letters were less than a column in length.) Furthermore, with economic stability gained from increased advertising revenues and larger circulations came new concepts of liberty of the press—one that included responsibility to society.

Although it can be said with some truth that letter essays evolved into the modern political or social columns often found on modern editorial pages rather than into the true editorial, short paragraphs of comment on a variety of topics found in the London news columns can be called without much equivocation editorials. Certainly by the time summaries of parliamentary debates were beginning to replace the political letters, it had become common for editors or editor-printers of the better-known English newspapers to insert in local news columns notices to the readers. And while it is also true that many such notices were concerned with boastful claims of circulation, announcements of new type faces, defenses against spurious imitations, and "puffs" favoring a candidate, an increasing number of them commented on economic or financial issues. Letters printed elsewhere in the issue sometimes evoked an editorial comment here also.[25] As has been noted earlier, such editorial paragraphs were already being used in some of the better provincial newspapers.

Such utterances were frequently italicized. This may have been originally a mere attention-getting device, but readers came to recognize italics as indicating the words of the editor. In addition, the use of the editorial "we" in this commentary was quite common and general.[26] As small and insignificant as some of these comments seemed, they were utterances of spokesmen for newspapers, and they appeared in the same location in each issue. Some newspapers did not use them every day or dropped them for a time, but the trend was set. The leader paragraph had arrived in England.

17. Colonial Organs of Revolution

The "leader" paragraph may have arrived in the English press; but its counterpart in the colonial press, the "editorial" paragraph, was still several years away. Instead, colonial newspapers became organs for the revolutionaries. And as Boston was the seat of the rebellion, publications there led the propaganda battle against English Tory rule.

Of course, political pamphlets were still popular. Such pamphleteers as James Otis, Samuel Adams, John Dickinson, and Thomas Paine have become legend in the political history of the United States. But these men, following in the footsteps of earlier English pamphleteers, also wrote letter essays for the scrawny little weekly newssheets. Often their pamphlets were printed in newspapers before they were published as pamphlets.

The printer was still the central figure in the colonial newspaper, but he was usually surrounded by a number of friends with creative ideas and ready pens to contribute semi-editorial comment in letters, essays, anecdotes, epigrams, poems, and even lampoons.[1] These formed the newspaper opinion literature of the "new politics."[2] Its theme was the rights of people. And although the printer may have written some of this commentary, his unpaid contributors—clergymen, lawyers, scholars—were glad to have a channel for expressing their individual opinions and for arousing people to action. The storms whipped up by these writers under a variety of pen names during the fading months of 1765 and early months of 1766 were only a foretaste of the passions which they aroused in the next ten years.

After news of the repeal of the Stamp Act reached the colonies and reports of resulting celebrations faded from the

little weeklies, colonists were soon embroiled in other controversies with the mother country. Trade problems remaining
after the Stamp Act crisis were made worse by the passage
in 1767 of the Townshend Acts, which imposed custom duties
on imports of glass, lead, paints, tea, and paper, including
newsprint. Resulting colonial unrest led to the Boston Massacre in 1770 and the Boston Tea Party in 1773. Passage of
the Quebec Act resurrected religious issues of a century earlier.
Then came the meeting of the First Continental Congress in
1774 and of the Second Continental Congress, which created
a Continental Army and adopted the Declaration of Independence. Indeed newspaper letter writers and printers of these
years had a plethora of news events on which to base their
semieditorial comments.

The role of colonial newspapers in awakening in Americans a sense of indignation over their wrongs and in keeping
alive their resentment in order that cohesive action could repel
Tory acts is well known. Still there were many colonials who
believed that England would recognize their rights and that
an open break would not be necessary. But the work of determined newspaper letter writers and printers in viciously
criticizing each event and administrative act was successful in
changing a preponderance of this attitude.

Thomas Green, printer of the *Connecticut Courant* in
Hartford, was typical. In early 1766 he wondered how those
who wished to unseat Governor Thomas Fitch reconciled
political meddling with the spirit of liberty.[3] But letters signed
with such names as "Cato," "Eucrates," and "Alexander
Windmill" and letters reprinted from other newspapers with
Patriot leanings soon showed that Green was using his editorial
powers of selection and rejection to make his paper an organ
of the revolutionaries.

Down in Philadelphia, William Bradford, grandson of
the first William Bradford, was printer-editor of the *Pennsylvania Gazette*. His increasing use of letters advocating the
rights of colonies was to make his newspaper a power on the
side of the Sons of Liberty. Late in August and early in
September 1766, he had printed several letters signed by John
Hughes. A member of the Pennsylvania Legislature, Hughes,
who had been appointed a stamp-tax collector, declared the

letters forgeries and brought action against Bradford and his son, Thomas. The action was ultimately dropped when Hughes, possibly fearing violent recriminations by the Sons of Liberty, refused to appear before the magistrate. Bradford's rather factual news account of what actually happened was preceded and followed by adjective-riddled commentaries, designed undoubtedly to inflame sentiment against British actions and arouse sympathy for the colonies.[4] Such comments in leads and in paragraphs following a news story were definite forerunners of the American newspaper editorial which was to develop in a separate form.[5]

One of the freedoms always in the minds of printers was that of the press. It was a frequent topic of discussion in letter essays. Typical was a letter addressed to the printers of the Boston *Gazette or Country Journal,* a recognized organ for presenting colonial grievances of all kinds.[6] The writer commented that political liberty consisted "in a freedom of speech and action so far as the laws of a community will permit, and no farther." All beyond was criminal and tended to the destruction of liberty itself.[7] Perhaps the most cogent statement in this letter, "The society whose laws least restrain the words and actions of its members, is most free," has come to be the basic philosophy underlying the continuing fight for a free press.

Passage of the Townshend Acts brought an avalanche of letters and essays to colonial printers. The most outstanding of these is now known as "Letters of a Farmer in Pennsylvania." Written by John Dickinson, a Pennsylvania lawyer-politician, the twelve letters were addressed to "Inhabitants of the British Colonies." They appeared first in the *Pennsylvania Chronicle and Universal Advertiser* from December 2, 1767, to February 15, 1768. Later, in what amounted to a continent-wide circulation, twenty-one of the twenty-five other colonial newspapers, including the Tory-minded Boston *Chronicle,* reprinted the letters.[8] Several editions in pamphlet form were widely stocked by bookshops.

In these letters, Dickinson, by discussing the foreign policy of the colonies, helped prepare public opinion for the coming revolution. He criticized the Townshend Acts, but recommended conciliation with the British. He viewed with contempt the rabble-rousing tactics of the Sons of Liberty, but he wanted "no taxation without representation." In reality, Dickinson was a middle-of-the-roader. His letters were "angled" to the businessman's interests. "If once we are separated from our mother country," he asked in his third letter, "what new form of government shall we accept, or will we find another Britain to supply the loss?" But it was Dickinson's eleventh letter, printed on the inside page of the *Pennsylvania Chronicle,* that must have changed the minds of many moderates and made Patriots of them. In this, he argued that colonists could not afford to let Parliament in London regulate their economy.[9] The persuasiveness of his utterances and his sporadic use of the editorial "we" brought his letters close to the realms of the newspaper editorial.

Samuel Adams, leader of a stable of writers for the Boston *Gazette,* set the pace for the extremists—the Patriots. He was particularly effective with his use of questions. In a salvolike propagandistic letter aimed at jarring the complacency of the British rule, Adams, as "Vindex," asked:

> What else is it but saying the greater part of the people of Britain are slaves? For if the fruit of all their toil and industry depends upon so precarious a tenure as the will of a few, what security have they for the utmost farthing. What are they but slaves, delving with the sweat of their brows . . . for their masters? After all the fine things have been said of the British Constitution and the boasted freedom and happiness of the subjects who live under it, will they thank these modern writers . . . for reducing them to a state inferior to that of indentured servants?[10]

Patriot newspapers became vituperative and scurrilous in their letters of comment. Printers were always in danger of prosecution. Even the Boston *Evening-Post,* printed by the Fleet brothers who had opened their journal to British supporters, dared in 1767 to print letters that commented on decisions of court.[11] Although no action was taken at the time, two months later the court in Springfield declared the letters had "divers injurious and scandalous Reflections on several Justices of the court."[12] Author of the letters, Joseph Hawley, a lawyer, was disbarred.

Perhaps the most outstanding attempt by British authorities to silence the press occurred in New York. Two broadsides, another print form often used by Patriots to influence opinion, were labeled "false, seditious," and an "infamous libel" by the New York Assembly. With devious methods, comparable to those used by Parliament under similar circumstances, an assembly committee discovered that the publications had been printed in the shop of James Parker's New York *Gazette, or, Weekly Post-Boy*. Threatened with losing his position as secretary of the post office, Parker revealed the author to be Alexander McDougall.

In turn, McDougall was arrested on a bench warrant; and when he refused to admit the fact, he was imprisoned. Thereupon, the colonial press had its own Wilkes case. Because the incident was recorded on the forty-fifth page of the Assembly Journal and John Wilkes in England had been arrested on a general warrant for No. 45 of the *North Briton,* "forty-five" became a watchword for the Sons of Liberty.[13] And newspaper letter writers had more coal for their propagandistic fires. Patriot newspapers reprinted the No. 45 *North Briton* and the Junius letter addressed to the King. Accounts of McDougall's trial with accompanying commentary in letters-to-the-printer traveled up and down the Atlantic seaboard. A letter to the printer of the New York *Gazette* blasted the assembly actions as Star Chamber tactics. Its author ended by saying that if "the *Star Chamber Trumpery*" passed "for the Law of the land, a kind father ought to tremble at the thought of sending his children to a Writing-School." Furthermore, no country would "be safe for a month, from the wicked aim of oppression; a silent press would be immediate Perdition to Liberty." [14]

Administrative officials were favorite targets for abusive letters, particularly in Edes and Gill's Boston *Gazette* and Isaiah Thomas's *Massachusetts Spy*. Boston Tories called the former publication the "weekly dung barge" [15] and the latter the "sedition factory." [16] Printers of both newssheets were called before the council, but Patriot feelings ran so high in Boston that no action was taken.

Meanwhile the Tory administrations, aware that they, too, needed press outlets to counterattack the liberty-minded colonials, were using certain newspapers in the same way that the Sons of Liberty were. In Boston, the old Boston *News-*

Letter, now the *Massachusetts Gazette and Post-Boy* (also known as Draper's *Gazette*), the Boston *Weekly Advertiser,* and the government-subsidized Boston *Chronicle* were Loyalist organs. Two of the most important letter writers for these publications were Governor Thomas Hutchinson and Attorney General Daniel Leonard.

As "Massachusettsensis," Leonard defended the actions of the English government in a series of seventeen letters printed in the *Massachusetts Gazette and Post-Boy.* He attacked measures adopted by the First Continental Congress. These provoked John Adams, as "Novanglus," to answer with a series of letters printed in the Boston *Gazette.* In one letter, Adams criticized the "candalous license of the Tory presses." To him, freedom of the press was a one-way street, or at least, like all effective propagandists, he was not interested in a balanced presentation.

As early as 1770 Governor Hutchinson had engaged several writers to aid the Loyalist cause by writing letter essays for the Draper journal. He had even provided this publication with a new press. One of the "hired" Loyalist writers was Jonathan Sewell, who as "Philanthrop," [17] exchanged a series of letters with Samuel Adams as "Vindex." Subject was the trial of British soldiers involved in the Boston Massacre. Josiah Quincy, Jr., as "Hyperion," had helped agitate this crisis with a series of letter essays in the Boston *Gazette.*[18]

In New York, James Rivington became the spokesman of the Loyalists with his *Rivington's New-York Gazetteer or the Connecticut, New Jersey, Hudson's River and Quebec Weekly Advertiser.* Theme of the letter essays in this publication was the retention of the structure of a colonial society, with the governing power in the hands of property owners and of those who by heredity and tradition were born into an authoritative position. Although in early issues Rivington opened his columns to both sides, his letter essays were so pro-British that in November 1775 the Sons of Liberty burned and destroyed his newspaper shop.[19]

News accounts of events published in the colonial press were so riddled with biased comment and invective that they became more semieditorial than news story. Reports of the Boston Massacre and the Boston Tea Party were typical. The

Boston *Gazette* printed the story of the massacre with turned rules as mourning for those who were killed and in the last column used Paul Revere's engravings of three caskets with skull and crossbones and the initials of those killed—an early example of editorial cartoons. According to the account, widely reprinted in other colonial newspapers, the event was a "melancholy demonstration of the destructive consequences of quartering troops among the Citizens in a time of peace, under a pretence of supporting the Laws and aiding Civil Authority." Two introductory paragraphs of comment and an editorial notice preceded the account. And two paragraphs of comment ended the story. Here the writer called the massacre a "more dreadful tragedy" than "was sometimes exhibited in St. George's Field, in London, in Old England."

Newspaper printer-editors prepared their readers for the Tea Party by openly sympathizing with smugglers and by increasingly abusive references to the tea tax. News of tea ships about to sail from England reached the colonies in early fall, 1773, and evoked the comment that men who could use "large sums, for the purpose of seduction," were "apt to conclude that true Virtue and Patriotism" were "mere names without any real existence." The printer hoped that Americans would "convince Lord North that they are not yet ready to wear the yoke of slavery" and that they would "send back the teas from whence it came." [20]

Samuel Adams's account of the Boston Tea Party, printed in the Boston *Gazette,* December 20, 1773, under the pseudonym, "An Impartial Observer," ended with the hope that American virtue would defeat every attempt to enslave the people. The next day in Hartford, the printer of the *Connecticut Courant,* wrote in a rumorlike lead for the account that "we" heard the tea "by some ACCIDENT, which happened in an attempt to get it on the shore, fell overboard" and "was swallowed up by the [vast] Abyss!"

Patriots were so enamored of Isaiah Thomas's account of the Battle of Lexington with its impassioned opening and closing comments that they resented any newspaper that did not print it. Thomas, who had sneaked a press and type from Boston before the famous battle, had established himself in Worcester. His first issue from the new location, May 3, 1775, contained the battle account, which began:

AMERICANS! forever bear in mind the BATTLE OF LEXINGTON!—where British Troops, unmolested and unprovoked, wantonly, and in most inhuman manner fired upon and killed a number of our countrymen, then robbed them of their provisions, ransacked, plundered and burnt their houses! nor could the tears of defenseless women, some of whom were in the pains of childbirth, the cries of helpless babes, not the prayers of old age, confined to beds of sickness, appease their thirst for blood!— or divert them from their DESIGN of MURDER and ROBBERY!

This was not the first time that Thomas's eyewitness account had appeared in print. On April 25, six days after the battle, Samuel Hall's *Essex Gazette* in Salem had contained the same story but with a different editoriallike lead, in which the British cruelty was described as "not less brutal than which our venerable Ancestors received from the vilest Savages of the Wilderness."

Early in 1775, however, utterances of another political commentator appeared in colonial newspapers to bolster the cause of the Patriots. Thomas Paine had arrived in the colonies from England in 1774. His first newspaper writing was printed in the *Pennsylvania Journal*, January 4, 1775. Taking a lesson from political writers for English journals nearly a century earlier, Paine wrote an essay in dialogue form. It purported to be a conversation between General James Wolfe and General Thomas Gage, in which the former rebuked the latter for leading the British against the Americans.

A year later Paine's famous pamphlet, *Common Sense,* was published. In it, the Englishman argued that reconciliation with England was impossible, rebellion was folly, and formation of a new nation was necessary. It went through several editions and in three months time, it had sold 120,000 copies.[21] More than any other single piece of writing, it was said to have crystallized in the popular mind the idea of independence for the colonies. Paine himself was later to say that as soon as this pamphlet spread throughout the colonies, the Continental Congress declared independence.[22]

Common Sense marked the beginning of a new school of political writers. Paine's extensive use of the pamphlet or broadside in the Revolutionary years may have indicated that colonial newspapers were still too small in size and too limited in circulation for lengthy discussions of current issues to reach a large reading public. But his use of shrewd illustrations, the force of his homely remarks, and the conciseness and vigor of his wordage, which appealed to the rank and file, gave a new dimension to the editorial as it was to develop.[23]

As was to be expected, the pamphlet, which was reprinted in many Patriot newspapers, elicited a rash of comments in letters to printers. The Reverend William Smith, president of the University of Pennsylvania, wrote a series of letters in answer to *Common Sense*. Signed Cato, these letters were reprinted in the *Pennsylvania Gazette*. As "Forrester," Paine replied to Cato in the *Pennsylvania Packet or the General Advertiser*. The Cato-Forrester exchanges in March and April 1776 were widely reprinted and were some of the most significant discussions of the pre-Revolutionary years.[24]

As a matter of fact, *Common Sense* supplemented the call for independence that for some time had been appearing in letters to printers. As early as December 1765, five letter essays addressed to the "Freemen of the Colony of Connecticut" and printed in the New London *Gazette* had predicted a bloody revolution. Three months later "F. L." in a two-thousand-word letter to the printer of the *Pennsylvania Journal and Weekly Gazette* discarded the idea of colonial representatives in Parliament as too expensive, too ineffective, and too unworkable for a growing country, where there were no peers to represent the colonies in the House of Lords. "F. L." ended his letter with this plea: "Let us steadily persist in maintaining our freedom, and though the struggle may be hard, let us not doubt of coming off victorious at last." [25]

Then in September 1773 Samuel Adams, as "Observations" had proposed "a CONGRESS OF AMERICAN STATES be assembled," and a "Bill of Rights be drawn up and published." [26] Two weeks later, a letter writer in the Boston *Gazette* took cognizance of Adams's plan and hoped it would be promulgated in order to "preserve the rights of America." [27] Then in his last "Novanglus" letter, printed two days before the Battle of Lexington, John Adams wrote a "masterly commentary" on the history of American taxation and on the rise of the American Revolution.[28] After the battle, letter writers, such as "Juridicus" and "Humanus" were saying that God was in favor of constitutional liberties for Americans.[29]

Printer-editors of newspapers in the ten years prior to the signing of the Declaration of Independence, also found space for moralistic comment in obituaries, for recommendation of means for enticing medical doctors to smaller towns, and for remarks on education and schools. But their greatest contribution to the developing editorial did not come from new trends or forms of commentary. Rather it lay in their printing propagandistic political commentaries, influential enough to play a powerful role in swaying colonials to form a new nation.

18. Waning of English Influence

Hostilities with England brought almost to an end the influence that English journalism was exerting upon the development of opinion writing in American newspapers. This was particularly true of the Patriot press. After 1776, the American newspaper editorial would grow from such concepts as were already adopted from the English press and from those advanced by farsighted and inventive-minded United States newspaper printers, publishers, and writers.

In the pre-Revolution years, colonial newspapers had waged an argumentative and propagandistic war of opinions through pseudonymous letters addressed to printers or to the public and through opinions of printers attached to the ends of news stories or infused into news accounts. Patriot newspapers during the war years used the same devices to hold those who were sympathetic to the cause, to increase the number of Patriots, and to attack Tories, who were said to be weakening the patriotic ranks through circulation of falsehoods.[1] The Tory press, often with more logical than emotional reasoning, argued and pleaded with their readers to return to the folds of sanity.

Publications of printers who could not move fast enough to evade advancing British forces became war casualties. Those who could move fast darted from hole to hole like chipmunks or fled to smaller cities and towns as the war action shifted back and forth. The battle between Tory and Patriot newspapers was as fierce as the ground action.[2] Denunciation and challenge seemed to be the keynote of almost all newspaper opinion during these war years.

A large proportion of space in Patriot newspapers, which were often reduced in size and printed on brown or yellow paper, was still devoted to letter essays signed by pen names. Printers, such as Isaiah Thomas, may have occasionally written such letters; but, in general, printers confined their opinions to introductory remarks before these letters, to lead paragraphs of news accounts, or to patriotic or flattering utterances at the ends of such accounts. During this period, however, an increasing number of these printers began setting their remarks in italics or using such typographical devices as the pointing finger to indicate their opinions. The practice of placing such editorializing utterances under the local heading also became more general. For example, Richard Goodwin, who by 1777 was calling himself the editor of the *Connecticut Courant,* commented on events, even of a national nature, and on letters printed elsewhere in his newspaper under the Hartford heading.

The most forceful opinion writer for the Patriot press was Thomas Paine, whose *Common Sense* early in 1776 had already made his reputation. His "Crisis" papers, appearing from December 1776 to January 1781, were brilliant wartime editorials designed to uphold military and civilian morale.

Paine volunteered as an aide-de-camp to General Nathaniel Greene, but he was probably more public relations man than anything else. His first Crisis paper—the now-famous "These are the times that try men's souls" essay—was first published in the *Pennsylvania Journal,* December 19, 1776;[3] and on the eve of Washington's attack on Trenton, it was read to the general's soldiers. The *Pennsylvania Packet* printed it on page one of its December 27 issue; and other Patriot newspapers reprinted it as soon as their printers obtained a copy, some as late as February. As were Paine's later Crisis arguments, this one was also printed as a broadside on one side of a sheet folded in half.

Primarily it was a call to service, a bolstering of pride. "The summer soldier and the sunshine patriot will, in this crisis, shrink from the service of his country; but he that stands it NOW, deserves the thanks of man and woman" were words that must have stirred the souls of many. The second Crisis paper was an address to Lord William Howe, commander-in-chief of the British forces. Thereafter, whenever Patriot interest seemed to flag, Paine wrote another Crisis paper—sixteen in all. Some were no longer than a short editorial. Others were pamphlet-size. Paine's vigorous, direct, and simple style and his ability to write timely arguments and to interpret events in a language that appealed to the average man placed his utterances notches closer to the modern editorial than the political disquisitions of Junius, whose more theoretical arguments were relished by comparatively few readers.[4] Paine was at his best when he was commenting on financial affairs, as in his "Crisis Extraordinary," which argued for funds for Washington.[5]

Center of the Tory press was New York after that city was occupied by the British. Leading Tory newspaperman was James Rivington, who, after his press was destroyed by a Patriot mob, fled to England, but returned with a new press. From this, he issued a new publication, *Rivington's Royal Gazette.* In it, his frequent news editorials addressed "To the Public" set forth his opinions and acted as a stimulating irritant to the Patriot press. His belittling references to the ragtail army and to an ineffective Congress increased editorial utterances in Patriot newspapers.

Another Tory newspaper, Gaine's New York *Gazette and Weekly Mercury,* was confiscated by the British when Gaine fled to New Jersey. Even after the printer returned to New York, the British retained control of the content of the publication. Two other Tory newspapers in New York were Robertson's *Royal American Gazette* and Lewis's New York *Mercury and General Advertiser.* Since each of these four newspapers was published on a different day, New Yorkers could read almost a daily outpouring of venom against the Patriots or Whigs, as they were sometimes called.

Subject matter of pungent, italicized or bracketed comments in news stories and of letters to the printers of both sides ranged from optimistic words of encouragement and calls for unity and perseverance to hostile and indignant utterances against opposing generals and atrocities of the enemy forces. In between were comments on the unpatriotic action of merchants in raising prices, on the bias of committees of inspection, and on currency speculation.[6]

News accounts of battles gave newspaper printers the opportunity of adding a few lines of comment that either made light of an evident defeat or boasted of an accomplishment. An account of an attack by the British fleet on Norfolk, Virginia, ended: "The tide is now rising, and we expect, at high water another cannonade. May it be as ineffectual as the last, for we have not one man killed, and but few wounded." [7] And a report of an engagement at Widow Moore's Creek Bridge ended: "This, we think will effectually put a stop to Toryism in North Carolina." [8]

"An American" in a letter to the printer of the *Virginia Gazette* apparently had this in mind when he wrote that he hoped the country would "not be all dispirited at the destruction of Norfolk, but rather rejoice" that "our enemies" had "done their worst." They had succeeded only in hardening "our soldiers" and in teaching "them to bear without dismay all the most formidable operations of a war carried on by a powerful and cruel enemy." They had given "the world specimens of British cruelty and American fortitude." [9]

Tory comment could turn a Patriot win into an inglorious performance. In an Ambrose Serle edition[10] of Gaine's New York *Gazette and Weekly Mercury,* an account of the arrival of the British fleet in New York ended by calling the "burning of the city by the New England incendiaries" a "lasting monument of inveterate malice against the trade and prosperity" of the colony as well as a "rooted disaffection of British law and government." The incendiaries had "long threatened the performance of this villainous deed," and this was "the best return that the people of property in this city, who have espoused their cause," could expect for their "heedless credulity." [11]

Such comment was often designed to throw fear into the hearts of those who were still riding the fence between the Tories and the Patriots. It had been observed, wrote one Tory newspaper commentator, that in the beginning of a war British power generally made "but feeble, and oftentimes unsuccessful exertions." But "in the prosecution of hostilities her force gradually" increased "like a gathered torrent" and became "almost irresistible." Then using the editorial we, he commented further that in the course of the summer, "we have seen a powerful army cross over the Atlantic," and "we have heard of other considerable armaments arriving safely." Opposed to all this was only "the *wisdom* of a Congress consisting of men either of new and doubtful character, or of none at all," "a wretched paper currency" which would "only eat up the prosperity of the continent," and "a vagabond army of ragamuffin, with paper pay, bad clothes, and worse spirits." [12]

Even more outspoken was the Londoner who wrote to the printer of *Freeman's Journal* and called for the "poor, deluded, misguided, bewildered, cajoled, and bamboozled whigs" and the "dumfounded, infatuated, back-bestridden, nose-led-about, priest-ridden, demagogue-beshackled, and Congress-becrafted independents" to "fly, fly, oh fly, for protection to the royal standard." [13]

Yearly celebrations on the anniversary of American independence gave Patriot newspaper printers another opportunity for editorializing. In 1776, the printer of the *Pennsylvania Journal* ended his account of this celebration by commenting that the people were now convinced "of what we ought long since to have known, that our enemies have left us no middle road between perfect freedom and abject slavery." Both in the field and in the council, he hoped "the inhabitants of New Jersey" would "be found ever ready to support the freedom and independence of America." [14] A year later the same printer hoped that July 4, "the glorious and ever memorable day," would "be celebrated through America by the sons of freedom, from age to age, till time shall be no more. Amen and Amen." [15]

Printers used news reports detailing atrocities to malign opposing generals or to "puff" their own. General John Burgoyne was called "stark mad" in the *Pennsylvania Evening Post*,[16] while General Washington was "puffed" as "our great and illustrious commander, the prop and glory of the western world" in the *Pennsylvania Journal*.[17] And the printer of the New York *Packet* called up his best literary efforts when he capped a news story about the burning by the British of "defenseless" Kingston, N.Y., with this near editorial: "Britain, how art thou fallen! Ages to come will not wipe away the guilt, the horrid guilt, of these and such like deeds, lately perpetrated by thee." [18]

James Humphreys, printer of the *Pennsylvania Public Ledger and Market Day Advertiser* at Philadelphia during the British occupation of that city, wrote in his column quasi-editorials, commenting on letters printed elsewhere in the news-paper. In the February 11, 1778, issue he reprinted a letter from the *New-Jersey Gazette,* a Patriot newspaper in Burling-ton. In the same issue under the Philadelphia heading, Humphreys wrote:

> The town of Philadelphia not being as fully acquainted with the subject of the letter taken from a Burlington paper, as the ingenious author would have his readers believe them to be, it may be necessary to relate them the fact. At the time it happened, it was so trifling as not to be thought worthy of notice in this paper; and we do not doubt our readers will allow this letter-writer full credit for the fertility of his invention. The case was, that on the fifth of January last, a barrel of an odd appearance came floating down the Delaware . . . when it blew up, and either killed or injured one or more of [some boys]. So far the matter was serious, and the fellow who invented the mischief may quiet his conscience . . . as well as he can. Some days after, a few others of much the same appearance . . . came floating in a like manner, and a few guns, we believe, fired at them from some of the transports lying along the wharves. Other than this no notice was taken of them, except, indeed, by our author, whose imagination, perhaps as fertile as his intentions, realized to himself in the frenzy of his enthusiasm the matters he has set forth.

Such semieditorials were sometimes printed several days after the letter to the printer was used. In the May 2, 1778, issue of the *Pennsylvania Gazette,* a letter detailed some of the contents of the new nation's treaty with France. In the May 13 issue, the printer commented about the contents of this letter. We do not doubt, he wrote, that "our readers will think as we do—that we have good reason to suspect" that the letter was "what many publications from the same quarter" had been, "a *seasonable* piece of *mis-representation.*" There was an art, he said, "of *mixing* truth and falsehood, or of conveying falsehood in the vehicle of truth." And he asked whether we *now* wished "for a final separation from Britain, the ancient and chief support of the Protestant religion in the world," merely to uphold, "at the expense of our lives and fortunes, the arbitrary power that Congress, who without even asking our consent," had "*disposed* of us," had "*mortgaged* us like vassals and slaves," by making "a treaty with that ambitious and treacherous power, whose religious and political maxims" had "so often disturbed peace and invaded the rights of mankind."

By 1779, the use of incipient editorials had spread to almost all of the thirty-eight newspapers. Isaac Collins, whose *New-Jersey Gazette* at Burlington was only two years old, commented at the end of an account about an entertainment to mark the first anniversary of the alliance with France that "the principles of the alliance" were "founded in true policy and equal justice." It was highly probable, he said, that mankind would "have cause to rejoice in this union" between two nations, one of which was "the most puissant in the old world, and the other the most powerful in the new world." [19]

And Shepherd Kollack, whose *New-Jersey Journal* at Chatham was even younger than Collins's paper, wrote in the lead paragraph of a story about the cruelty and deviousness of the British troops that "arguments at this period of the war to prove the justice of our cause, or the importance of the controversy, would be useless, nay, would be insults to our understanding." And he warned that "our success in arms and in gaining the powerful alliances of foreign nations" may have "lulled us into a dangerous security." [20]

Printers also found time to comment on events close to their homes. At a time when Hartford was thronged with British and Tory prisoners and hardened criminals, the printers of the *Connecticut Courant* called for a nightly patrol of that city's streets "not only for the security of private property, but for the safe keeping of what nearly and deeply concerns the public." [21] But they considered a letter from "J. W." that had proposed a method "to raise and establish the credit of our currency" too "plain to need publication." [22]

In a discussion of a title for the chief administrator of the new nation, the printer of the *Pennsylvania Evening Post* advised leaving "the titles of excellency and honorable to the abandoned servants" of the tyrant king of England. "We" should "satisfy ourselves" he wrote, "with beholding our senators, governors, and generals rich in real excellence and honor." [23]

But letters addressed to the printer remained the medium for long political harangues, whether the writer attacked the opposition press, a political event, or action by the enemy. Tory "Candidus" addressed "Mr. Printer" in the August 16, 1779, issue of the New York *Gazette and Weekly Mercury*. "Candidus" wrote that he had "just met with a rebel newspaper" that contained "a very curious article relative to the late attack on Stony Point." The rebel article was "written in that turgid style, and in that spirit of triumph" characteristic of all rebel publications. It was, he said, "a just sample of the eloquence and temper of the rebels." It took "Candidus" only one short paragraph to detail the battle story, but it took him nine long paragraphs to criticize the "rebel" writer.

Across the river, a letter in the *New-Jersey Gazette* was critical of British writers. The British government, the letter writer said, had spent "upwards of fifty thousand Guineas on hirelings employed to tell lies in pamphlets and news-papers in Europe and America" and this year they would probably spend "double that sum, as their affairs were "in a more critical state." He predicted "redoubled industry in the trade of misrepresentation and falsehood" because newspapers were beginning "to abound with the species of intelligence." [24]

"A Whig" in a letter in the *Pennsylvania Packet* addressed "To the Public," abhorred the leniency shown the Tories. In fact, this leniency was one of the greatest errors America had made, and no other error had been attended with "more fatal consequences." In a kind of forewarning of Benedict Arnold's defection, he wrote that "at first it might have been right, or perhaps political"; but it was not surprising that, "after repeated proofs of the same evils resulting therefrom," no notice was taken of the Tories, "who are one principal cause of our depreciation" and who were allowed "to live quietly among us." "America," he said, "your danger is great—great from the quarter where you least expect it." The Tories would yet "be the ruin of us." No spark of virtue was "to be found in one Tory's breast." He called Tories wretches and bosom vipers who would sell their souls to subject their country "to the will of the greatest tyranny the world at present produces." [25]

A year later Arnold's defection was called "treason of the blackest dye" in this same newspaper.[26] And John Dunlap, its printer, wrote that the hanging of Major John André showed that "we are not deterred by great menaces, but determined to extirpate our enemies one by one until peace is restored to our country." [27]

By this time, however, another type of near editorial had made a brief appearance in the *Maryland Journal and Baltimore Advertiser*. At this time this publication was being printed by Mary Katherine Goddard although William Goddard and Eleazer Oswald were closely connected with its contents. In the July 6, 1779, issue a series of questions were addressed to Washington. Under the heading "Some Queries, Political and Military Humbly Offered for the Consideration of the Public," the questions were, in reality, a vicious attack on Washington. They were written by General Charles Lee, who had sent them to Goddard and Oswald for publication. Lee was trying to vindicate "his reputation by tainting" Washington's name.[28] But Washington had become something of a hero to the common man, and Goddard's home was attacked by a mob. Although a recantation was printed, Goddard was forced to request protection for himself and his press. Probably because of this reception, other printer-editors did not experiment with this particular type of editorializing.

The surrender of Cornwallis on October 17, 1781, brought a variety of continuing commentary to the pages of the weekly press. The announcement of his surrender in the October 25 issue of the New York *Packet* ended with "Laus Deo!" Up in Connecticut, George Goodwin and Barzillai Hudson noted in their *Connecticut Courant* of November 20 that "all New-York papers" had at long last acknowledged the surrender and that even the articles of capitulation had been inserted verbatim from the "Philadelphia gazettes." Women were in tears, soldiers in panic, merchants selling goods at less than their cost in Europe, Tories in consternation, and Benedict Arnold was trembling "like an aspen leaf." Furthermore, the demagogues of New York were "publishing in their gazettes contents of rebel mails and criticisms" of poems by the king of Prussia. To the printers of the *Courant,* such content was "as ridiculous and stupid as if a criminal on his way to the gallows . . . should at the same time be amusing himself with Ben Johnson's jests."

At the end of the war, the Loyalist press disappeared.

But the Patriot press, strengthened by the ordeal and vitalized by its enhanced influence, emerged to establish the fundamental characteristics of United States newspapers. Not the least among these was the opinion-making function of the press, which was inextricably involved in the issue of freedom of the press. Although the greatest contribution to this role of the newspaper during the Revolution years had been the emphasis by printer-editors on letters and essays by contributors of similar political beliefs, the first strains of the editorial had appeared occasionally. With a newspaper reading habit instilled in the people of the thirteen states, the first years of peace would find printer-editors entering zestfully into local and national political controversies. They would become embroiled with rival printer-editors. These "newspaper battles" would lead rather quickly not only to libel court cases and duels but also to an established practice of editorial writing as it is known today.

19. THE 1780's: CRAWLING STAGE

WHEN WAR ENDED, forty-three newspapers survived in America. Of these the most outstanding were the *Connecticut Courant,* the Boston *Gazette,* and the *Pennsylvania Packet.*[1] But it was from the *Connecticut Courant* that the concept of the editorial as an opinion of the newspaper conductor, to be printed apart from an attached news story, would crawl forth and slowly be adopted by other newspaper conductors.

In spite of the depression that inevitably followed the war, newspaper presses multiplied rapidly. Before the war, weekly publications were found only in seaports or colonial capitals. By 1783, however, they were moving westward. Printers of these inland newspapers looked to week-old city papers for their content, much as earlier colonial printers had waited for English newspapers. In small villages with no newspapers, ministers read the latest news publications to the adult population.[2] In this way it was the city semiweekly or triweekly newspaper that set patterns for content and style in the expanding press and that trained a readership to expect certain content elements.

And the main content of newspapers after the war was opinion. Citizens of the 1780's were assuming an interest in public issues as a patriotic duty to their fledgling nation. They looked to newspapers, which had championed their cause during the war, to supply information on state and national questions and to voice opinion on these issues.[3]

The first postwar decade was a period of unrest—an unrest that would lead to the political agitation in the press of the 1890's. At first, the chaotic, almost anarchic conditions of the country seemed to emphasize two great factions in society —the rich and the poor.[4] And the discussions in the press of various new issues, as grave as those that precipitated the war, seemed to turn on whether the rich, or aristocrats, would be benefitted more than the poor, or the mechanics. With political parties not yet formed in that period from 1783 until 1789 when the federal government established under the Constitution began to function, the new nation was governed by public opinion voiced through the press.[5]

In one respect, newspaper development retrogressed in the 1780's. Reporting of local news events, such as accounts of battles printed during the war, was eliminated from many newspapers. Foreign news, as in earlier colonial newspapers, was considered the staple diet. But foreign items made up only a small portion of the contents of many newspapers. Printers and newspaper conductors who had learned to include such political utterances as would promote their own beliefs filled their publications with long essays and letters. Signed with Latin names, they were usually written by local contributors in the same coarse satire and bitter tone of the wartime letters to printers. Generally, newspaper conductors seemed content to leave the shaping of opinion to the political essayists and letter writers, although they were quick to exclude contributions which opposed their own views.

Among the many eco-socio-political issues discussed in these letters were the depreciated currency and the funding of the national debt; the status of Loyalists who had remained in the country and were refugees; land grants and land speculation; the Society of the Cincinnati, an organization believed by many to be the beginning of an American aristocracy; the Constitution; the powers of Congress; and the framing of the state constitutions.

The fight for the adoption of the Constitution, by far the most controversial issue of the 1780's, occasioned the customary war of pamphlets. By this time, however, newspapers could give a faster and wider distribution to such political arguments than before the Revolution. Consequently, many pamphlets on the Constitution question were printed as letter essays in newspapers. Among those writing against adoption were Patrick Henry, Richard Henry Lee, George Mason, George Clinton, Samuel Chase, Elbridge Gerry, and James Monroe. Important pro-Constitution pamphleteers were Noah Webster, John Dickinson, and Alexander Hamilton.

The most noted series of letter essays was "the Federalist," a group of eighty-five letters written by Alexander Hamilton, James Madison, and John Jay. Printed first in New York newspapers from October 27, 1787, to April 1788, these brilliant political arguments for adoption of the Constitution were reprinted widely by other newspapers. Twenty-three of the "Federalist" letters appeared first in the New York *Independent Journal;* fifteen in the New York *Packet*; two in the *Daily Advertiser*; and six appeared simultaneously in two or more of these newspapers.[6] Later they were printed in pamphlet and book form.

Hamilton, as "Publius," wrote more than half of the letters. It is believed that Madison wrote fourteen and coauthored with Hamilton two others. John Jay wrote five.[7] In a clear, concise style, the letters explained the philosophy of the Constitution. The tenth letter, by Madison, gave the gist of this philosophy. The eighty-fourth letter, by Hamilton, was first published May 28, 1788, and explained the omission of a bill of rights in the Constitution. In it, Hamilton contended that to place a provision in the Constitution against restraining liberty of the press would imply that the national government could prescribe proper regulations for the press. To him, liberty of the press could not be defined without leaving latitude for evasion. It was, therefore, impracticable to include a provision for freedom of the press. Its security should depend on public opinion and on the prevailing spirit of the people and of the government.

The "Federalist Papers," generally conceded by historians to have awakened the populace to the possibilities of the new form of government, were greatly influential in securing the adoption of the Constitution. Not only did the Federalist Papers have the desired effect of the editorial—that of influencing opinion—but they also had other similarities to the daily editorial as it was soon to evolve. They were written with haste, scratched out as an editorial writer pounds out his utterances on the typewriter today. They were politically sound, persuasive arguments, and as near good literature as any modern editorial writer could hope to achieve.

Partly because of the Federalist Papers, Hamilton has been called one of the fathers of the American editorial.[8] Indeed his newspaper letters that preceded the Federalist Papers

—from "A Farmer Refuted" in 1772 to his "Continentalist" letters in 1780—could easily have won him this title. His insight into public issues and his ability to condense and to write quickly and clearly are qualifications of the best modern editorial writers. Hamilton was to contribute even more directly to the evolving editorial in the 1890's.

The letter essay, however, was only one strain of editorial parentage; and, as has been pointed out, another strain was already developing in the local column headings of newspapers. Up in Hartford, Connecticut, the co-printer-conductors of the *Connecticut Courant,* who by 1784 were calling themselves editors, in their Hartford column had occasionally printed paragraphs of their own opinion on local, national, and regional events and on letters printed elsewhere in their newspaper. The local column was the space reserved by these men for their own reporting. These opinion paragraphs were usually composed as the printers set type. Probably, it seemed natural to the editors to lump all of their own writings in the same column. After the war, such expressions of opinion came more often in the Hartford column. When the paper's owners, Barzillai Hudson and George Goodwin, were stirred by particular events or decided to defend themselves against charges of partiality, which came frequently, they expressed their opinions in this column.[9] It was a practice that other newspaper printer-conductors would come to use. Down in New Jersey, Isaac Collins was using an occasional paragraph of opinion in his Trenton column.[10]

Increasingly often, Hudson and Goodwin spoke out in favor of the passage of the Constitution and for a strong federal government. Shortly after the Constitutional Convention met in Philadelphia in May, 1787, they used the Hartford column to explain that "various opinions" were "propagated respecting the probable result of the federal convention," but it seemed "to be unanimously agreed that a strong and efficient power must be somewhere established." The character of the Union would have been "widely different" if Congress had the "power to control the selfish interests of a single state." Experience, they said, should "instruct us that little can be left to the voluntary disposition of the people." [11]

On occasions, it is now known, Hudson and Goodwin

called on recognized letter writers to compose a paragraph of opinion for inclusions in their Hartford column. The most noted of these was Noah Webster, who can be called, as it will be seen, the father of the editorial column. In one such paragraph, in which he defended the newspaper's partiality, Webster used the editorial "we" as if he were Hudson and Goodwin. "It has been repeatedly reported," he wrote, "especially in remote towns, where such reports" were "most likely to go uncontradicted, that we have been partial—that we have published everything in favour of commutation, and either delayed or suppressed essays" of the opposite side. This, Webster, in the name of the editors, denied. Then he added: "As we ever have, so we ever shall conduct ourselves with the strictest impartiality, and sooner than deviate from this resolution, we will suffer every misfortune slander can produce." [12]

It is known that Webster wrote this because he labeled it as his in his personal copies of the *Courant* now in possession of the New York Public Library and Yale University Library. What is not known and what cannot now be ascertained is whether Webster volunteered to write these utterances or whether Hudson and Goodwin asked him to write them. Webster at this time was contributing to the *Courant* his "Honorius" letters on regulating commerce, conduct of foreign relations, and taxation; and it seems probable that the decision to write such editorial paragraphs for the Hartford column grew from conferences between Webster and the two printer-conductors. However the idea was conceived and whoever was responsible, Webster was to expand it later in his own newspaper.

Either Webster, the *Courant* printers, or possibly other letter writers, such as Joel Barlow, John Trumbull, or Oliver Wolcott, Jr., speaking for the printers in the Hartford column, also praised the new constitution and advised their readers "to shun" Patriots who wanted to reject the new federal government.[13] The Convention, *Courant* readers were told, would be composed "of the most respectable men in the state—men venerable for their age and abilities, and possessed of the public confidence." [14] The letter writers expressed their joy over the ratification of the Constitution.[15] And frequently *Courant* readers were made aware of the printers' views on the convention issues through a paragraph in the Hartford column.

But the convening of the Constitutional Convention and the issues there being discussed brought forth opinions from other newspaper printers. Not far away in Boston, Major Benjamin Russell, who had learned newspapering from Isaiah Thomas, and William Warden had founded the *Massachusetts Centinel* in March 1784. Although conceived as a mercantile paper, the *Centinel* by 1786 had become as political as other newspapers of the era. After Warden dropped out as a partner, Russell enlarged the publication and changed its name to *Columbian Centinel*. He joined the political newspaper battles over the adoption of the Constitution on the side of the Federalists and stoutly advocated a strong unified government.

In his Boston column, Russell, who by 1790 was also referring to himself as an "editor," sometimes inserted subheadings to indicate his editorials, although this term in its modern sense had not then been coined. In the issue of December 11, 1784, he devoted a little more than one short column under the subheading "Unity and Peace" to the promotion of a unified country. "All mankind," he wrote, "seems to be agreed that some kind of unity is absolutely necessary," and he pleaded for "condescension, mutual forbearance, harmony of mild benevolent effection" to make America strong. Two years later under the subheading "Sentiment," he stressed "virtue" as being "essential to preserve government of the American States." [16] Sometimes he signed his editorial "Centinel" to distinguish it from contributed letters or essays.[17] Russell's editorial comment ranged over a wide variety of subjects. Once he commented on the opening of the Shakespearean Gallery in London. Here he used both I and the editorial we to indicate his opinions.[18]

Bold, vigorous, and incisive in his opinion writing, Russell was one of a new breed of journalists who had firm political convictions and who did not hesitate to use their truculent pens to record their views and interpret public sentiment. In a sense, Russell was a prototype of Horace Greeley and James Gordon Bennett of the next century in that the *Centinel* began to represent his own personality and viewpoints.[19] Russell attacked trade with England on the premise that it would drain America of currency. He was against the Commutation Act because antipathies bred by the war were too deep-seated for a liberal treatment of the Tories. He was against the Society of Cincinnati until he learned Washington was one of the founders of that organization. Then he recanted his position and became a strong supporter of the society.[20] Russell's admiration for General Washington was frequently evident. In June 1787 when the Constitutional Convention was in session, Russell in one of his editorial paragraphs called on the men of America to "banish from your bosums those daemons, suspicion and distrust," and he assured them that "the men whom ye have delegated to work out, if possible, your natural salvation" were men whose "extensive knowledge, known abilities, and approved patriotism" warranted confidence. "Consider, they have at their head a Washington, to describe the amiableness of whose character would be unnecessary." [21]

Russell also used the political cartoon to further his Federalist viewpoints. In the same vein as the early snake cartoons, he added a new column to a picture of a federal building every time another state ratified the Constitution.[22]

As Russell probably expected, he soon was in the midst of a newspaper feud. The Boston *Independent Chronicle and Universal Advertiser* was acquired by the Adams brothers, Thomas and Abijah, in 1788. They were strongly Antifederalist in that they violently opposed the Society of Cincinnati on grounds that it was an opening wedge to the establishment of a hereditary monarchy; they wanted foreign relations with England to improve trade; they favored importance of state over a strong centralized federal government; and they objected to any system of government on a permanent Republican basis. Because the Adams brothers were not adept at writing, they depended for twenty years on the vicious pen of Benjamin Austin, Jr. As "Honestus" or as "Old South," Austin tackled Russell. And the two newspapers, locked in a feud of editorial utterances, soon pushed the Patriot Boston *Gazette or Country Journal* of Edes and Gill into the background.

Meanwhile in Philadelphia, the old *Pennsylvania Packet or General Advertiser,* under the name of the *Pennsylvania Packet and Daily Advertiser,* had become in 1784 the first successful daily publication. As a mercantile publication, the daily *Packet* was a financial success for its owners, John Dunlap and David C. Claypool. More than half of its sixteen columns was devoted to advertising. But on either page two or page three, these two enterprising and innovating newspaper conductors printed in nearly every issue a column headed "America" with smaller subheadings that listed various cities from which the news article or essay had originated. This was in addition to their local column. In the America column, which varied in length from one to three columns, Dunlap and Claypool summarized news from other cities. And not infrequently editorial-like material, either written by the printer-conductor or re-printed from another newspaper without credit, was included.

One such editorial paragraph, for example, appeared in the America column under the smaller heading, "Boston." The writer, noting that Rhode Island had "at length acceded to impost and supplementary aid," said that there was little doubt now that "the same national spirit" would animate "every other government this side of the Hudson." All "eyes of the friends of the union" would now "be turned to the State of New York, which," it was hoped, would soon exhibit "this last proof of its attachment to our federal interest." It seemed strange to the writer that "the influence of Congress should be least regarded in the place of their immediate residence." If reluctance to accede to the impost on the part of New York came from "any little benefit" which that state might "derive from its peculiar situation as to commerce," then "we must hope it will soon give place to a mode of procedure more consonant to their past glory and the present hopes of every real friend of America." [23]

While it may be and probably is true that Dunlap and Claypool were using their "exchanges" for news summaries, still they seemed careful to include only those paragraphs that advanced their own viewpoints. And they were definitely pro-Constitution.

Fourth of July celebrations nearly always brought patriotic editorial utterances from newspaper printer-editors. In 1787, during the Constitutional Convention, Matthew Carey, publisher of the short-lived *Pennsylvania Evening Herald* ended his description of the day's events with this hopeful comment:

> With zeal and confidence we expect from the federal Constitution a system of government adequate to the security and preservation of those rights which were promul-

gated by the ever-memorable Declaration of Independence.[24]

Printer-editor-publishers of successful mercantile newspapers had found it impossible to remain neutral during the fight for the ratification of the Constitution. They seemed more frequently to be indicating a Federalist or Antifederalist stand through letter essays and through their own news accounts and in local columns. At the same time, there were other purely political newspapers. In the autumn of 1786 during Shay's Rebellion, for example, William Butler in Northampton established the weekly *Hampshire Gazette,* which contained little or no news. Its main purpose was to impress on its readers the importance of preserving law and order. Later the *Gazette* became a typical weekly filled with a few items of foreign news and political and patriotic essay letters contributed by Caleb Strong and Joseph Hawley.[25] Another such publication, the *Falmouth Gazette,* was established in 1785 to further the movement to separate the Maine settlement from Massachusetts and make it a separate state.[26]

By 1789, the Federalists had won, but the fight over the adoption of the Constitution had singled out newspapers and newspaper writers who would become outstanding leaders of public opinion. The omission of free press guaranteed in the Constitution not only helped introduce party strife, but it also opened the way for the bitter licentiousness in political newspaper utterances. Benjamin Franklin, now an old man, in a satirically bitter essay in the *Pennsylvania Gazette,* censured the libelous and scandalous press attacks that were already beginning.

> If by *Liberty of the Press* were understood merely the *Liberty* of Discussing the Propriety of Public Measures and political opinions, let us have as much of it as you please: But if it means Liberty of affronting, calumniating and defaming one another, I, for my part, own myself willing to part with my share of it . . . and shall cheerfully consent to exchange my *Liberty* of abusing others for the *Privilege* of not being abused myself.[27]

Meanwhile in New York in 1787, Thomas Greenleaf bought John Holt's New York *Journal,* changed its name to the New York *Journal and Daily Patriotic Register,* and made it a daily. He printed the Brutus series of letters in opposition to Hamilton's Federalist letters. Strongly Antifederalist, Greenleaf devoted one entire local column to ridiculing the festivities that celebrated New York's adoption of the Constitution and to animadverting those who had taken part in the celebration.[28]

Another outspoken Antifederalist printer-editor-publisher was Eleazer Oswald, of the Philadelphia *Independent Gazette*. Oswald, a leader against the adoption of the Constitution, printed a series of twenty-four articles, signed "Centinel," that denounced the Constitution with vigorous and incisive language.[29]

The arrival on the American newspaper scene of the semi-weekly *Gazette of the United States* on April 15, 1789, however, marked the beginning of the political party newspaper. Its editor was John Fenno, a Boston schoolteacher, who was probably financed, at least in part, by Alexander Hamilton. Until then, New York, which was at the time the new nation's capital, had no newspaper with strong Federalist convictions. Conceived as a national paper, the *Gazette* stated that its purpose was to promote the "people's own government." Fenno defended the Federalist viewpoints with such overzealousness that the Antifederalist printer-editors were soon attacking him in their newspapers.[30] Hamilton probably dictated political articles to Fenno, as in the next decade he would dictate political paragraphs to other editors.

At this time, Governor George Clinton, leader of the anti-Hamilton forces in New York was using Francis Child's *Daily Advertiser* to promote Antifederalist viewpoints. But it was not until the return of Thomas Jefferson from France in March of 1790 that the *Gazette of the United States* and Hamilton would have a formidable editorial foe.

Interestingly, the editorial in its modern concept would emerge in the 1790's in political newspapers backed by leading politicians and edited by men who, like Fenno, were not printers. The sporadic editorial commentary in local columns of the 1780's would blossom into what could be called an editorial column.

20. The 1790's: Young Adulthood

The new breed of hired editors for many of the leading American newspapers in the 1790's were so busy hurling abuses at the opposition that they came to use the editorial, in the modern sense of the word, possibly without being aware that they were creating a new journalistic form. A specific date can almost never be given for the birth of such a trend as that of the newspaper editorial; but the decade of the 1790's can certainly be called the period of the popularization of the shorter paragraphs of opinion written by editors, or the young adulthood years of the editorial. The writing of opinions about public issues and news events, which had begun with handwritten newsletters more than two centuries earlier, had now gone through its gestation period. By 1800, the culminating form of the newspaper editorial had arrived unheralded and with little or no fanfare. It emerged, as most such stylistic devices, from a welter of various forerunners and from a necessity created by other advances and other movements.

To understand what happened to newspaper opinion writing in the last decade of the eighteenth century, it will be necessary to look first at this rising breed of newspaper conductors who were calling themselves editors. Since the turbulent years of the Revolution, a few newspaper printer-conductors had come to call themselves editors—a word that to them must have been a prestigious name for their profession. Very possibly, this tag differentiated them as men who selected and sometimes wrote what they printed in their publications from the mere printer of a newspaper, who was a hired mechanic, or from a one-man conductor of a newspaper who printed his columns from his "exchanges." Among users of this epithet in the 1780's, it will be remembered, had been Barzillai Hudson and George Goodwin of the *Connecticut Courant* and Major Benjamin Russell of the *Columbian Centinel.*

Then came John Fenno of the *Gazette of the United States.* As has been noted, he was one of the few conductors of an American newspaper who was not a trained printer. His main duties were to select and write content. A printing company was employed to produce the publication. He was, in this sense, a newspaper conductor—but a conductor who also wrote opinions. He was called the editor. So common had this term become that by 1792, letters to newspapers were being addressed "To the Editor" rather than "To the Printer."

With the political climate what it was, Fenno was quickly followed by others. On October 31, 1791, Philip Freneau founded in Philadelphia the *National Gazette,* a semiweekly organ in opposition to the Fenno paper. Like Fenno, Freneau was paid to conduct the newspaper by subsidization through government printing or government jobs. Also in Philadelphia, Benjamin Franklin Bache founded October 1, 1790, the *General Advertiser and Political, Agricultural and Literary Journal,* which by late 1794 had become the *Aurora.* Also calling himself an editor, Bache was a printer; but he did more writing for, than printing of, his publication. Fenno, who moved his newspaper to Philadelphia when the seat of the national government was moved to that city, Freneau, and Bache today would be called editorial writers because they dashed off abusive paragraphs at each other and at the political opposition. Bache's newspaper came to be recognized as the chief Antifederalist, or Republican, newspaper in Philadelphia. When Bache died of yellow fever, William Duane, a native-born American who had spent most of his life out of the country and who had enjoyed a rather successful newspaper career in India, took over the editorial reins of the *Aurora* and continued the bitter invective writing of Bache.

Meanwhile, Noah Webster had migrated to New York to found early in December 1793 the brilliant *American Minerva.* Backed financially by Alexander Hamilton and Rufus King, Webster wrote not only paragraphs of comment for the local column but also political letters for other columns of the *Minerva.* He, too, was an editor in the rigid sense because he was no printer. His contributions to the newspaper editorial form, as will be seen, were outstanding.

Another vituperative newspaper editor appeared on the Philadelphia scene on March 4, 1797, when William Cobbett as Peter Porcupine founded *Porcupine's Gazette*. Though this political organ lasted only a short two years, Cobbett's extravagant ideas and personal abuse and billingsgate would color opinion writing for at least another quarter of a century.

At the beginning of the decade the line between editors of these scrawny-looking political newspapers and political pamphleteers was still blurred. But by the turn of the century, the pamphleteer was rapidly fading into the background and the editor was emerging as a man who not only selected what opinions were printed but also contributed his views of political issues in the form of shorter, more concise paragraphs. His rise to prominence on the American journalistic scene at this particular time was due as much to the contributions of the mercantile press as to that of the political press. Political papers put views first and news second, their editors often shaping news to fit their political views. Mercantile newspapers, such as the *Connecticut Courant, Columbian Centinel,* Philadelphia *Packet,* and Samuel Loudon's New York *Mercantile Advertiser* with their larger circulations, put news first but views became a prominent feature. Their editors, unable to remain aloof from the political struggle of the time, often wrote their views for the local column. The use by both types of newspapers of the shorter editorial-like paragraph probably was influential in creating a demand for this form of opinion writing and may have helped establish it as a permanent feature of the newspaper.

Other elements also contributed to the emergence of the editorial at this time. One was the increase in the number of dailies. By 1800, 24 of the 235 existing newspapers were dailies. Many others were semiweeklies and triweeklies. These were made possible by newer and better printing equipment and by demand for advertising on the part of the business establishment. But an increase in the number of issues of a publication meant an increase in the amount of space that could be allotted to the letter essays on the inside pages. Too, the advent of magazines took away from newspapers some of the literary efforts—essays, poetry, art, and theater criticism—and gave the newspapers more space for news and comment by editors.

The opinionated pamphlet like contributions of political leaders, which, of necessity, had to be cut into daily install-ments for newspapers, had begun by 1795 to bore party lead-ers, businessmen, and readers. Although use of these long political diatribes would continue into the next century, some editors, such as Webster and Duane, began to show a marked preference for the short editoriallike paragraph, which they themselves wrote. Often filled with denunciatory epithets and invective accusations, these shorter, livelier comments some-times were sprinkled among the pamphlet-style essays.[1]

In the smaller cities and in the boondocks, the printer was still the key figure of the weeklies. But, he, too, was soon known as an editor. Often a local group would supply the necessary funds for a newspaper by giving a lien or a mortgage on the printing equipment. Or a group of men with political aspira-tions would decide to publish a newspaper, would hire a printer, and name one of the members as editor. In either event, the printer was expected to promote his patrons and their causes. And he did, although, by so doing, he left himself open to the charge that his press was not his own.[2]

By 1800, conductor-editors of country newspapers, fol-lowing in the footsteps of Fenno, Webster, Freneau, and Bache, had attached their publications to a political party and were helping to mold the nation's opinion. They did this partially by clipping letter essays from their favorite city newspapers and partially by serving as a grass-roots sounding board for party leaders. But in this era, comparatively few country edi-tors were capable enough to write their own editorial para-graphs.[3]

The very nature of the political climate of the 1790's, however, provided the most conducive influence in the upsurge of the invective paragraph. The split into parties which had begun over the fight for the adoption of the federal Constitu-tion deepened with each succeeding national crisis. The cleavage was complete in Washington's second term. On the one side was Alexander Hamilton, secretary of treasury, who headed the Federalist party. On the other side was Thomas Jefferson, secretary of state, who led the antifederalists forces, or Repub-lican party. Each of these statesmen used the press to shape public opinion in support of his theory of government or his side of an issue. Generally speaking, the Federalists, the conservatives of the time, were the business and propertied classes of the coastal towns, while Republicans, the liberals, were the agrarian Southerners, small farmers, and working men.

Both Hamilton and Jefferson needed editors who could write ably and who could support vigorously the ideas of each man, Hamilton found Fenno and Noah Webster. Jefferson used Freneau and Bache. Among the events that caused comment in newspapers were Washington's proclamation of neutrality following the British declaration of war against France in 1793; the attempt by Charles Genêt, French minister to the United States, to use American ports for repair of his country's war ships; the John Jay treaty; the excise law of 1791; Washington's retirement in 1796; the XYZ Affair in which the French foreign minister wanted a bribe to receive the U.S. diplomats; and the Alien and Sedition Acts of 1798.

It was known almost from the first issue of Fenno's *Gazette of the United States* that it was Hamilton's organ. As a matter of fact, Fenno told his readers on April 27, 1791, that for two years he had been assisted by "several distinguished literary characters." These were Hamilton and Vice-President John Adams, who wrote under pseudonyms. In printing their contributions, Fenno was carrying out one of the promises in his "Prospectus"—that he would publish "essays upon great subjects of Government in general." [4] In one of his own editorial contributions, the *Gazette* editor explained his view of the kind of utterances that should be included in his publication. Newspaper comment should "hold up the people's own government in a favorable light" and "impress just ideas of its administration by exhibiting FACTS." It was his patriotic duty "by every exertion, to endear the GENERAL GOVERN-MENT to the people" for "so long as the principles of the Constitution" were held "sacred, and the rights and liberties of the people," were "preserved inviolate." [5]

Whether this was one of the ideas dictated by Hamilton to Fenno cannot be determined. But when Hamilton himself wanted to propound his views of current political issues, he wrote under the name of "Catullus" long essay letters that sometimes ran three columns in length. In one such letter, he attacked Thomas Jefferson for his opposition to the Constitution.[6] When Hamilton, in turn, was criticized in the Freneau newspaper, the secretary of treasury wrote a letter signed "T. L." for the *Gazette of the United States*. "T. L." questioned Jefferson's policy of paying funds to an officeholder editor who was attacking the Washington administration.[7] The newspaper feud between Hamilton and Jefferson newspapers became so bitter that President Washington intervened, though with little success.[8]

On the front page of the *Gazette*, Fenno as early as 1790 was running a kind of editorial column as a regular feature. "The Tablet," as it was headed, carried long arguments for a strong government, for a monarchy, and for other Hamiltonian ideas. The first sentence was frequently italicized and appeared to be a kind of subhead. In the March 20, 1790, issue, for example, Fenno seemed to be advocating a king in a Tablet article that began (in italics) : "Take away thrones and crowns . . . and there will be an end of all dominion." He pointed out that there had to "be some adventitious properties infused into the government to give it energy and spirit, or the selfish, turbulent passions of men" could never be controlled. "In proportion as we become populous and wealthy must the tone of the government be strengthened."

The Tablet was the voice of the *Gazette of the United States*, which its readers understood to be that of Hamilton. Here was an editor writing for the man behind the newspaper, much as today's editorial writer voices the opinions of those who direct the editorial policies of his newspaper.

But this column apparently did not help make the *Gazette* the financial success its backers had hoped for. It lacked advertising. In the fall of 1793, when a yellow fever epidemic hit Philadelphia, the *Gazette* was suspended. Hamilton, however, still felt the need for an organ as an outlet for his political commentary. With the help of Rufus King and others, in December he backed Noah Webster in establishing the *American Minerva*, a New York daily. Webster was already well known for his newspaper contributions to the outstanding *Connecticut Courant* and for his political pamphlets, portions of which had appeared not only in the *Connecticut Courant* but also in the *State Gazette of South Carolina*, the *Maryland Gazette*, the *New-Hampshire Gazette,* and the Norwich (Connecticut) *Packet*.[9]

From the first issue of the *Minerva*, Webster spoke of

himself as an editor, and letters printed in the publication were often addressed "To the Editor." In this capacity, Webster added to his laurels as a news-opinion writer through his paragraphs in the "New York" column. He set the tone for his ideas on the role of commentaries in the daily press in the "The Editor's Address to the Public," which appeared on the front page of the first issue of the *Minerva*. In no other country, he wrote, had "newspapers so generally circulated among the body of the people." Because of their cheapness and the frequency of their circulation, they had assumed in America "an eminent rank in the catalogue of useful publications." And "in a great degree," they had superseded political pamphlets. "In view of their great importance in republican governments," newspapers should be "considered auxiliaries of governments," as "heralds of truth," and as "protectors of peace and good order." [10]

In his "Prospectus" which was printed alongside this "Address to the Public," and which itself was a statement of "editorial" policy, Webster promised that as "the Editor," he would "endeavor to preserve this paper *chaste* and impartial," would avoid "Personalities, if possible," and would make the *Minerva* a "Friend of Government, of Freedom, of Virtue, and of every species of Improvement." Webster, of course, was not always able to live up to his promises, although the *Minerva* was as nearly a fair newspaper as could be found in that decade. But it definitely was a Federalist organ, which favored the French Revolution and deprecated Genêt in letters and in editorial paragraphs. Webster, however, did not indulge in personalities as much as did other editors of the time.

As the *Minerva* editor, he wrote pseudonymous letters for his publication. In 1795 as "Curtius," he defended Jay's Treaty with England in a series of twelve letters. He also published in his columns a similar series of thirty-eight letters, written by Hamilton and King as "Camillus." In their purpose and content, all fifty letters could be termed editorial utterances. But because the Curtius letters were written by an editor, they can be called editorial opinions. Furthermore in these letters, in a series of essays which he labeled "The Times," and in other letters and essays under various other names, Webster adapted the language of his comments to the ordinary reader.

But Webster's greatest contribution to editorial writing was to help popularize the practice of printing paragraphs of his own opinions in the local column. Sometimes he started these with "The Editor . . ." and he frequently used the editorial we. The "New York" column was really, like other "local" columns of other newspapers of that era, a summary of news, mostly local, but often with items of the latest foreign and national news. Webster frequently included interpretation and backgrounding on the news and sometimes out-and-out editorial comment because it was understood by the readers to be written by the editor. He himself wrote these news summaries and often used brackets to enclose his own commentary. Sometimes, he was able to localize his comments on a foreign event. About a story on pirates in the Mediterranean Sea, for example, he pointed out that pirates damaged not only sailors and merchants, but also farmers. New York harbor might be hard to defend from pirates, although two or three ships of the line could do it. "But the expense! We like the *protection* but *who pays?*" he asked.[11]

Of course, this device of lacing news summaries in the local column with short editoriallike paragraphs was not new. But Webster was using it more frequently and discussing more diverse subjects than other editors. For example, on July 4, 1796, he commented in this column on the twentieth anniversary of the American Revolution; on July 28, 29, and 30 of that year, he discussed the corporation's recommendations for improving the New York harbor. With short sentences, liberally decorated with exclamation points, he criticized the corporation's plan to fill in part of the East River because of the threat of pollution.

These editorial paragraphs appeared under the "New York" column through May 18, 1796. On the next day, May 19, Webster began using a masthead or "flag," consisting of the words "The Minerva," over this local column. This was, of course, an editorial column in the modern sense because Webster's commentaries on the news represented the voice of the *Minerva*.

However, Webster was not the first editor to use over his own comments a flag, or miniature nameplate in the same family of type as, but in a smaller size than, that used in the title on the front page. Up in Boston, the *Independent Chroni-*

cle, a partisan Republican rival of Russell's *Columbian Centinel*, had earlier used a small nameplate, "The Chronicle," over its Boston columns on November 8, 1792. Thomas Adams, editor of the *Independent Chronicle*, used the flag sporadically until late in 1793, when he used it regularly. Sometimes a subhead "Remarks" was used under "The Chronicle," [12] and here Adams printed his personal commentaries. He often animadverted on Russell and the *Centinel*. The regular use of "The Chronicle" over Adam's editorial paragraphs preceded Webster's use of "The Minerva" by at least three years.

Not even Webster's semiweekly edition of the *Minerva*, which he called the *Herald*, was an original idea with him. Intended for countywide distribution, the *Herald*, which carried no advertising and used only material already carried in the *Minerva*, came to be known as Webster's *Herald*. This device had been used earlier by Thomas Greenleaf whose daily *Journal* had lasted only a short time. But if Webster was not always original with his journalistic innovations, he can be credited with popularizing them. Probably because he could write so much better than other editors and because he kept the *Minerva* notches above most other newspapers of the time, he set the pace for other inventive editors. And certainly he was more adept than others in taking ideas dictated, in this case by Hamilton, and developing them into short one-argument forms for his editorial comment.

Webster left the *Minerva* as editor in 1798, about a year after a more virulent Federalist newspaper had been established in Philadelphia by William Cobbett—*Porcupine's Gazette and United States Advertiser*. Cobbett, an Englishman, was less than thirty years old when he fled in 1792 to the United States to escape a court martial. Self-educated, he first made a name for himself as a political pamphleteer whose tracts viciously attacked haters of England. Because of the sharp barbs in his pamphlets, someone likened him to a porcupine.[13] This must have pleased Cobbett because he immediately began writing under the name of "Peter Porcupine," and he called his newspaper *Porcupine's Gazette*.

Cobbett wasted no time in letting his readers know that he would conduct a Federalist publication. "Professions of impartiality I shall make none," he proclaimed in his first issue. He wished his paper "to be a rallying point for the friends of government." His duties as an editor were also explained in the same decisive manner: "As to the other articles that compose a paper, he that does not exercise his own judgment, either in admitting or rejecting what is sent to him, is a poor passive fool, and not an editor." Furthermore, he did not intend to be one of those editors "who look on the conflict [Federalist vs. Republican] with perfect indifference, and whose only anxiety is the strongest side." *Porcupine's Gazette* would never "be an instrument of destruction to the cause I espouse." [14]

In the 778 issues of *Porcupine's Gazette,* Cobbett minced no words in his daily barrage of coarse, pithy, often witty editoriallike utterances against the French and anything tinged with French influence. With a penchant for writing in the first person singular, Cobbett filled his newspaper with scurrilous paragraphs in which he attacked his opponents with personal virulence. Frequently before and after a story, or a contribution to his publication, he printed a paragraph of his own comment in brackets.

When Cobbett really wanted to lash out at his opponents, he attacked them in long sarcastic diatribes on page one. His favorite target was usually the *Aurora,* the Philadelphia daily edited by Benjamin Franklin Bache, whom Cobbett tagged "Lightning Rod, Jr." In his first issue of *Porcupine's Gazette,* Cobbett called the rival *Aurora* a "vehicle of lies and sedition." [15] Two days later he charged Bache and William Duane, Bache's assistant, with being in the pay of France.[16] So abusive were Cobbett's attacks that other Federalist editors chided him. Webster reproved him in the *Minerva;*[17] and when later Cobbett attacked President Adams,[18] Benjamin Russell took him to task in the *Columbian Centinel.*[19]

Cobbett had the ability to use small current incidents as "lead-ins" to his attacks. For his most abusive assault on Bache, he used the publication of a calendar (almanac) by Bache as an excuse for calling the *Aurora* editor "the Market Street Scoundrel," "an impudent scoundrel," "an atrocious wretch (worthy descendant of Old Ben)," "an abominable liar," "a tool and a hireling," and a "miscreant." The calendar had noted that in 1788 Louis XVI had eight thousand people murdered in France, and Cobbett wrote: "Who ever heard of this before? Who ever heard of a sacrifice at Paris, while poor old Louis retained his power of King?" Louis never authorized "the shedding of a drop of blood." Instead, if it had not "been for this unconquerable aversion to shedding blood," he would still be king of France. Then Cobbett thought it would be proper to characterize Bache for his many readers. Bache was "an evil-looking devil," whose eyes never "get above your knees." He had "a sallow complexion, hollow cheeks, dead eyes"; and altogether, he was like a "fellow who has been about a week or ten days on a gibbet." [20]

But Cobbett could be just as sarcastic at things as at people. Once in a long, page two commentary, he attacked lotteries, even though he was not averse to advertising them. In the third paragraph he advised readers to make a lottery if they had "an itching propensity to use your wits to an advantage." Lotteries were splendid schemes—baits "that cannot fail to catch the gulls." Then he advocated advertising rich prizes but printing so many blanks that they could not all be sold and the drawing would never be held. At the end Cobbett added a postscript in which he said this was the "most sure, safe, and easy way of getting money." Of course, there were other ways, "such as fingering your neighbour's strong box or borrowing from a friend on the highway." In a second postscript he promised to write again, "not by way of apology, upon the *expedition* used by the managers of the Canal Lottery now drawing in Philadelphia." [21] Here the current event was tied into the last paragraph. With all of his vituperativeness, Cobbett was using what was to become an accepted editorial writing device—the immediate event as an illustration of a general principle.

Cobbett's opinions and language gave offense to many, among them Dr. Benjamin Rush, a Philadelphia physician and politician. Rush sued for libel; Cobbett was convicted, and rather than pay the five-thousand-dollar fine, he returned to England. But his "strong personality and vigorous controversial style were potent influences in strengthening the bitterness" of opinion writing in the next two decades.[22]

On the other side of the political fence, Freneau in the

National Gazette and Bache and Duane in the *Aurora* were also making contributions to the new form for writing views of news. Thomas Jefferson, whose ideas of government opposed those of Hamilton, wanted an organ to combat Fenno's *Gazette of the United States.* He gave Philip Freneau, better known today as the Revolutionary poet, a job as a State Department translator at $250 a year so that Freneau could establish the semiweekly *National Gazette* in Philadelphia on October 31, 1791. It became the leading Republican organ of the early 1790's. Jefferson also gave Freneau access to all of his correspondence, and information gleaned from this source must have added grist to the *National Gazette* political opinion mill.

One of the best printed journals of the time, Freneau's newspaper was filled with the usual letter essays to the editor. The editor often used brackets to indicate utterances that he wrote. Occasionally he inserted bracketed comments within letter essays or within items reprinted from other publications. Such bracketed comment sometimes followed excerpts from foreign newspapers. Lesser Republican newspapers were soon reprinting Freneau's partisan utterances. Just as Fenno was echoing the opinions of Hamilton, so Freneau was echoing Jefferson's liberal ideas and his sympathies with France, although Jefferson wrote Washington that he never by himself or through anyone else "directly or indirectly" wrote, dictated, or procured "any one sentence or sentiment to be inserted in Freneau's or "in any other gazette" which he had not signed in his official capacity.[23]

Freneau attacked Hamilton's funding plan, his national bank, his proposed public debt, and his advocacy of extending the powers of the federal government under the "general welfare" clause of the Constitution. He criticized Washington and denounced, often with ridicule, the monarchial tendencies of Hamilton and Vice-President John Adams. Freneau set down his ideas of the role of the newspaper in government in early issues of the *National Gazette.* "Public opinion," he wrote, "sets the bounds to every government and is the real sovereign of every free one." [24] A rather early advocate of the "watchdog" role of the press, he told his readers that "perpetual jealousy of the government" was necessary against "the machinations of ambition." He warned that "where jealousy does not exist in reasonable degree, the saddle is soon prepared for the back of the people." [25]

Freneau's brash ridicule and savage attacks on Hamilton in letters signed "Brutus" so goaded Hamilton that he felt compelled to write his famous "T. L." letter in which he said that Freneau had no right to criticize the government which paid him. Freneau reprinted this letter in his newspaper, and beneath it, in brackets, his jibing reply. In part, he said that an editor who received "a small stipend for services to the Department of State" was more likely to admit "into his publication impartial strictures on the proceedings of government" and "to act an honest and disinterested part toward the public than a vile sycophant," who attempted "to poison the minds of the people by propaganda" and to disseminate "principles and sentiments utterly subversive of the true republican interests of the country." [26]

This exchange between Hamilton and Freneau continued for several more letters, and the following year another verbal war via newspapers erupted between the two. The Genêt affair was the underlying cause of this exchange. Freneau espoused Genêt's cause and, as "Veritas," impudently addressed several letters to President Washington on the issue. In one, he accused the President of underhanded dealings in his neutrality proclamation when the people did not want neutrality.[27] In another, the editor reminded the President that he was not a hereditary ruler. He warned that "some court satellites may have deceived" Washington about "the sentiment" of his "fellow citizens." The chief of a country seldom knew "the real state of a nation, particularly if he be so buoyed up by official importance as to think it beneath his dignity to mix occasionally with the people." The editor cautioned not to "view the state of the public mind through a fallacious medium" and not to mistake "the little buzz of the aristocratic few" for "the exalted and generous voice of the American people." [28] Hamilton answered this charge as "No Jacobin" in the New York *Daily Advertiser* and in Fenno's *Gazette of the United States*.[29] Scurrilous attacks and abusive assaults on politically prominent men and on editors had begun in earnest by this time.

Freneau's *National Gazette* lived only two years. It was unsuccessful financially, although Jefferson took subscriptions for it. But when Jefferson retired from his cabinet post and the yellow fever epidemic hit Philadelphia, Freneau and his printers, who were bankrupt, shut down the publication. In his brief sojourn as editor of the *National Gazette,* however, Freneau, through his bracketed utterances, had been influential in opening sessions of the United States Senate to reporters.[30] And Jefferson later gave Freneau's newspaper credit for having "served our constitution which was galloping fast into monarchy." [31]

The controversial editor, however, had learned much about news-opinion writing that helped him when he founded in 1797 the New York *Time Piece and Literary Companion* which would soon become the fastest growing newspaper in the nation. He stayed with this publication only a year. Using the editorial we, Freneau commented, in direct and telling prose, on inside pages of the *Time Piece* on current events that were reported on the first page of the publication. Of a bill before the Pennsylvania legislature that proposed to drive settlers from their estates and burn their homes, he wrote that the "severity of the proposed measure" called forth "pointed animadversions in that state." If the bill passed and was enforced, "a civil commotion would probably be the consequence." Freneau predicted bloodshed, but hoped "the dreadful alternative" would "be avoided." [32]

To alert his readers that his commentary referred to an event reported elsewhere in the *Time Piece,* the editor inserted such information in his inside-page utterances. For example, in a criticism of the system of slavery, his lead sentence read: "Mr. Rushton's address to the late President of the United States (see the first page of this paper) is an awesome appeal to the moral sentiment of the world on the injustice and cruelty of man in bondage." [33]

But the death of Freneau's *National Gazette* may have been due partially to the surging *Aurora,* which was fast becoming the leading spokesman for the Republican party. Founded in late 1790 by "Lightning Rod, Jr." Bache as the *General Advertiser and Political Commercial, Agricultural and Literary Journal, and Literary Journal,* it soon became known as the *Aurora* when Bache centered that word in the nameplate. At first the editor was sympathetic to Washington, but his years in France gave him natural sympathies toward that country. By the time of the Genêt incident, he was making the *Aurora* the mouthpiece for French interests in the country. His abuse of Washington in his newspaper is a well-known scurrilous black mark in American journalism. Bache was assisted in writing vituperative utterances for his newspaper by William Duane, who would become the *Aurora*'s editor when in 1798 Bache died.

As did most editors of political newspapers during this period, Bache and Duane filled the *Aurora* with letters to the editor. Under such pseudonyms as "Hancock," "Belisarius," "Pettachus," "Atticus," "Gracchus," and "Valerius," critics of Washington called the President everything from a "spoiled child" to a despotic counterfeit of England's King George.[34] Washington issued his famous "Farewell Address" on September 19, 1796, in Dunlap and Claypool's *Pennsylvania Packet,* a commercial daily which he considered more respectable than other Philadelphia newspapers. It was three months later, however, before Bache reprinted the address in the *Aurora* and followed it with his famous comment that if "ever a nation was debauched by a man, the American nation" had "suffered from the improper influence of Washington." And if "ever a nation was deceived by a man, the American nation" had "been deceived by Washington." The President's conduct should serve as "a warning that no man may be an idol and that a people may confide in themselves rather than an individual." [35]

The inauguration of President Adams provided Bache with another opportunity to blast Washington—this time with an irreverent prayer.[36] The *Aurora* editor soon grew disenchanted with President Adams and turned his vitriolic pen on the new administration.

Animosities naturally developed between the editors of the *Aurora* and those of Federalist publications. Bache and Cobbett carried on a running battle with each other in their publications. Bache once called Webster "an impious, disorganized wretch" [37] and a "jackall" and "devoted tool" of the British faction. "If ever a man prostituted the little sense that he had, to serve the purposes of a monarchial and aristocratic junto, Noah Webster, Esq. must be that man." [38]

After Bache's death, Duane continued the bitter attacks on administration leaders and on rival editors. He called J. W. Fenno, John's son who had become editor of the *Gazette of the United States* when after the yellow fever epidemic it had resumed publication, "a scoundrel and a liar." [39] Even though Duane was as versatile as Bache at name-calling, his audacious and virile political commentary in the *Aurora* has been credited with helping prevent imminent war with France and with helping to elect Thomas Jefferson to the presidency. [40]

Editors of these leading Federalist and Republican newspapers were not alone in their vituperative commentaries. Up in Boston, in the *Columbian Centinel,* Russell was bitterly attacking the Federalists, particularly Vice-President Jefferson. When Bache died, Russell's brother, editor of another Boston newspaper, wrote that the memory "of the vile Benjamin Franklin Bache" could not "be too highly execrated." [41] Among other editorial writers engaged in name-calling were James T. Callender of the Richmond *Examiner,* Thomas Adams of the Boston *Independent Chronicle,* Matthew Lyon, David Frothingham, and the Reverend William Bentley.

The wave of vituperation which swept through the personal utterances of editors after 1795 might easily be attributed to the influence once more of the English press. With the Revolution, it is true, the American and English press had diverged. The leading article had become a main attraction in the English press, and the editorial began slowly emerging in the American newspapers. But in the last half of the 1790's, many English and Irish political exiles migrated to the United States. Because some of these had been connected with the press in their homelands, they became journalists in the United States, where the demand for printers and editors could not be supplied from domestic sources. They brought with them the personal journalism then current in the Grub Street journals.

In America where newspapers were enjoying a greater freedom of comment than had ever been known anywhere in the world, these transplanted journalists soon became known for the vituperativeness of their writing. And native-born editors often equaled their venom. Typical of their name-calling were such phrases as "pert and prating popinjay," "hackneyed guttersnip," "maggot of corruption," "wad on a dungheap," and "sniveling sophisticated hound." [42]

Chief Justice McKean said in 1798 that everyone was offended at the scurrility that "has raged in pamphlets and newspapers in Philadelphia." For several years "our satire has been nothing but ribaldry and billingsgate; the contest has been who could call names in the greatest variety of phrases, who could mangle the greatest number of names, or who could excel in the magnitude of lies." [43] Even some editors themselves deplored the vilification in newspaper commentary. J. W. Fenno called American newspapers "the most base, false, servile and venal publications that ever polluted the fountains of society." And their editors were the most "ignorant, mercenary, vulgar automatons that ever were moved by continually rusting cries of sordid mercantile avarices." [44]

But this was after the passage in 1798 of the Alien and Sedition Acts, which were intended to shackle the press, particularly the opposition, or Republican, newspapers.[45] At the time there were about two hundred newspapers, of which twenty to thirty were violently opposed to the Adams administration and were edited and controlled by aliens. Although several prominent editors were victims of the Sedition Act, among them Matthew Lyon, James Callender, Bache, Anthony Haswell, Charles Holt, and William Durell, this move to throttle the press backfired on the Federalists, when they lost the 1800 presidential election to Thomas Jefferson.

The Alien and Sedition Acts were meant to be and were a restriction on the liberty of opinion writing. However, in selecting and in writing commentaries for their newspapers, partisan editors of the 1790's, as one historian has said, were no worse than "their readers who delighted in gall and wormwood." [46] Still there were others who contributed to a more wholesome type of opinion writing. The Reverend William Bentley, for example, wrote a weekly review of worldwide current events, with paragraphs of interpretative comment, and numerous paragraphs commenting on political questions for the Salem *Gazette,* as long as that publication remained neutral. But when its printer-editor became a Federalist mouthpiece, the Reverend Bentley transferred his weekly commentaries to the Salem *Register,* a newspaper that favored Jeffersonian policies.[47] Then there was Joseph Dennie, editor of the *Farmer's Weekly Museum,* as it came to be called. Now famous for his "Lay Preacher" articles and for his fluent, graceful, and spicy Addison-like essays, Dennie also used inserted comment in his brightly written news summaries.[48] He once wrote that every sentence in every paragraph in Republican papers was "a malicious lie." [49]

Editors liked to comment at the close of obituaries—long considered appropriate journalistic practice. The editor of the Salem *Gazette* attached a lengthy moralizing note to the obituary of a man who had died "in irons." [50] And down in Alexandria, Virginia, the editor of the *Times and District of Columbia Advertiser* was the first newsman to announce the death of George Washington. Following a short paragraph reporting the death, which was printed with turned rules for mourning, appeared this italicized paragraph:

> It was yesterday generally determined upon, and will no doubt be universally adhered to by the inhabitants of this town, to observe this day, as a day of mourning. It is of course expected that the stores and shops will be closed, and a suspension of business take place, in consequence of the lively sensibility which the sudden death of the "Father of his Country" has excited in the breast of his fellow-citizens.[51]

The italics were used here in conjunction with the pointing finger to indicate the editor's opinion—by this time a common device in many newspapers.

Increasingly, too, editors of this period were using a kind of "editorial notice" to give readers a better understanding of what was being printed. For example, the editor of the Salem *Gazette* preceded a lengthy series about China with this comment: "That our readers may not be at a loss in reading the recent intelligence from the East Indies, we give an explanation of terms used in those advices." Then followed definitions of such words as "pagoda," "pegoda," and "Koran." [52]

In the 1790's, then, the editorial syndrome was apparent. It had arrived almost simultaneously with and certainly because of the advent of the writing editor, as opposed to the mere "mechanic" printer-editor. And the writing editor was the product of partisan political turmoil when politicians of the time needed people who could write persuasively, and condense their views into simple language for newspaper readers. The writing editor was also the result of the need by owners of mercantile newspapers for someone to comment regularly on political issues and current events while they devoted their time to gathering advertising and shipping news for their expanding weeklies and dailies.

It must be remembered that the political essay letters, which filled the newspapers of the time, were themselves editorial in nature in that, if they were not written by the editor, they were selected by him because they fit his political views. And the opinion paragraph in the local columns or interspersed within the letters, the comment at the end of news stories, and the editorial notices represented the editor's views on the news. Though the word was as yet still "uncoined," the editorial, in a very real sense, was a part of the newspaper.

21. ASSESSMENT

THE MODERN EDITORIAL has been defined as a presentation of fact and opinion in a concise, logical, pleasing order for the sake of entertaining, of influencing opinion, or of interpreting significant news in such a way that its importance is clear to the average reader. It is an interpretation of events viewed from the standpoint of certain principles or policies adopted or advocated by the newspaper publishing it. In this sense the editorial, largely biased, becomes the mouthpiece, the very personality of the newspaper. If we accept this explanation of the editorial and if we recognize that the term "editorial" was originally an adjectival modifier of the word "article" and meant an article written by the editor, it becomes easier for us to understand its evolution. Origins and forerunners of the modern editorial begin to stand out from the welter of newspaper opinion writing before 1800.

We can see more clearly elements of the editorial in handwritten newsletters and ballads. Writers of those early newsletters, handwritten and printed, could not and did not differentiate between the fact of an event and opinions about the fact. The mere writing of an event was an opinion; the mere printing itself was news. Because these newsletters were intended for specific readers, writers "angled" what they wrote, or interpreted events for an elite few—for those leaders in government, business, and religion who could read.

More often than not, newsletter writers based their interpretations not so much on what they had observed as on what they had heard at the old marketplaces of rumor, and perhaps not so much on what they believed as on what they thought their readers wanted to believe. Thus in that religious-oriented period of history, we find almost every event infused with moralistic interpretations and opinions. Many events, similar in nature to those of today, were explained with much the same views as are found in modern editorials—economic effects of administrative changes, riots, wars, crimes, disasters, diseases, even unrest on university campuses.

The old news ballad or broadside interpreted and explained events, in moralistic and patriotic overtones, for the unlettered many. They tended toward the gory, or the sensational. And their writers worked into these popular songs fantastic interpretations of happenings. Singing rhymes came to be used to extol or to deride, and in them rumor became fact. But with them, the masses could be swayed. News ballads, however, eventually passed into literature, and doggerel verse took their place in newspapers.

Pamphlets, of course, were specifically meant, from their beginning, to explain and interpret, to persuade readers, to influence public opinion. They were highly biased opinions of one person. To be sure, early pamphlets and many later ones were concerned not so much with interpreting news events as with explaining religious theories. But with the controversial religious-governmental issues that plagued the English people and the early American colonists, pamphleteers, in actuality, were commenting on what at the time amounted to significant public affairs.

It is difficult today to pore over these early pamphlets with their long, verbose sentences, their abstract statements, and their frequent digressions and find anything of the modern editorial in them. Admittedly, there was little of the immediacy in them. But they did interpret and influence. And the time came when, instead of spending months in the preparations of his manuscript, a pamphleteer, in the stress of the moment, dictated his thoughts directly to the printer so that the finished product could be sold on the streets the next day. This, indeed, was an editorial writer meeting a "deadline."

Furthermore, before letter essays in newspapers began replacing the pamphlet as the prestigious form for opinion writing, significant news events and issues had replaced abstract theories as matter for discussion. And frequent pamphlet wars with their inflaming, derogatory, and libelous statements were not too unlike, especially in purpose, editorial battles of a much later date. Although crude in comparison with the polished output found on editorial pages of modern dailies, the pamphlet was perhaps as influential as today's editorial, if not more so.

With the rise of literacy levels, with less drastic restrictive measures against the press, and with development of larger and better newspapers, the need for long, cumbersomely-written pamphlets began to fade. By mid-eighteenth century, they had already split into two kinds—the more literary, which became magazine literature, and the relatively shorter, more spur-of-the-moment commentaries, which became the letter essay used by newspaper "authors" and "conductors" to foment dissent or to promote "in" policies and personnel. At first, such essays were printed as a pamphlet and then serially in newssheets. Later they were printed first in newspapers and then collected in pamphlet form. Progressively, these were closer steps to the editorial. In fact, we might easily call these writers maxi-editorial writers, just as we might call those who wrote letter essays entirely for newspaper consumption mini-pamphleteers.

Many early newsletters, ballads, and pamphlets had a common element that in itself was a progenitor of the editorial. This was the preface, added often by the printer, not the news compiler. Frequently filled with inflammatory adjectives and sparsely sprinkled with the editorial we, prefatory commentaries were designed either as additional interpretation or as a persuasive device for buyers. The preface became a more highly developed form of interpretative or persuasive commentary when newsletters became corantos and diurnals. Then, hired translators of foreign news wrote the prefaces, explained the news, and sometimes interpolated remarks in news accounts.

With the press-mad 1640's and its billingsgate diurnals and mercuries, prefaces grew into long introductory paragraphs of comment. The use of interpolated remarks increased in asides, remarks in or out of parenthesis, and shoulder notes, remarks printed in the margins. The first use of the question and answer as a form of comment on issues occurred in these publications. And the editorial we became more common. Almost all news stories were so infused with comment that they were quasi editorials themselves.

Ribald commentaries filling these newsbooks became only

an abortive attempt at newspaper editorial writing when the blackout news curtain dropped again. And further developments of the editorial form in news publications had to wait for the abolition of the licensing act toward the end of the seventeenth century. With the advent, at that time, of journals of commentary, the question and answer type of comment was improved. The "dear reader" prefaces and introductory paragraphs of commentary became "letters introductory" addressed to the printer. Opinion began to separate from news accounts. Some journals were divided into sections, with one part for news and two parts for comment. Survivors of the old authorized newspapers and new commercial newspapers began to issue side sheets of comment.

Meanwhile, essay papers were providing another stage of the slowly evolving newspaper editorial. They lent a delightfully entertaining side to commentary. And satiric tones began coloring opinion writing that was concerned with events, issues, and human frailties. But increased interest in immediate or "fresh" news drove essay papers from the journalistic scene. Such commentaries either passed into magazine literature or were retained in shorter form as letter essays to the printers of the developing dailies and weeklies.

During the political press era of the eighteenth century when newspapers attached themselves to one faction or another, letter essays came to be the mouthpieces for the political party behind the paper. Slowly the practice of printing these letters in the same place in the newspaper spread. Even the custom of choosing the most effective of these letters to head the column was adopted by many newspapers. The letter essay was to remain the most influential form of news-opinion writing at the end of the century.

But when the demand for advertising in newspapers increased and when newspaper business had developed economically to the point where a publication could be operated profitably without subsidization by the government or by political parties, editorials emerged as short paragraphs of comment on many and varied significant events and issues. But this happened only after the printer became merely a hired mechanic, and publishers who directed the newspaper's policy, employed someone to write their views. In England, these paragraphs were called leaders. They had become common in local news columns of dailies and some weeklies by 1775. In America, where these paragraphs would become known in the nineteenth century as editorials, their use did not become common until near the end of the eighteenth century.

And who were the journalistic writers, creative and daring enough to experiment with the various predecessors of the editorial paragraph? One of the earliest compilers and news commentators of note was Captain Thomas Gainsford. Although the preface had been used earlier, Gainsford appears to have used it in Bourne and Butter's coranto in the 1620's for much the same purposes as that of the modern editorial writer. In prefaces and concluding notes to "dear" or "courteous" readers, he offered advice about acceptance or rejection of news events in shallow, piously pro-Protestant platitudes. And in remarks, sometimes bracketed in parenthesis, he interpreted news events.

No other major contributors to editorial forms appeared on the journalistic scene until the 1640's when the Protestant-Catholic and inter-Parliamentary issues erupted in weekly diurnals and mercuries. Samuel Pecke and John Birkenhead, on opposing sides at first, delighted in animadverting on each other. Pecke made the "courteous reader" prefaces a common element in newsbooks. Birkenhead attempted to separate fact from opinion by dividing his mercury into three sections, the first-known attempt at departmentalizing newspapers. Two sections contained ribald comments on news and on the opposition. Both writers, with vigorous language, were attempting to sway public opinion, and both presented biased opinions.

Other newsbook compilers of these turbulent years contributed various forms and style elements to opinion writing. These included John Dillingham, Marchamont Nedham, George Smith, Gilbert Mabbott, Daniel Border, and John Crouch. John Dillingham used asides and shoulder notes. But his greatest contributions were the quasi editorials used to open his publication. Almost all other newsbook compilers came to use their opening paragraphs for editoriallike utterances.

All of these men were also influential pamphleteers, but to Nedham belongs the distinction of being the first to break up one of his previously published pamphlets into sections and use them as introductory quasi editorials. He also worked this device in reverse, that is, combined a series of introductory utterances into a pamphlet.

Smith contributed the question-and-answer form of news commentary. Mabbott rejected the popular verbosity for a clear and ordered simplicity. Daniel Border stands alone as the compiler who tried to present both sides of whatever issue he was explaining. Crouch added the entertainment purpose with commentaries filled with smut and caricature.

Both Henry Muddiman and Roger L'Estrange in the early 1660's did more to kill editorial comment than to develop it. Muddiman popularized news and omitted comment. L'Estrange tried to popularize comment and omit news. But an all-comment newspaper proved unpopular. It was no different from the pamphlet. Perhaps these years of newssheets with no editoriallike comment, aside from biased news reports, were needed as a period of rest from the earlier vulgar diatribes in diurnals and mercuries. Still, a bit later L'Estrange in the *Observator* improved upon and popularized George Smith's question-and-answer form of comment. With this he was effective in gaining public acceptance of governmental actions.

Toward the end of the seventeenth century, John Dunton improved on L'Estrange's questions and answers by having, or pretending to have, readers ask the questions. In his answers, Dunton foreshadowed essay papers by offering his advice on love, marriage, manners, and clothes. He followed in Birkenhead's footsteps by dividing his triweekly journal in sections. The last two segments avowedly were commentaries on news and political issues. This last was also a kind of extension of Harry Care's device of adding a side sheet of news commentary to his newssheet of foreign advices.

Early eighteenth-century newspaper authors were particularly effective in contributing to the evolution of the newspaper editorial. John Tutchin further developed the question and answer commentaries. Daniel Defoe used pungent and persuasive political and social criticism in his new form, the letter introductory. This was a vast improvement on the introductory quasi editorials that John Dillingham had used. His later use of the *Little Review* to answer questions reportedly from readers was an improvement on John Dunton's use of this form of opinion writing.

Addison, Steele, and Swift added refinements in style in their essays that foreshadowed the newspaper social editorial of today. They refined the entertainment purpose of opinion writing. Henry Fielding and George Smollett, as hired political commentators, contributed slashing vituperation and an occasional typographical innovation to make their utterances stand out.

In the political press era of the eighteenth century, newspapers came to be recognized as mouthpieces for political parties; writers of letter essays that criticized the government's policies were influential enough to unseat several administrations. Among the more outstanding letter essayists were John Trenchard and Thomas Gordon with their "Cato" letters, John Wilkes, and "Junius." Toward the end of the century, letter essays, addressed by that time to the printer, were still playing an important role in their editoriallike purposes of entertaining, interpreting significant events, and influencing readers who at that time wanted to be told what to believe.

In the American colonies, where newspaper development was always years behind that in the mother country, the influence of British press opinion was evident both in content and in form. As in England, evolution of editorial utterances went through the same stages—pamphlets, ballads, opinionated and moralistic news accounts, prefaces, asides, shoulder notes, quasi-editorial beginnings, letters introductory, letter essays, and finally the short editorial paragraphs. By 1880, these editorial paragraphs were found under a flag, and the editorial we had become common.

In spite of this imitativeness, there were leaders who added verve and creativity to opinion writing in the colonial and early American newspapers. These included James and Benjamin Franklin, Samuel and John Adams, the Bradfords, John Dickinson with his "Letters to a Pennsylvania Farmer," Thomas Paine, John Peter Zenger, Isaiah Thomas, even Hugh Gaine and James Rivington. Toward the end of the century, American newspapers, developing aside and apart from the

British press, played a quick game of "catch-up." John Fenno, Philip Freneau, and Noah Webster were outstanding "hired" editors, whose newspaper utterances influenced public opinion. Webster, Benjamin Russell, and the publishers of the *Connecticut Courant* were instrumental in popularizing embryo editorial columns in the 1790's. Benjamin Franklin Bache, James T. Callender, and William Cobbett added vicious vituperation that would color American newspaper opinion writing for years.

These men and their views of the news had established a recognizable editorial syndrome. In the next century, old interests would decline; new ideas and concepts would develop. The newspaper editorial would acquire its name and reach its golden age. But its progress and development after 1800 would not be as torturous as its birth which took more than two hundred years.

Notes / Bibliography / Index

Notes

1 In the Beginning

[1] Alexander Andrews, *The History of British Journalism* (London, 1859), I, 16; S. H. Steinberg, *Five Hundred Years of Printing* (Edinburgh, 1955), p. 37.

[2] Norman McClure, ed. *The Letters of John Chamberlain* (Philadelphia, 1939), I, 6–20. This two-volume collection of the letters provided excellent examples of infused comment.

[3] Ibid., p. 59.

[4] Ibid., p. 119.

[5] Ibid., p. 432.

[6] Ibid., pp. 138–39.

[7] Victor von Klarwill, ed. *The Fugger News-Letters—Being A Selection of Unpublished Letters from Correspondents of the House of Fugger During the Years 1568–1605,* trans. Pauline de Chary (New York, 1924), p. 6. This is one of several translations of this collection of letters. It provided many examples of infused comment.

[8] Ibid., p. 19.

[9] Ibid., p. 14.

[10] Ibid., p. 18.

[11] Ibid., p. 17.

[12] Ibid., pp. 52–53.

[13] Andrews, I, 24.

[14] Leslie Shepherd, *The Broadside Ballad: A Study in Origins and Meaning* (London, 1962), p. 26.

2 From Edict to Newsbook

[1] Harold Herd, *The March of Journalism—The Story of the Press from 1622 to the Present Day* (London, 1952), p. 11.

[2] S. H. Steinberg, *Five Hundred Years of Printing* (Edinburgh, 1955), p. 71.

[3] Leonard W. Levy, *Legacy of Suppression: Freedom of Speech in Early American History* (Cambridge, Mass., 1964), pp. 8–9.

⁴ Cyprian Blagden, *The Stationers' Company, A History, 1403–1959* (London, 1961), p. 25.

⁵ Matthias A. Shaaber, *Some Forerunners of the Newspaper in England* (Philadelphia, 1929), p. 51. This scholarly book has one of the better discussions of the opinion element in the precoranto era.

⁶ Ibid.

⁷ Ibid., p. 48.

⁸ Ibid., p. 70.

⁹ Ibid., p. 73.

¹⁰ Harry T. Baker, "Early English Journalism," *Sewanee Review,* XXV (Oct. 1917), 399.

¹¹ Shaaber, pp. 75–79.

¹² Blagden, p. 50.

¹³ Shaaber, p. 204.

¹⁴ Ibid., pp. 205–6.

¹⁵ Steinberg, p. 38.

¹⁶ Shaaber, p. 11; Alexander Andrews, *The History of British Journalism* (London, 1859), p. 25.

¹⁷ Shaaber, p. 53.

¹⁸ Ibid., p. 53.

¹⁹ Ibid., p. 54.

²⁰ W. P. Trent, *Daniel Defoe: How to Know Him* (New York, 1916), p. 150.

²¹ Shaaber, pp. 48–49.

²² Ibid., p. 44.

²³ Ibid., pp. 137–67

²⁴ Ibid., p. 155.

²⁵ Ibid., p. 159.

²⁶ Ibid., p. 23.

²⁷ Ibid., p. 293.

²⁸ Ibid., pp. 189–97; Leslie Shepherd, *The Broadside Ballad* (London, 1962), pp. 47–54; Hyder Edward Rollins, *The Pack of Autolycus, or Strange and Terrible News of Ghost, Apparition, Monstrous Births, Showers of Wheat, Judgments of God, and Other Prodigious and Fearful Happenings As Told in Broadside Ballards of the Years 1624–1692* (Cambridge, Mass., 1927). Ballards in this collection show the kinds of commentary used in songs of passing events.

²⁹ Fred S. Siebert, "The Regulation of Newsbooks, 1620–1640," *Journalism Quarterly,* XVI (June 1932), 152; Blagden, p. 25; Shaaber, pp. 257–58.

³⁰ Shaaber, p. 310; Herd, p. 13.

³¹ Herd, p. 12.

³² James Frank, *The Beginning of the English Newspaper, 1620–1660*

(Cambridge, Mass., 1961), p. 3. This excellent book is particularly outstanding for the 1640–60 years.

[33] Shaaber, quoted, p. 207.

[34] Ibid., pp. 278–79, 285.

[35] Ibid., quoted, p. 236.

[36] Ibid., quoted, p. 238.

[37] Frank, p. 1.

[38] Siebert, pp. 153, 156; Frank, p. 6.

[39] Shaaber, pp. 288–89; H. R. Fox Bourne, *English Newspapers: Chapters in the History of Journalism* (New York, 1877: reissue), I, 4.

3 Corantos

[1] Folke Dahl, *A Bibliography of English Corantos and Periodical Newsbooks, 1620–1642* (London, 1952), p. 22. This is the most complete bibliography available for those years.

[2] Ibid., p. 20.

[3] Matthias A. Shaaber, "The History of the First English Newspaper," *Studies in Philology,* XXIX (Oct. 1932), 587.

[4] Ibid., p. 587; James Frank, *The Beginning of the English Newspaper* (Cambridge, Mass., 1961), p. 9; Dahl, p. 192.

[5] Shaaber, p. 569; Frank, p. 3.

[6] Frank, p. 9.

[7] Lawrence Hanson, "English Newsbooks, 1620–1641," *The Library,* XVIII (4th ser., 1937–38), quoted, 367.

[8] *A continuation of the newes . . . ,* Nov. 16, 1622.

[9] *More Newes of the Affaires of the World . . . ,* June 10, 1623.

[10] *The Affaires and generall Businesse of Europe . . . ,* Feb. 24, 1624.

[11] *The Continuation of our Weekely Newes . . . ,* Jan. 18, 1626.

[12] H. R. Fox Bourne, *English Newspapers* (New York, 1877), quoted I, 6–7.

[13] Frederick Seaton Siebert, *Freedom of the Press in England, 1476–1776* (Urbana, 1952), pp. 155–56.

4 Diurnals and Mercuries

[1] James Frank, *The Beginning of the English Newspaper* (Cambridge, Mass., 1961), p. 14; Folke Dahl, *A Bibliography of English Corantos and Periodical Newsbooks* (London, 1952), p. 203.

[2] Matthias A. Shaaber, "The History of the First English Newspaper," *Studies in Philology,* XXIX (Oct. 1932), 584; Dahl, p. 223; Fred S. Siebert, "The Regulation of Newsbooks, 1620–1640," *Journalism Quarterly,* XVI (June 1932), 30.

[3] Quoted in Dahl, p. 251, and Alexander Andrews, *The History of British Journalism* (London, 1859), I, 30.

[4] *The Continuation of the most remarkable passages* . . . , June 4, 1642.

[5] Frank, pp. 23–25.

[6] J. B. Williams, "The Beginnings of English Journalism," *Cavalier and Poet,* Vol. VII: *Cambridge History of English Literature* (New York, 1933: reissue), p. 394.

[7] *A Perfect Diurnall* . . . , Nov. 13, 1642.

[8] Frank, p. 67.

[9] *Perfect Diurnall* . . . , Nov. 13, 1642.

[10] Ibid.

[11] Frank, p. 38.

[12] *Mercurius Aulicus,* April 9 and 23, 1643.

[13] Frank, quoted, p. 51.

[14] *Kingdomes Weekly Intelligencer,* June 24, 1645.

[15] Ibid., May 12, 1646.

[16] R. H. Griffith, "Some Unrecorded Newsbooks," *Times Literary Supplement,* Dec. 11, 1924, p. 849.

[17] Frank, pp. 42–48.

[18] *Parliamentary Scout,* June 29, 1643.

[19] Ibid., July 6, 1643.

[20] Williams, p. 396.

[21] *Parliamentary Scout,* Dec. 1, 1643.

[22] *Moderate Intelligencer,* May 28, 1648.

[23] *Weekly Account,* May 8, 1644.

[24] William M. Clyde, *The Struggle for Freedom of the Press from Caxton to Cromwell* (London, 1934), p. 70; Frank, p. 50.

[25] *Mercurius Britanicus,* Feb. 3, 1645.

[26] *Compleate Intelligencer and Resolver,* Nov. 28, 1643.

[27] *Spie,* Jan. 30, 1644.

[28] Ibid., Feb. 13, 1644.

[29] Frank, p. 81; Williams, pp. 399–400.

[30] *Mercurius Civicus,* Feb. 26, 1646.

[31] *Mercurius Pragmaticus,* Oct. 9, 1647.

[32] Ibid., Nov. 21, 1648.

[33] *Mercurius Elencticus,* June 20, 1648.

[34] *Aulicus,* Sept. 14, 1644.

[35] *Moderate Intelligencer,* Oct. 31, 1648.

5 Pamphlets and Ballads

[1] Harry T. Baker, "Early English Journalism," *Sewanee Review,* XXV (Oct. 1917), 399; James Frank, *The Beginning of the English Newspaper* (Cambridge, Mass., 1961), p. 136.

[2] William M. Clyde, *The Struggle for Freedom of the Press* (London, 1934), pp. 40–47.

[3] Frank, p. 41.

6 Death of the Embryonic Editorial

[1] Clyde Augustus Duniway, *The Development of Freedom of the Press in Massachusetts* (New York, 1906), pp. 36–37.

[2] James Frank, *The Beginning of the English Newpaper* (Cambridge, Mass., 1961), pp. 200–201.

[3] William M. Clyde, *The Struggle for Freedom of the Press* (London, 1934), p. 189.

[4] J. B. Williams, "The Beginnings of English Journalism," *Cavalier and Poet,* Vol. VII: *Cambridge History of English Literature* (New York, 1933: reissue), p. 167; Frank, p. 202.

[5] *Severall Proceedings,* Jan. 19, 1654.

[6] Clyde, p. 197; Frank, pp. 202, 238; Williams, p. 403.

[7] Harold Herd, *The March of Journalism* (London, 1952), p. 21; J. Milton French, "Milton, Needham, and *Mercurius Politicus,*" *Studies in Philology,* XXXIII (April 1936), 236.

[8] French, p. 239; Frank, pp. 208–9.

[9] *Mercurius Politicus,* Sept. 26, 1650.

[10] Ibid., Sept. 25, 1651.

[11] Williams, pp. 407–8; French, pp. 242–44; Frank, pp. 208, 225; Elmer A. Beller, "Milton and *Mercurius Politicus,*" *Huntington Library Quarterly,* V (1941–42), 480–82.

[12] *Mercurius Politicus,* May 6, 1652.

[13] Frank, p. 225.

[14] Frank, pp. 226, 254.

[15] French, pp. 261–63; Williams, p. 411.

[16] Frank, pp. 210–11, 259.

[17] Clyde, pp. 243–51; Herd, p. 24; Frank, p. 218.

[18] *Weekly Intelligencer,* March 16 and March 25, 1652.

[19] Ibid., Sept. 14, 1652.

[20] *Faithfull Scout,* Dec. 16, 1653.

[21] Frank, pp. 259–60.

[22] *French Intelligencer,* March 2, 1652.

[23] *Man in the Moon,* June 27, 1649, and Aug. 30, 1659.

[24] Frank, p. 196.

[25] Ibid., pp. 203–4; 229–32; 242–43.

[26] Ibid., pp. 247–51; 259–60.

[27] *Weekly Post,* Nov. 8, 1659.

[28] *Perfect Account,* Aug. 4, 1562.

7 Enter the Pamphlet

[1] Harold Herd, *The March of Journalism* (London, 1952), p. 31; J. B. Williams, "The Beginnings of English Journalism," *Cavalier and Poet,* Vol. VII: *Cambridge History of English Literature* (New York, 1933: reissue), pp. 410–11; James Frank, *The Beginning of the English Newspaper* (Cambridge, Mass., 1961), p. 266.

[2] Williams, p. 412; Frank, p. 266.

[3] *Kingdomes Intelligencer,* April 12, 1661; quoted, Herd, p. 23.

[4] Ibid., p. 28; Williams, p. 411.

[5] Herd, pp. 33–34; Alexander Andrews, *History of British Journalism* (London, 1859), I, 65.

[6] George Kitchin, *Sir Roger L'Estrange: A Contribution to the History of the Press in the Seventeenth Century* (London, 1913), pp. 67–141; Herd, p. 28.

[7] Harold V. Routh, "The Advent of Modern Thought in Popular Literature," *Cavalier and Puritan,* Vol. II: *Cambridge History of English Literature* (New York, 1933: reissue), pp. 439–40.

[8] John T. Winterich, *Early American Books and Printing* (Boston, 1935), p. 35; Clyde Augustus Duniway, *The Development of Freedom of the Press in Massachusetts* (New York, 1906), pp. 38–43.

8 The Editorial Pamphlet

[1] George Kitchin, *Sir Roger L'Estrange* (London, 1913), p. 166.

[2] George Orwell and Reginald Reynolds, eds. *British Pamphleteers,* Vol. I: *From the Seventeenth Century to the French Revolution* (London, 1948), p. 9. George Orwell's introduction to this volume contains invaluable information on the general characteristics and uses of the early pamphlets.

[3] Ibid.

[4] George Macaulay Trevelyan, *England under the Stuarts* (London, 1961), pp. 164–65.

[5] Harold Herd, *The March of Journalism* (London, 1952), p. 7.

[6] Kitchin, p. 167.

[7] Ibid., p. 165.

[8] Ibid., p. 184.

[9] Ibid., pp. 164–65.

[10] Ibid., p. 230.

[11] Ibid., pp. 186–88.

[12] Quoted in *British Pamphleteers,* I, 141–42.

[13] Quoted, ibid., pp. 182–87.

¹⁴ Kitchin, p. 233; Alexander Andrews, *The History of British Journalism* (London, 1859), I, 75.

¹⁵ *Cambridge History of English Literature* (New York, 1933: reissue), IX, 3.

¹⁶ Ibid.; Kitchin, p. 270.

¹⁷ H. R. Fox Bourne, *English Newspapers* (New York, 1877: reissue), I, 46–47; Kitchin, pp. 270–71; 302–3.

¹⁸ *Cambridge History of English Literature*, IX, 3; Herd, pp. 35–36.

¹⁹ Kitchin, p. 303.

²⁰ Herd, p. 36.

²¹ Kitchin, pp. 280–343.

²² Ibid., p. 283.

²³ Ibid., p. 284; Herd, pp. 35–36.

²⁴ Herd, p. 32; *Cambridge History of English Literature*, IX, 34; Kitchin, p. 347.

²⁵ Bourne, I, 52–53.

²⁶ *Cambridge History of English Literature*, IX, 4–5; Herd, p. 36.

²⁷ *Cambridge History of English Literature*, IX, 4–5.

²⁸ Quoted, Stanley Morison, *The English Newspaper: Some Accounts of the Physical Development of Journals Printed in London Between 1622 and the Present Day, 1932* (Cambridge, Eng., 1932), p. 51.

9 Early Colonial Tracts and Pamphlets

¹ Vernon Louis Parrington, *Main Currents in the History of American Thought: An Interpretation of American Literature from Beginning to 1920* (New York, 1927), p. 127.

² Quoted, Edwin H. Ford, "Colonial Pamphleteers," *Journalism Quarterly*, 13 (March 1936), 29–30.

³ Ibid., pp. 28–29.

⁴ Quoted, S. N. D. North, "The Newspaper and Periodical Press," *The Miscellaneous Documents of the House of Representatives*, Department of Interior, Census Office (Washington, D.C., 1884), p. 4.

⁵ John T. Winterich, *Early American Books and Printing* (Boston, 1935), pp. 49–56.

⁶ Ibid.

⁷ North, p. 5.

⁸ Ibid., p. 4.

⁹ Clyde Augustus Duniway, *The Development of Freedom of the Press in Massachusetts* (New York, 1906), pp. 64–66.

¹⁰ Winterich, p. 54.

¹¹ Lawrence C. Wroth, *The Colonial Printer* (Charlottesville, 1964: 2d ed., reprint), p. 31.

[12] Ibid., p. 32 ; Winterich, pp. 54–55.

[13] Frank Luther Mott, *American Journalism, A History: 1690–1960* (New York, 1962), p. 10.

[14] Ibid., reproduced opp. p. 10.

[15] Duniway, pp. 68–69.

[16] Ibid., pp. 69–70.

[17] Ibid., pp. 71–72.

10 Experimental Era

[1] George Orwell and Reginald Reynolds, eds. *British Pamphleteers* (London, 1948), I, 13.

[2] Harry T. Baker, "Early English Journalism," *Sewanee Review,* XXV (Oct. 1917), 406, 409; *Cambridge History of English Literature* (New York, 1933 : reissue), I, 30.

[3] *Cambridge History of English Literature,* IX, 27–31.

[4] Baker, p. 406.

[5] W. E. H. Lecky, "The Evolution of the Leader," *Living Age,* CCXXXVI (Jan., Feb., March 1903), 596.

[6] T. H. S. Escott, *Masters of English Journalism: A Study of Personal Forces* (London, 1911), p. 95; *Cambridge History of English Literature,* IX, 125–26.

[7] William Lee, *Daniel Defoe: His Life and Hitherto Unknown Writings* (London, 1869), I, xxv.

[8] Frederick Seaton Siebert, *Freedom of the Press in England* (Urbana, 1952), pp. 326–30.

[9] Ibid., p. 327; *Cambridge History of English Literature,* IX, 8–9.

[10] *Cambridge History of English Literature,* IX, 9–10; Siebert, pp. 278, 330; Alexander Andrews, *The History of British Journalism* (London, 1859), I, 95.

[11] *Cambridge History of English Literature,* IX, 12–23; Edwin H. Ford, "Colonial Pamphleteers," *Journalism Quarterly,* 13 (March 1936), 25.

[12] William L. Payne, comp. and ed. *The Best of Defoe's Review* (New York, 1951), p. xi.

[13] Stanley Morison, *The English Newspaper* (Cambridge, Eng., 1932), pp. 83–84.

[14] Payne, *The Best of Defoe's Review,* p. xii.

[15] Andrews, I, 96–97; Harold Herd, *The March of Journalism* (London, 1952), pp. 32–33.

[16] H. R. Fox Bourne, *English Newspapers* (New York, 1877 : reissue), I, 63.

[17] Most authorities now agree that Defoe did not start the *Review* while he was still in prison.

[18] Herd, p. 47; Payne, *The Best of Defoe's Review,* p. xi.

[19] "Preface," *Review,* Vol. I.

[20] Lee, *Daniel Defoe,* p. 84; Payne, *The Best of Defoe's Review,* pp. xiv–xvi.

[21] *Review,* July 7, 1705.

[22] Ibid., April 19, 1709.

[23] Ibid., July 19, 1712.

[24] Ibid., Jan. 3, 1706; March 10, June 18, and 23, July 7 and 9, Aug. 11, 1709; Jan. 8 and Feb. 3, 1713.

[25] Herd, p. 19.

[26] Escott, p. 70.

[27] Reproduction, Baker, p. 408; Herd, opposite p. 48.

[28] Herd, pp. 52–53; *Cambridge History of English Literature,* IX, 37–41, Baker, p. 409.

[29] Escott, pp. 90–91.

[30] Escott, p. 90; Baker, p. 409.

[31] Morison, p. 87.

[32] Bourne, I, 106.

[33] Lee, *Daniel Defoe,* II, 13.

[34] Ibid., II, viii–ix, and III, v; Bourne, I, 108.

[35] *Mist's Journal,* Dec. 28, 1717.

[36] Paul Dattin, *The Life and Surprising Adventures of Daniel Defoe,* trans. Louise Ragan (New York, 1929), p. 188; Lee, *Daniel Defoe,* I, 307.

[37] Dattin, p. 188.

[38] Morison, p. 99.

[39] Lee, *Daniel Defoe,* I, 337.

[40] Ibid., I, 250–51, 338.

[41] Dattin, pp. 188–89.

[42] Morison, p. 101.

11 Colonial Imitations of English Polemics

[1] Edwin H. Ford, "Colonial Pamphleteers," *Journalism Quarterly,* 13 (March 1936), 6.

[2] Boston *News-Letter,* April 2, 1705.

[3] Ibid., Aug. 6, 1705.

[4] Ibid., Oct. 1, 1705.

[5] Boston *Gazette,* Dec. 28, 1718.

[6] Cited in Elizabeth C. Cook, *Literary Influences in Colonial Newspapers, 1704–1750* (New York, 1966: reissue), p. 15. This has an excellent discussion of letters and essays in colonial newspapers for the years indicated.

[7] *American Weekly Mercury,* Feb. 14, 1720.
[8] Ibid., Jan. 2, 1721.
[9] Cook, p. 15.
[10] Boston *Gazette,* Jan. 22, 1722.
[11] *New-England Courant,* June 4, 1722.

12 Political Editorializing and Biased News Stories

[1] R. L. Haig, *The Gazetteer, 1735–1797* (Carbondale, 1960), p. 5.
[2] G. A. Cranfield, *The Development of the Provincial Newspaper, 1700–1750* (Oxford, 1962), pp. v, vi. This book has an excellent discussion of the development of the provincial press. See also R. M. Wiles, *Freshest Advices: Early Provincial Newspapers in England* (Columbus, 1965), pp. 288–98.
[3] T. H. S. Escott, *Masters of English Journalism* (London, 1911), pp. 71, 84.
[4] Wiles, p. 274.
[5] Stanley Morison, *The English Newspaper* (Cambridge, Eng., 1932), p. 131.
[6] Ibid., p. 126.
[7] Alexander Andrews, *The History of British Journalism* (London, 1859), I, 132.
[8] "Evolution of the Leader," *Living Age,* CCXXXVI (Jan., Feb., March 1903), 602.
[9] Cited, Andrews, I, 132.
[10] Escott, p. 83.
[11] Ibid., p. 84.
[12] *Craftsman,* Sept. 6, 1735.
[13] *Daily Gazetteer,* Sept. 10, 1735
[14] Cranfield, p. 128; Andrews, I, 132; Wiles, pp. 288–89.
[15] Wiles, pp. 270–84.
[16] Ibid., cited, p. 270.
[17] Ibid., cited, p. 271.
[18] Ibid., cited, p. 273.

13 News Commentary Grows in the Colonial Press

[1] H. B. Parkes, "New England in the Seventeen-Thirties," *The New England Quarterly,* 3 (July 1930), 401–2.
[2] Cited, Edwin H. Ford, "Colonial Pamphleteers," *Journalism Quarterly,* 13 (March 1936), 30–31.
[3] Elizabeth C. Cook, *Literary Influences in Colonial Newspapers, 1704–1750* (New York, 1966: reissue), pp. 37–56.

4 Cited, S. N. D. North, "The Newspaper and Periodical Press," *The Miscellaneous Documents of the House of Representatives* (Washington, 1884), pp. 14–15.

5 Cited, Alfred McClung Lee, *The Daily Newspaper in America: The Evolution of a Social Instrument* (New York, 1937), p. 37.

6 Boston *Evening-Post,* March 30, 1741.

7 Ibid., Dec. 15, 1742.

8 *American Weekly Mercury,* April 15, 1724.

9 Ibid., Feb. 28, 1727.

10 Ibid., Feb. 4, 1729.

11 Ibid., Feb. 25, 1729.

12 Cook, p. 84.

13 *American Weekly Mercury,* Sept. 18, 1729.

14 Ibid., Sept. 25, 1729.

15 Ibid., April 24, 1734.

16 *Pennsylvania Gazette,* June 26 and July 3, 1732.

17 Ibid., April 4, 1734.

18 Ibid., Jan. 4, 1733.

19 Ibid., June 10, 1731.

20 Ibid., Nov. 7 and Dec. 8, 1734.

21 New York *Weekly Journal,* Dec. 17, 1733.

22 Ibid.

23 Ibid., Nov. 23, 1733.

24 Ibid., Jan. 14, 1734.

25 Ibid., March 25, 1734.

26 Ibid., Nov. 4, 1734.

27 Cook, pp. 177–78.

28 *Maryland Gazette,* Oct. 20, 1730.

29 *South-Carolina Gazette,* Jan. 8, 1732.

30 Ibid., Jan. 29, 1732.

31 Ibid., Feb. 26, 1732.

14 Fighting Progenitors, 1750–1765

1 R. L. Haig, *The Gazetteer* (Carbondale, Ill., 1960), pp. 36–37, 65.

2 Ibid., p. 72.

3 Ibid., pp. 44, 65.

4 T. H. S. Escott, *Masters of English Journalism* (London, 1911), pp. 103–4.

5 Ibid., pp. 101–3.

6 Ibid., p. 105.

7 *Universal Chronicle or Weekly Gazette,* April 8, 1758.

8 Robert R. Rea, *The English Press in Politics, 1760–1774* (Lincoln,

1963), p. 17. Rea's valuable study gives political background of these critical years in the legal battle for privileged reporting.

[9] Ibid., p. 22.

[10] George Nobbe, *The North Briton: A Study in Political Propaganda* (New York, 1939), pp. 19, 31. This book has an excellent discussion of the Wilkes Case.

[11] Rea, pp. 29–30; Nobbe, p. 32.

[12] Nobbe, p. 32.

[13] Rea, p. 30.

[14] Rea, p. 30; Nobbe, pp. 32–33.

[15] See *St. James's Chronicle,* June 5, 1762.

[16] Rea, p. 35.

[17] Nobbe, pp. 160–61. William Hogarth in 1763 made Wilkes one of the subjects for his satirical engravings—forerunners of the political cartoon, so much a part of the modern editorial page. Hogarth depicted him as a sharp-eyed, leering dandy. The print is reproduced in Rea.

[18] Rea, p. 35.

[19] Nobbe, pp. 143–45.

[20] Nobbe has an entertaining account of this hoax.

[21] *North Briton,* June 1, 1762.

[22] Ibid., Dec. 4, 1762.

[23] Rea, p. 37.

[24] *North Briton,* March 27, 1763.

[25] Alexander Andrews, *The History of British Journalism* (London, 1859), I, 164, 179.

[26] *North Briton,* April 2, 1763.

[27] Rea, p. 43.

[28] Ibid., p. 59.

[29] "Evolution of the Leader," *Living Age, CCXXXVI* (Jan., Feb., March 1903), 602.

[30] Rea, p. 92.

[31] Ibid., p. 99.

15 Colonial Printers Discover Propaganda

[1] Lawrence C. Wroth, *The Colonial Printer* (Charlottesville, 1964: reissue), pp. 23–24; Livingston Rowe Schuyler, *The Liberty of the Press in the American Colonies* (New York, 1905), pp. 16–17.

[2] Schuyler, pp. 58–59.

[3] Boston *Gazette,* Jan. 21, 1765.

[4] *Pennsylvania Gazette,* May 9, 1764.

[5] Boston *Gazette,* Oct. 1, 1754.

[6] Cited, Leonard W. Levy, *Legacy of Suppression: Freedom of Speech*

and *Press in Early American History* (Cambridge, Eng., 1964), pp. 141–42.

[7] *Cambridge History of American Literature* (New York, 1943), p. 119.

[8] Ibid., p. 118; Alfred McClung Lee, *The Daily Newspaper in America* (New York, 1937), p. 39.

[9] Edwin H. Ford, "Colonial Pamphleteers," *Journalism Quarterly,* 13 (March 1936), 36.

[10] Edmund S. Morgan and Helen M. Morgan, *The Stamp Act Crisis, Prologue to Revolution* (Chapel Hill, 1953), p. 74.

[11] *Pennsylvania Journal,* Aug. 23, 1764; *Massachusetts Gazette and Boston News-Letter,* Sept. 6 and 13, 1764.

[12] Boston *Post-Boy and Advertiser,* Oct. 1, 1764; Newport *Mercury,* Aug. 20, 1764.

[13] *Massachusetts Gazette and Boston News-Letter,* July 5, 1764; Boston *Post-Boy and Advertiser,* Oct. 1, 1764; Newport *Mercury,* Aug. 20, 1764.

[14] Newport *Mercury,* Sept. 17, 1764.

[15] Providence *Gazette,* Feb. 23, 1765.

[16] *Connecticut Courant,* Oct. 29, 1764.

[17] New York *Gazette,* June 13, 1765; *Pennsylvania Journal,* June 20, 1765; *Maryland Gazette,* Aug. 1, 1765.

[18] New York *Mercury,* Oct. 21, 1765.

[19] *New-Hampshire Gazette,* May 19, 1765.

[20] Arthur M. Schlesinger, "The Colonial Newspapers and the Stamp Act," *Journalism Quarterly,* VIII (March 1935), 70.

[21] *Connecticut Courant,* Aug. 26, 1765.

[22] Morgan and Morgan, pp. 121–22.

[23] *Connecticut Gazette,* Aug. 30, 1765.

[24] Ibid., Sept. 13, 1765.

[25] *Connecticut Courant,* Sept. 23, 1765.

[26] Cited, Levy, p. 179, and Schlesinger, p. 70.

[27] Schuyler, p. 62.

[28] New York *Mercury,* Oct. 14, 1765.

[29] Allen Nevins, "The Editorial as a Literary Form," *Journalism Quarterly,* V (March 1928), 21.

16 Arrival of "Leaders"

[1] For a discussion of the effects of the nonimportation policy on British industry, see Dora Mae Clark, *British Opinion and the American Revolution* (New Haven, 1930), pp. 1–93.

[2] Ibid., p. 41.

[3] Ibid., p. 39.

⁴ Robert R. Rea, *The English Press in Politics, 1760–1774* (Lincoln, 1963), p. 123.

⁵ London *Chronicle,* Jan. 23 and 28, Feb. 13, 1766.

⁶ Rea, p. 122.

⁷ Clark, p. 48.

⁸ Ibid., p. 83.

⁹ R. L. Haig, *The Gazetteer* (Carbondale, Ill., 1960), p. 139.

¹⁰ Ibid., p. 91.

¹¹ *Publick Advertiser,* Feb. 3, 1767. See also Rea, p. 148.

¹² *Gazetteer and London Daily Advertiser,* Feb. 4, 1767; see also Rea, pp. 148–49, and Clark, p. 6.

¹³ Ibid., March 13, 1767.

¹⁴ Cited, Rea, p. 166.

¹⁵ Clark, pp. 6–7; Rea, pp. 201–10.

¹⁶ Rea, p. 200.

¹⁷ Cited, Haig, p. 115.

¹⁸ T. H. S. Escott, *Masters of English Journalism* (London, 1911), p. 110.

¹⁹ Alexander Andrews, *The History of British Journalism* (London, 1859), I, 186.

²⁰ Harold Herd, *The March of Journalism* (London, 1952), p. 70.

²¹ Escott, p. 111.

²² Stanley Morison, *The English Newspaper* (Cambridge, Eng., 1932), p. 143.

²³ Lucyle Werkmeister, *The London Daily Press, 1772–1792* (Lincoln, Nebr., 1963), pp. 221–22.

²⁴ Ibid., p. 22.

²⁵ Ibid., p. 137.

²⁶ Ibid., p. 74; Morison, p. 148.

17 *Colonial Organs of Revolution*

¹ James Melvin Lee, *History of American Journalism* (Garden City, N.Y., 1923: rev. ed.), p. 81.

² Charles A. Beard and Mary R. Beard, *The Rise of American Civilization* (New York, 1930), I, 187.

³ *Connecticut Courant,* March 31, 1766.

⁴ *Pennsylvania Gazette,* Sept. 11, 1776.

⁵ Frank Luther Mott, *American Journalism, A History: 1690–1960* (New York, 1962), p. 102–3.

⁶ Clyde Augustus Duniway, *The Development of Freedom of the Press in Massachusetts* (New York, 1906), p. 123.

⁷ Boston *Gazette,* Dec. 19, 1768.

[8] Lee, *History of American Journalism,* p. 39.

[9] *Pennsylvania Chronicle,* Feb. 1, 1768.

[10] Boston *Gazette,* Dec. 19, 1768.

[11] Boston *Evening-Post,* July 6 and 13, 1767.

[12] Duniway, pp. 125–26.

[13] George Henry Payne, *History of Journalism in the United States* (New York, 1931), pp. 88–89; Livingston Rowe Schuyler, *The Liberty of the Press in the American Colonies* (New York, 1905), pp. 64–68.

[14] New York *Gazette,* April 9, 1770.

[15] Maurice R. Cullen, Jr., "The Boston *Gazette*: A Community Newspaper," *Journalism Quarterly,* 36 (Spring 1959), p. 204.

[16] Leonard W. Levy, *Legacy of Suppression: Freedom of Speech and Press in Early American History* (Cambridge, Mass., 1964), p. 72.

[17] Willard Grosvenor Bleyer, *Main Currents in the History of American Journalism* (Boston, 1927), p. 83; William Vincent Wells, *The Life and Public Services of Samuel Adams* (New York, 1911), I, 439, 442.

[18] Payne, *History of Journalism in the United States,* p. 104.

[19] Isaiah Thomas, *The History of Printing in America* (Albany, N.Y., 1874: 2nd ed.), II, 120–24.

[20] *Connecticut Courant,* Oct. 12, 1773.

[21] Bleyer, p. 92.

[22] "Tom Paine's First Appearance in America," *Atlantic Monthly,* IV (Nov. 1859), 568.

[23] Ibid., pp. 569–70; Bleyer, p. 93.

[24] Bleyer, p. 92.

[25] *Pennsylvania Journal and Weekly Gazette,* March 13, 1766.

[26] Boston *Gazette,* Sept. 27, 1773.

[27] Ibid., Oct. 11, 1773.

[28] Ibid., April 17, 1775; see also Payne, *History of Journalism in the United States,* p. 105.

[29] *Connecticut Courant,* May 8, 1775; *Pennsylvania Journal and Weekly Gazette,* Oct. 18, 1775.

18 Waning of English Influence

[1] George Henry Payne, *History of Journalism in the United States* (New York, 1931), pp. 117–18.

[2] Charles A. Beard and Mary R. Beard, *The Rise of American Civilization* (New York, 1930), I, 504.

[3] Moncure D. Conway, *Writings of Thomas Paine,* ed. Philip S. Foner (New York, 1945), I, 57.

⁴ "Tom Paine's First Appearance in America," *Atlantic Monthly,* IV (Nov. 1859), 570.

⁵ Ibid., p. 572.

⁶ Eugene J. Smith, *One Hundred Years of Hartford's Courant from Colonial Times through the Civil War* (New Haven, 1949), pp. 34–35.

⁷ *Pennsylvania Evening Post,* Jan. 16, 1776; New York *Packet,* March 29, 1776.

⁸ *Pennsylvania Evening Post,* March 23, 1776; New York *Packet,* March 29, 1776.

⁹ *Virginia Gazette,* Jan. 5, 1776.

¹⁰ Serle was the conductor of this newspaper while Gaine was in New Jersey on the Patriot side for several weeks. The New York *Gazette and Weekly Mercury* issued from New York at this time is here called Serle edition.

¹¹ Reprinted in *Freeman's Journal,* Oct. 29, 1776.

¹² New York *Gazette and Weekly Mercury,* Serle edition, Oct. 14, 1776.

¹³ *Freeman's Journal,* March 22, 1777.

¹⁴ *Pennsylvania Journal,* July 17, 1776.

¹⁵ Ibid., July 9, 1777.

¹⁶ *Pennsylvania Evening Post,* Aug. 28, 1777.

¹⁷ *Pennsylvania Journal,* Sept. 10, 1777.

¹⁸ New York *Packet,* Oct. 23, 1777.

¹⁹ *New-Jersey Gazette,* Feb. 17, 1779.

²⁰ *New-Jersey Journal,* Aug. 2, 1780.

²¹ *Connecticut Courant,* Feb. 3, 1778.

²² Ibid., Sept. 8, 1778.

²³ *Pennsylvania Evening Post,* July 13, 1776.

²⁴ *New-Jersey Gazette,* July 4, 1781.

²⁵ *Pennsylvania Packet,* Aug. 5, 1779.

²⁶ Ibid., Oct. 10, 1780.

²⁷ Ibid.

²⁸ Joseph Towne Wheeler, *The Maryland Press, 1777–1790* (Baltimore, 1938), p. 25.

19 The 1780's: Crawling Stage

¹ George Henry Payne, *History of Journalism in the United States* (New York, 1931), p. 138.

² Ibid.

³ Lawrence C. Wroth, *The Colonial Printer* (Charlottesville, 1964: re-issue), p. 234.

⁴ Payne, *History of Journalism in the United States,* p. 139.

⁵ Ibid., p. 135.

⁶ Paul Leicester Ford, ed. *Pamphlets on the Constitution of the United States* (New York, 1968: reprint), p. 395.

⁷ Ibid.

⁸ Claud G. Bowers, *Jefferson and Hamilton* (Boston, 1925), p. 26.

⁹ Eugene J. Smith, *One Hundred Years of Hartford's Courant from Colonial Times through the Civil War* (New Haven, 1949), p. 124.

¹⁰ Richard F. Hickson, *Isaac Collins, A Quaker Printer in 18th Century America* (New Brunswick, 1968), p. 101.

¹¹ *Connecticut Courant,* May 28, 1787.

¹² Ibid., Jan. 6, 1784.

¹³ Ibid., Oct. 1, 1787.

¹⁴ Ibid., Nov. 26, 1787.

¹⁵ Ibid., Jan. 23 and 30, 1788.

¹⁶ *Columbian Centinel,* Oct. 18, 1786.

¹⁷ Ibid., June 16, 1790. This "Centinel" is not to be confused with the "Centinel" essays against the Constitution which were written by Samuel Bryan and appeared in the *Independent Gazette* of Philadelphia.

¹⁸ Ibid, July 24, 1790.

¹⁹ Payne, *History of Journalism in the United States,* p. 142.

²⁰ Ibid., p. 113.

²¹ *Columbian Centinel,* June 13, 1787.

²² Frank Luther Mott, *American Journalism, A History: 1690–1960* (New York, 1962), p. 132.

²³ *Pennsylvania Packet,* March 22, 1786.

²⁴ Cited, Catherine Drinker Bowen, *Miracle at Philadelphia—The Story of the Constitutional Convention, May to September 1787* (Boston, 1966), p. 139.

²⁵ S. G. W. Benjamin, "Notable Editors between 1776 and 1800—Influence of the Early American Press," *Magazine of American History,* XVII (Feb. 1887), 108.

²⁶ Wroth, pp. 27–28.

²⁷ *Pennsylvania Gazette,* Sept. 12, 1789.

²⁸ Payne, *History of Journalism in the United States,* pp. 145–46.

²⁹ Joseph Towne Wheeler, *The Maryland Press, 1777–1790* (Baltimore, 1938), p. 31

³⁰ Payne, *History of Journalism in the United States,* pp. 154–56.

20 The 1790's: Young Adulthood

¹ Nevins, Allan, *American Press Opinion, Washington to Coolidge—A Documentary Record of Editorial Leadership and Criticism* (Bos-

ton, 1928), p. 5; A. M. Lee, *The Daily Newspaper in America* (New York, 1937), p. 604.

2 Milton W. Hamilton, *The Country Printer, 1785–1830* (Port Washington, Long Island, 1964: 2d ed.), pp. 53–54, 110–11.

3 Ibid., pp. 98–99.

4 *Gazette of the United States,* April 15, 1789.

5 Ibid., April 27, 1791.

6 Ibid., Sept. 19, 1792.

7 Cited, Willard G. Bleyer, *Main Currents in the History of American Journalism* (Boston, 1927), p. 110.

8 George Henry Payne, *History of Journalism in the United States* (New York, 1931), pp. 162–63.

9 See Edwin H. Carpenter, Jr., ed. *A Bibliography of Writings of Noah Webster* (New York, 1958).

10 *American Minerva,* Dec. 9, 1793.

11 Ibid., Dec. 18, 1793.

12 See, e.g., Boston *Independent Chronicle,* Jan. 31, 1793.

13 Bleyer, p. 117.

14 *Porcupine's Gazette,* March 5, 1797.

15 Ibid.

16 Ibid., March 7, 1797.

17 *American Minerva,* March 21, 1797.

18 *Porcupine's Gazette,* Sept. 9, 1797.

19 Bleyer, p. 119.

20 *Porcupine's Gazette,* Nov. 14, 1797.

21 Ibid., Aug. 25, 1797.

22 Bleyer, p. 119.

23 Paul Leicester Ford, ed. *Writings of Thomas Jefferson* (New York, 1892), VI, 106.

24 *National Gazette,* Dec. 9, 1791.

25 Ibid., Feb. 9, 1792.

26 Ibid., July 28, 1792.

27 Ibid., June 1, 1793.

28 Ibid., June 5, 1793.

29 Payne, *History of Journalism in the United States,* p. 166.

30 Lee, *The Daily Newspaper in America,* p. 479; Frank Luther Mott, *American Journalism, A History: 1690–1960* (New York, 1962), p. 143.

31 *Jefferson's Writings,* I, 198–99.

32 New York *Time Piece,* March 20, 1797.

33 Ibid., May 26, 1797.

34 James E. Pollard, *The Presidents and the Press* (New York, 1947), p. 19.

[35] *Aurora,* Dec. 23, 1797.

[36] Ibid., March 6, 1798.

[37] Ibid., Nov. 12, 1796.

[38] Ibid., Dec. 2, 1796.

[39] Ibid., April 1, 1800.

[40] Mott, p. 129.

[41] *Russell's Gazette,* Sept. 21, 1798.

[42] "Thomas Paine's Second Appearance in the United States," *Atlantic Monthly,* IV (July 1859), p. 7.

[43] Cited S. N. D. North, "The Newspaper and Periodical Press," *Miscellaneous Documents of the House of Representatives* (Washington, 1884), pp. 32–33.

[44] *Gazette of the United States,* March 4, 1799.

[45] For an excellent discussion of press involvement in the Alien and Sedition Acts, see James Morton Smith, *Freedom Fetters—The Alien and Sedition Laws and Civil Liberties* (Ithaca, 1967: emended ed.), pp. 159–418.

[46] S. N. D. North, p. 35.

[47] G. G. W. Benjamin, "Notable Editors between 1776 and 1800," *Magazine of American History,* XVII (Feb. 1887), 115.

[48] Mott, p. 143.

[49] Cited, James Morton Smith, p. 178.

[50] Salem *Gazette,* Nov. 29, 1799.

[51] *Times and District of Columbia Advertiser,* Dec. 16, 1799.

[52] Salem *Gazette,* Nov. 23, 1799.

Bibliography

BOOKS

Adams, Charles Francis. *Works of John Adams.* 10 vols. Boston, 1956.

Andrews, Alexander. *The History of British Journalism.* 2 vols. London, 1859.

Beard, Charles A. and Mary R. *The Rise of American Civilization.* New York, 1930.

Blagden, Cyprian. *The Stationers' Company—A History, 1403-1959.* London, 1960.

Bleyer, Willard Grosvenor. *Main Currents in the History of American Journalism.* Boston, 1927.

Bourne, H. R. Fox. *English Newspapers: Chapters in the History of Journalism.* 2 vols. Reissue. New York, 1966.

Bowen, Catherine Drinker. *Miracle at Philadelphia—The Story of the Constitutional Convention, May to September, 1787.* Boston, 1966.

Bowers, Claude G. *Jefferson and Hamilton.* Boston, 1925.

Buckingham, Joseph T. *Personal Memoirs and Recollections of Editorial Life.* 2 vols. Boston, 1852.

Burton, K. G. *The Early Newspaper Press in Berkshire, 1723-1855.* Reading, Eng., 1954.

Cambridge History of American Literature. 3 vols. New York, 1943.

Cambridge History of English Literature. Vols. II, VII, IX. New York, 1933.

Carpenter, Edwin H., Jr. *A Bibliography of Writings of Noah Webster.* New York, 1958.

Clark, Dora Mae. *British Opinion and the American Revolution.* New Haven, 1930.

Clyde, William M. *The Struggle for Freedom of the Press from Caxton to Cromwell.* London, 1934.

Conway, Moncure D. *Writings of Thomas Paine,* ed. Philip S. Foner. Vol. I. New York, 1945.

Cook, Elizabeth C. *Literary Influences of Colonial Newspapers, 1704-1750.* Reissue. New York, 1966.

Cooper, Charles A. *An Editor's Retrospect: Fifty Years of Newspaper Work*. New York, 1896.

Cranfield, G. A. *The Development of the Provincial Newspaper 1700–1750*. Oxford, 1962.

Curti, Merle. *The Growth of American Thought*. 3d ed. New York, 1964.

Dahl, Folke. *A Bibliography of English Corantos and Periodicals Newsbooks, 1620–1642*. London, 1952.

Dattin, Paul. *The Life and Surprising Adventures of Daniel Defoe*, trans. Louise Ragan. New York, 1929.

Davis, Norman. *Paston Letters*. Oxford, 1958.

De Armand, Anna Janney. *Andrew Bradford, Colonial Journalist*. Newark, 1949.

Duniway, Clyde Augustus. *The Development of Freedom of the Press in Massachusetts*. New York, 1906.

Emery, Edwin, Philip H. Ault, and Warren K. Agee. *Introduction to Mass Communications*. 2d ed. New York, 1965.

Emery, Edwin. *The Press and America, An Interpretative History of Journalism*. 2d ed. Englewood, N.J., 1962.

—— ed. *The Story of America as Reported in Its Newspapers to 1965*. New York, 1965.

Escott, T. H. S. *Masters of English Journalism: A Study of Personal Forces*. London, 1911.

Fay, Bernard. *Franklin, The Apostle of Modern Times*. Boston, 1929.

Flint, Leon Nelson. *The Editorial: A Study of Effectiveness in Writing*. New York, 1926.

Ford, Edwin H. and Edwin Emery, eds. *Highlights in the History of the American Press*. Minneapolis, 1954.

Ford, Paul Leicester, ed. *Pamphlets on the Constitution of the United States*. New York, 1968.

——. *Writings of Thomas Jefferson*. 10 vols. New York, 1892–99.

Frank, James. *The Beginnings of the English Newspaper, 1620–1660*. Cambridge, Mass., 1961.

Graham, Walter James. *English Literary Periodicals*. New York, 1930.

——. *The Beginnings of English Literary Periodicals, A Study of Periodical Literature 1665–1715*. New York, 1926.

Haig, Robert L. *The Gazetteer: 1735–1797: A Study in the Eighteenth-Century English Newspaper*. Carbondale, 1960.

Hamilton, Milton W. *The Country Printer, New York State, 1785–1830*. 2d ed. Empire State Historical Publication, Vol. XXIX. Port Washington, Long Island, 1964.

Herd, Harold. *The March of Journalism—The Story of the British Press from 1622 to the Present Day*. London, 1952.

Hickson, Richard F. *Isaac Collins, A Quaker Printer in 18th Century America.* New Brunswick, 1968.

Junius: including Letters by the Same Writer under other Signatures. Reissue. Philadelphia: Walker, 1836.

Kitchin, George. *Sir Roger L'Estrange: A Contribution to the History of the Press in the Seventeenth Century.* London, 1913.

Kobre, Sidney. *Foundations of American Journalism.* Tallahassee, 1958.

Lee, Alfred McClung. *The Daily Newspaper in America: The Evolution of a Social Instrument.* New York, 1937.

Lee, James Melvin. *America's Oldest Daily Newspaper.* New York, 1918.

———. *History of American Journalism.* Rev. ed. Garden City, N.Y., 1923.

Lee, William. *Daniel Defoe: His Life and Hitherto Unknown Writings.* 3 vols. London, 1869.

Levy, Leonard W. *Legacy of Suppression: Freedom of Speech and Press in Early American History.* Cambridge, Mass., 1964.

——— ed. *Freedom of the Press from Zenger to Jefferson: Early American Libertarian Theories.* Indianapolis, 1966.

McClure, Norman, ed. *The Letters of John Chamberlain.* 2 vols. Philadelphia, 1939.

Miner, Ward L. *William Goddard, Newspaperman.* Durham, N.C., 1962.

Moore, Frank. *The Diary of the Revolution.* Hartford, 1876.

Morgan, Edmund S. and Helen M. *The Stamp Act Crisis: Prologue to Revolution.* Chapel Hill, 1953.

Morgan, Edmund S., ed. *Prologue to Revolution: Sources and Documents on the Stamp Act Crisis, 1764–1766.* Chapel Hill, 1959.

Morison, Stanley. *The English Newspaper: Some Accounts of the Physical Development of Journals Printed in London Between 1622 and the Present Day, 1932.* Cambridge, Eng., 1932.

Mott, Frank Luther. *American Journalism: A History, 1690–1960.* 3d ed. New York, 1962.

Mott, Frank Luther and Chester E. Jorgenson, eds. *Benjamin Franklin —Representative Selections, with Introduction, Bibliography, and Notes.* New York, 1936.

Nelson, Harold L., ed. *Freedom of the Press from Hamilton to the Warren Court.* Indianapolis, 1967.

Nevins, Allan. *American Press Opinion, Washington to Coolidge— A Documentary Record of Editorial Leadership and Criticism, 1785–1927.* Boston, 1928.

Nobbe, George. *The North Briton: A Study in Political Propaganda.* New York, 1939.

Orwell, George and Reginald Reynolds, eds. *British Pamphleteers.* Vol. I. London, 1948.

Parrington, Vernon Louis. *Main Currents in American Thought: An Interpretation of American Literature from Beginning to 1920.* 3 vols. New York, 1927.

Payne, George Henry. *History of Journalism in the United States.* New York, 1931.

Payne, William L., comp. *The Best of Defoe's Review.* New York, 1951.

Pollard, James E. *The Presidents and the Press.* New York, 1947.

Rea, Robert R. *The English Press in Politics, 1760–1774.* Lincoln, 1963.

Reynolds, Reginald, ed. *British Pamphleteers.* Vol. II. London, 1951.

Rollins, Hyder E., ed. *Cavalier and Puritan: Ballads and Broadsides Illustrating the Period of the Great Rebellion, 1640–1660.* New York University, 1923.

————. *The Pack of Autolycus or Strange and Terrible News of Ghost, Apparition, Monstrous Births, Showers of Wheat, Judgments of God and other Prodigious and Fearful Happenings as Told in Broadside Ballads of the Years 1624–1692.* Cambridge, Mass., 1927.

Salmon, Lucy Maynard. *The Newspaper and Authority.* New York, 1923.

————. *The Newspaper and the Historian.* New York, 1923.

Schlesinger, Arthur M. *Prelude to Independence: The Newspaper War on Great Britain.* New York: Alfred A. Knopf, 1958.

————. *The Rise of Modern America—1865–1951.* New York, 1951.

Schuyler, Livingstone Rowe. *The Liberty of the Press in the American Colonies.* New York, 1905.

Scott, John Anthony, ed. *The Diary of the American Revolution.* New York, 1967.

Shaaber, Matthias A. *Some Forerunners of the Newspaper in England.* Philadelphia, 1929.

Shepard, Leslie. *The Broadside Ballad: A Study in Origins and Meanings.* London, 1962.

Siebert, Frederick Seaton. *Freedom of the Press in England, 1476–1776.* Urbana, 1952.

Smith, Eugene J. *One Hundred Years of Hartford's Courant from Colonial Times through the Civil War.* New Haven, 1949.

Smith, James Morton. *Freedom's Fetters—The Alien and Sedition Laws and Civil Liberties.* Emended edition. Ithaca, 1967.

Steinberg, S. H. *Five Hundred Years of Printing.* Edinburgh, 1955.

Thomas, Isaiah. *The History of Printing in America.* 2d ed. 2 vols. Albany, 1874.

Trent, W. P. *Daniel Defoe: How to Know Him.* Indianapolis, 1916.

Trevelyan, George Macaulay. *England under the Stuarts.* 21st ed. London, 1961.

Tyler, Moses Coit. *Literary History of the American Revolution, 1763–1783.* New York, 1897.

von Klarwill, Victor, ed. *The Fugger News-Letters—Being a Selection of Unpublished Letters from Correspondents of the House of Fugger during the Years 1568–1605,* trans. Pauline de Chary. New York, 1924.

Wells, William Vincent. *The Life and Public Services of Samuel Adams.* 3 vols. New York, 1911.

Werkmeister, Lucyle. *The London Daily Press 1772–1792.* Lincoln, 1963.

Wheeler, Joseph Towne. *The Maryland Press, 1777–1790.* Baltimore, 1938.

Wiles, R. M. *Freshest Advices: Early Provincial Newspapers in England.* Columbus, 1965.

Winterich, John T. *Early American Books and Printing.* Boston, 1935.

Writings of George Washington. Bicentennial edition. 34 vols. Washington, D.C., 1931–44.

Wroth, Lawrence C. *The Colonial Printer.* Reissue. Charlottesville, 1964.

PERIODICALS

Baker, Harry T. "Early English Journalism," *The Sewanee Review,* XXV (October 1917), 396–411.

Beller, Elmer A. "Milton and *Mercurius Politicus,"* *The Huntington Library Quarterly,* V (1941–42), 479–87.

Benjamin, G. G. W. "Notable Editors Between 1776 and 1800—Influence of the Early American Press," *Magazine of American History,* XVII (February 1887), 97–127.

Cullen, Maurice R., Jr. *"The Boston Gazette:* A Community Newspaper," *Journalism Quarterly,* XXXVI (Spring 1959), 97–127.

Ford, Edwin H. "Colonial Pamphleteers," *Journalism Quarterly,* XIII (March 1936), 24–36.

French, J. Milton. "Milton, Needham, and Mercurius Politicus," *Studies in Philology,* XXXIII (April 1936), 236–52.

Griffith, R. H. "Some Unrecorded Newsbooks," *Times Literary Supplement,* December 11, 1924, p. 849.

Hanson, Lawrence. "English Newsbooks, 1620–1641," *The Library,* 4th ser., XVIII (1937–38), 355–84.

Lecky, W. E. H. "The Evolution of the Leader," *Living Age,* CCXXXVI (January February March, 1936), 596–606.

Nevins, Allan. "The Editorial as a Literary Form," *Journalism Quarterly,* V (March 1928), 19–27.

Parker, H. B. "New England in the Seventeen-Thirties," *New England Quarterly,* III (July 1930), 379–419.

Kuo, Ping-Chia. "Canton and Salem," *New England Quarterly,* III (July 1930), 420–42.

Rosenberg, Marvin. "The Rise of England's First Daily Newspaper," *Journalism Quarterly,* XXX (Winter 1953), 3–14.

Schlesinger, Arthur M. "The Colonial Newspaper and the Stamp Act," *Journalism Quarterly,* VIII (March 1935), 63–83.

Shaaber, Matthias A. "The History of the First English Newspaper," *Studies in Philology,* XXIX (October 1932), 551–87.

Siebert, Frederick Seaton. *"The Regulation of Newsbooks, 1620–1640,"* *Journalism Quarterly,* XVI (June 1932), 151–64.

Sirlock, Ernest. "Shakespeare and Jonson Among the Pamphleteers of the First Civil War: Some Unreported Seventeenth Century Allusions," *Modern Philology,* LII (November 1955), 88–99.

Spaulding, E. Wilder. *"The Connecticut Courant,* A Representative Newspaper in the Eighteenth Century," *New England Quarterly,* III (July 1930), 443–63.

"Tom Paine's First Appearance in America," *Atlantic Monthly,* IV (November 1859), 565–75.

"Tom Paine's Second Appearance in the United States," *Atlantic Monthly,* IV (July 1859), 1–17.

OTHER SOURCES

Nelson, William. "The American Newspapers of the 18th Century on Sources of History," *Annual Report of American Historical Society,* I, 211–22.

North, S. N. D. "The Newspaper and Periodical Press," *Miscellaneous Documents of the House of Representatives.* Department of Interior, Census Office. Washington, D.C., 1884.

Stamford Mercury. University of Missouri Bulletin, Journalism Series 165. 66:38, October 28, 1965.

NEWSPAPERS

Frank Collection of 3000 Microfilmed Early English Newspapers. Rochester, University Library. Rochester, New York.

Readex Microprints of Early American Newspapers. American Antiquarian Society. Morris Library, Southern Illinois University. Carbondale, Illinois.

Index